CANNES

Of related interest from Faber and Faber

ADVENTURES OF A SURBURBAN BOY
By John Boorman

ALTMAN ON ALTMAN
Edited by David Thompson

COPPOLA
By Peter Cowie

DOUBLE VISION
By Andrzej Wajda

FELLINI ON FELLINI
Edited by Constanzo Constantini

FRANÇOIS TRUFFAUT: LETTERS
Edited by Gilbert Adair

MALLE ON MALLE
Edited by Philip French

MY TIME WITH ANTONIONI
By Wim Wenders

THE NAME OF THIS BOOK IS DOGME 95
By Richard Kelly

REVOLUTION!
THE EXPLOSION OF WORLD CINEMA IN THE 60S
By Peter Cowie

TRIER ON VON TRIER
Edited by Stig Bjorkman

CANNES

*Inside the World's Premier
Film Festival*

KIERON CORLESS & CHRIS DARKE

ff

faber and faber

First published in 2007
by Faber and Faber Limited
3 Queen Square London WC1N 3AU

Typeset by Faber and Faber Limited
Printed in England by Mackays of Chatham plc, Chatham, Kent

All rights reserved
© Kieron Corless & Chris Darke, 2007

Kieron Corless and Chris Darke are hereby identified as authors
of this work in accordance with Section 77 of the Copyright,
Designs and Patents Act 1988

*This book is sold subject to the condition that it shall not, by way
of trade or otherwise, be lent, resold, hired out or otherwise
circulated without the publisher's prior consent in any form of binding
or cover other than that in which it is published and without a
similar condition including this condition being imposed on the
subsequent purchaser*

A CIP record for this book
is available from the British Library

ISBN 978–0–571–23046–4
ISBN 0–571–23046–6

2 4 6 8 10 9 7 5 3 1

Contents

Introduction
page 1

I
To Serve the Cinema
page 11

II
Avoiding Offence
page 25

III
That Riviera Touch
page 49

IV
Sacred Monsters
page 71

V
'Our mere presence here makes them die'
page 95

VI
'Beneath the paving stones . . . the beach'
page 121

VII
Adventures in Cinema
page 145

VIII
The Jury Speaks
page 167

IX
Selection
page 193

X
Festivalworld
page 211

Appendix 1
Timeline
page 231

Appendix 2
List of Palme d'Or Winners
page 237

Notes
page 241

Select bibliography
page 255

Acknowledgements
page 259

Introduction

A dinosaur, a brothel, a vacuous PR-driven spectacle? A vital commercial showcase, a critical barometer, a cinematic cornucopia? Take your pick, but one thing is unarguable: the Cannes Film Festival never fails to compel strongly held, often deeply polarised views of its worth and importance.

Since its inception in 1946 (following an aborted first attempt which saw it open literally on the eve of the Second World War), Cannes has slowly but surely asserted itself in the popular imagination. Now, each May, we are accustomed to Cannes dominating TV and newsprint coverage all over the world, thanks to the stars and starlets it attracts, to its annual outbreaks of scandal and outrage, and, occasionally, to the calibre of the films laurelled on the final prize-giving night at the festival's Grand Palais. After the World Cup and the Olympics, Cannes is probably the most mediated event on the planet.

The publication of this book is occasioned by the milestone of the festival's sixtieth edition in May 2007. With such seasoned maturity comes a moment for looking back and taking stock. At the festival itself there will, of course, be a huge jamboree along the lines of the previous fiftieth birthday party, when every past and living winner of the Palme d'Or (arguably the most coveted prize on Planet Cinema) was flown in for a celebratory photo-call on the Palais stage – thus providing further fuel for the nay-sayers quick to seize on any evidence of Cannes's attention-grabbing *amour propre*. Nevertheless, reaching sixty has been quite a journey, and no small achievement, so a degree of self-congratulation is doubtless in order. The festival sailed very close to the wind in its early years, and didn't even manage to open in 1948 or 1950 owing to lack of funds. So precisely how did a small 'free' festival – set up to rival Mussolini's fascist equivalent in Venice and based in a small town on the Côte d'Azur – come to exercise such dominion in the world of film, rivalling the Oscars for glamour, star allure, and cinematic cachet?

Part of the answer lies in the question. The now-fabled location on the shores of the Mediterranean has supplied a ready-made iconography that photographers, journalists and the festival authorities themselves have not been slow to exploit: the mile-long Croisette under clear blue May skies, with its beautiful hotel facades and palm trees (immortalised in the design of the Palme d'Or), and, above all, the beach, where not even the most sanguine festival organiser in its early days could have foreseen the impact of topless starlets and young bikini-clad ingénues such as Brigitte Bardot frolicking in the surf.

Of course, there is very much more to Cannes than the annually renewable pageant of red-carpet glamour, photo-ops, and endless parties. Though vital in themselves, these splashy happenings tend to obscure and distract from other significant elements of the festival's present and past. This book attempts to redress the balance and probe beneath the surface by telling another story – a counter-history of Cannes, if you will. We believe that what happens at the festival each year over twelve frenzied days tells us all a great deal, not only about the state of cinema, but more broadly about the changing tastes of the times. By virtue of its sheer size and importance, Cannes is able to shape the film world – setting agendas, influencing other festivals, unearthing new talent, and propelling selected directors to global attention. But Cannes also provides a stage on which certain dramas are enacted, some of them purely cinematic, others that reflect – or have repercussions in – the wider world.

It's no surprise that with so much at stake – both for those charged with maintaining the festival's pre-eminence as well as for the film-makers and financiers who arrive there with dreams of glory – that the atmosphere during Cannes fortnight can be somewhat combustible. Frequently there are scandals, bust-ups, walk-outs, premieres of movies that instantly stand accused of bringing cinema into disrepute. At times the festival itself has been charged with encouraging such controversies, as a sure-fire means of garnering media coverage and so perpetuating its top-dog reputation. Guilty or not guilty? We will weigh the evidence herein.

This book does not attempt to be a dogged blow-by-blow account of the festival's incident-packed first sixty years. Instead, we have chosen to highlight a multitude of revealing moments and resonant incidents which, carefully unpacked, can lay bare those wider issues. The history of Cannes is replete with such 'flashpoints' (a word suggestive of conflict, but also illumination and clarity). In other words, this is not one of those anecdotal and slightly self-indulgent Cannes memoirs, of which there are several available in English and French. Rather, it is anchored by an overarching thesis, and by the anecdotal evidence of numerous influential people closely involved with the festival down the years, who agreed to be interviewed especially for this volume. These range from current festival director Thierry Frémaux and his predecessor Gilles Jacob, to prominent and prizewinning film-maker-jurors such as Bernardo Bertolucci, Robert Altman, Mike Leigh, and John Boorman, among others. It is their expert testimony, above all, that informs the debates and analyses herein.

Our account is heavily tinged with politics, for the simple reason that politics have been rife throughout the festival's history. For all Cannes' official rhetoric down the years (tending to elevate the ideas of 'film culture' and 'auteur directors' to a quasi-religious level), it has been deeply embroiled in the cut-and-thrust of national and international politics – never more so than during the Cold War years, or when attempting to cope with the upheavals of 1968 and its aftermath, or when making a stand against censorship by showing films banned in their home countries, to name but three general instances. And we should never forget that Cannes is a French festival – indeed 'a French state business', as the eminent scholar and film producer Colin MacCabe puts it. Does Cannes simply peddle French cultural and political agendas? Certainly the presence of French films in competition is never a pure or simple matter. Political considerations often seem pertinent to the decision of which films win prizes – think of the furore in 2004 that greeted the Palme d'Or award to Michael Moore's *Fahrenheit 9/11*. Indeed, accusations of corruption have dogged the festival throughout its history, as we shall see, particularly in the areas of film selection and the awarding of honours. Cannes is, and always has been, a volatile nexus of aesthetic idealism, commercial opportunism and hard-nosed geopolitics. It is these tangled skeins of oft-conflicting interests that we hope to unravel for the reader.

* * *

Cannes has sometimes appeared as a sort of battleground for combating notions of art versus commerce, auteur cinema versus the multiplex, politics versus culture, et cetera. Naturally, the reality is always a little more complex than these simplified oppositions suggest. One antagonism stands out above all others, however, and that is the encounter between France and America. This is often depicted in terms of the two august republics squaring up to each other across the Atlantic, the elder standing up for the auteur theory (France was, after all, its birthplace) and art-for-art's-sake, its ruder, younger cousin for the coarse pleasures of mass entertainment and consumption. In his 2005 memoir *My Lives*, the American writer Edmund White (an ardent Francophile who lived for many years in Paris) succinctly captures Americans' perceptions of France in the late 1950s and early 1960s: 'The French knew much more about American B-movie directors than we did and lamented our lack of "film culture". We weren't sure we thought "film" and "culture" belonged in the same sentence.'

INTRODUCTION

More than any other forum, Cannes has thrown into sharp relief the tensions provoked by these different versions of what constitutes cinema; at certain periods they have been mutually enriching, at others deeply adversarial.

One amusing vignette of same was revealed to director Mike Leigh when he attended Cannes in 1993 to present his bold and bruising drama *Naked* in the official competition. Leigh sets the scene:

> It's our gala night, a big deal for us. We get into the cars, we arrive at the Grand Palais – the red carpet up the stairs, the paparazzi and all the rest of it. We get out, a very nice French publicist meets us, and she says, 'Look, do you mind standing to one side? Because Arnold Schwarzenegger is coming and he's going to go in first.' We said, 'Great, fantastic, Arnie's going to see our film!' So we stood aside, and the next thing we know the cars pull up and out gets Arnie with three or four of his henchmen. We went up the stairs behind them, and there was a massive roar of approval and applause from the crowd and the paparazzi. Once we were inside we discovered that Arnie's lot had gone in, left through a side door, and buggered off for the night . . .

Some readers might be surprised to hear that 'Arnie' was invited to the festival in the first place. But such is the curious schizophrenia of Cannes. In 2005, George Lucas and Paris Hilton independently brought the place to a standstill, but it was a low-budget art film by the Dardennes brothers of Belgium that carried off the top prize. There is a case to be made that the 'sizzle' added to Cannes by big Hollywood stars – the marquee value, the massive crowds, the sheer column inches – is of benefit to everyone, especially to the related exposure of lesser-known auteurs. For others, it seems like a pact with the devil, fatally undermining the festival's integrity. But it is by no means a recent phenomenon. As we shall see, right from the start the festival organisers pragmatically set out to court Tinseltown glamour, realising that it could guarantee success and survival. For their part, the Hollywood studios have recognised the usefulness of Cannes as a launch platform for their product, while remaining nervous of the potential damage to their commercial prospects in the event of taking a beating from the French critics. As such, a delicate *pas de deux* has taken place down the years between France and America, revealing mutual dependence and a degree of affection, but also a mutual suspicion.

* * *

The history of Cannes is best considered in three distinct phases. The first runs from the start-up of the festival in 1946 through to May 1968, that near-numinous date, when Cannes' share of worldwide upheavals resulted in the festival being terminated by the young turks of the *nouvelle vague*. Between those years, several themes are key:

- the festival as often unwitting platform for, and mediator of, Cold War tensions, making for many moments of unintended comedy but also for a dark side to proceedings;
- the notion of the democratic 'free' festival, and how that squared with the festival's undeniable social elitism;
- the competition with Venice and Berlin, which continues to this day;
- the rise of great auteurs such as Bergman, Fellini and Buñuel;
- the start of sixties libertarianism, as reflected in censorship battles with the Catholic Church;
- and the delicious presence of starlets, alongside the attendant early stirrings of 'youth culture'.

Factor in the magnificently lavish parties and the presence of such luminaries as Cocteau and Picasso, and it's small wonder so many people look back nostalgically on this period as representing the festival's golden age, one of unrecoverable innocence and joy, as the world gradually emerged from the agonies of war.

INTRODUCTION

The second phase runs from 1968 to the opening of the festival's new Palais headquarters in 1983. The closure of '68 is the single most dramatic event in Cannes history, and the one with the most far-reaching consequences. The reverberations would be felt for years afterwards, as Cannes realised it had to properly reform to keep pace with a changing world, throwing open its doors to previously excluded or overlooked constituencies. What followed, in the period to 1983, was the inauguration of new strands to run alongside the main competition – in particular the *Quinzaine des Réalisateurs* – dedicated to filmic innovations such as the New German Cinema of Herzog, Fassbinder and Wenders that began to make itself felt from the early seventies. As struggles against oppressive dictators, state censorship and colonial masters gained momentum all over the world, particularly in Latin America and Africa, Cannes also provided a forum for more politicised national cinemas represented by directors such as Ousmane Sembene and Glauber Rocha. It should be noted, though, that France's dirty war with Algeria barely registered in the programme at Cannes until Algerian director Mohammed Lakhdar-Hamina walked off with the Palme d'Or in 1975, sparking a predictable furore.

The opening of the monumental (and many would say monumentally hideous) Grand Palais in 1983, replacing the charming and more modestly scaled version further down the Croisette, signals the start of another new era and guides us toward the present day – characterised by the festival's corporate gigantism and ambition, the courting of a ravenous media (especially TV) and sponsorship partners, and above all the development of the Cannes *Marché* or Market, today by some distance the biggest in the world. During the same period, there has also been an explosion of film festivals internationally, creating a self-sustaining network in which context Cannes now has to be seen, and which has given rise to the phenomenon of the 'festival film' (one whose existence may never register outside of these specialised surroundings). Cannes is still the biggest and most important festival in the annual calendar, but it is now only one of a huge number provid-

8 CANNES

ing a platform for so-called 'quality cinema'. Relations among the festivals are on the whole mutually supportive, but Cannes has to fight off cut-throat competition to acquire the top directors and films from other 'A-list' festivals, particularly Venice and Berlin.

The festival's capacity to reinvent itself through the vicissitudes of its history is exemplary, but the one constant has been glamour, and no account of Cannes is complete without consideration of it. Here as elsewhere, though, there is a deeper story, behind the bikinis and beauty spots and beguiling smiles. There is, for instance, a great deal more to the tale of Brigitte Bardot than mere pulchritude. Bardot embodied the contradictions and birth-pangs of a completely new attitude, one that travelled from the beaches of the Côte d'Azur throughout France and the rest of the world. Bardot's presence, proudly atop a pile of myriad other hopeful young starlets, helped to trigger useful associations of Cannes with excess and licentious behaviour – which is as it should be. This is a festival after all, and by all accounts nowhere lays on a party quite like Cannes. Ultimately, very few of us are immune to such excitement, even the most austere highbrow. We are all just a bit curious to see how a true star deports his or her self en route up the red carpet, whether it be Madonna or Jean-Luc Godard. Clearly, for the elite, the adoration poured out by the public in the course of this short walk is the finest experience Cannes can offer.

For mere mortals, such as the press pack behind the cordon ropes, Cannes can be rather more of an ordeal. Everyone accredited to the festival is weighed in the balance, 'placed' in a hierarchy determined by the colour of badge they will wear for the fortnight. Some are found wanting – the lowest pass in the pecking order can confer a near-invisibility upon its wearer. Only the festival's ubiquitous security goons seem immune to distinctions, trampling with relish on any available ego in alarmingly democratic fashion. 'I've been fucking *manhandled* by those guys,' one eminent American producer told us, clearly still smarting at the slight. If we choose to be kind, we could surmise that the festival's colossal growth since the 1980s requires an

INTRODUCTION

assiduous security force to police it. Those unable to bear the thought of receiving such discourtesy have little choice but to stay away, or else take up martial arts. But this pervading sense of caste at Cannes can make the festival feel ritualised and exclusive to an oppressive degree. It is very easy for the initiate stumbling through Cannes to feel, as Milan Kundera put it, that 'life is elsewhere' – at a cooler party, a finer restaurant, a more scintillating premiere, a more exclusive press conference. Even at the C-list party it is likely that everybody will be looking over everybody else's shoulder for someone more interesting to talk to.

A chief obstacle to having a nice time is the sheer number of bodies that Cannes attracts. 'You *have* to be here,' one distributor told us, 'otherwise people assume you've gone bust.' According to Cannes lore, there was a time when a journalist really could just sit down and have a coffee with Cary Grant or Alfred Hitchcock without first chivvying a phalanx of publicists for the privilege. Nowadays, the entire experience of being at Cannes can be encapsulated in two words: *hustling* and *waiting*. Waiting in queues to get into screenings or parties. Waiting ages to be served in overcrowded bars and restaurants. Waiting outside the Palais for '*la montée des marches*' when the stars ascend the red-carpeted steps. Such 'dead' time is punctuated by sudden flurries of excitement and agitation, lots of shouting and camera flashes and mounting hysteria as a star is driven slowly by, followed by a gradual melting back into the habitual state of glazed, listless anticipation.

The hot-house, semi-hysterical atmosphere at Cannes produces a condition known as 'festival fever'. It's apparent at other festivals too, but with nothing like the intensity of Cannes, where ultimately so much more is at stake. And it manifests itself in all kinds of ways. If you're Spike Lee, you might threaten to take a baseball-bat to jury president Wim Wenders, for not bestowing a prize on *Do the Right Thing* in 1989 ('I have a Louisville slugger with Wim Wenders' name on it.'). In the midst of a typical Cannes audience, you might find yourself stamping and cheering at the end of a projection, or else baying and hissing like a feral dog when the lights go up, much as you might have done had you been in a Roman amphitheatre circa 100 BC. 'The cathedral of cinema' is how producer Jeremy Thomas described the Grand Palais to these authors – but such ritualised savagery suggests something altogether more pagan. Nevertheless (to stretch Thomas's metaphor just a little) Cannes these days is more than ever a broad and growing church, complete with its own rituals and semi-reverent multitudes. And this book should perhaps be read as a sort of church history, with more than sufficient in the way of revered saints, principled splits, and bitterly disputed heresies.

Let us begin the story, then, in 1946: Europe in ruins after six years of anguish and bloodletting, France in particular struggling to recover its national pride and identity after the Nazi occupation. The war was over, but in a gorgeous little town on the Côte d'Azur, modestly unsuspecting of its destiny, other battles were about to commence . . .

Kieron Corless & Chris Darke
December 2006

I

To Serve the Cinema

He asks not to be expected to spend nine hours a day in a cinema where, outside,
the sun shines, the hills beckon, and the golden sands whisper alluringly. Hold the
festival in Calais or Lille or Lyons, or even in what is left of the Maginot Line.
Anonymous film critic reported in December 1946

It is tempting to imagine the first Cannes film festival as a Jacques Tati
film, or an early misadventure of the hapless Inspector Clouseau: a
catalogue of cock-ups culminating in unlikely success. Barely two
years after the Liberation, still reeling from the Occupation, racked by
shortages and internal political strife, France called on the 'seventh
art' to semaphore its national grandeur to the world, staging a glitter-
ing jamboree in celebration of the peace. In so doing, it set the template for future festivals, where opulence would strain (not always
successfully) to contain the combined forces of artistic dissent, diplomatic tussles and political wiles. Failure, as they say, was not an
option. 'The festival must be a victory for France,' declared an official
government communiqué of the time. But victory had to be snatched
from the jaws of defeat.

Technical mishaps provoked Great Power spats. Eleventh-hour crisis management narrowly averted meltdown. Even for a gathering of
film people there was more than the usual complement of hustlers and
chancers in attendance. Worse, the public were invited. (The official
post-mortem would fulminate against 'ill mannered and extraordinarily undisciplined' locals.) The great unwashed of Cannes not only had
the nerve to 'refuse to refrain from smoking' during screenings, they
freely nabbed the best seats. Worse still, it was discovered that organ-

ised scams were being operated to smuggle three or four people into the cinema on a single invitation (so loaning proceedings the flavour of an austerity-era crime caper – *To Catch a Thief* with rationing). Two days in, and under the headline 'HOLLYWOOD PLEASE NOTE', an English newspaper reassuringly reported jewels and money being stolen from hotel rooms, as well as the theft of thirty cars. A couple of days later, and all ticket reservations were cancelled, leaving uninvited *Cannois* to make their own entertainment.

Between 20 September and 5 October 1946, fifty-two features and seventy-five shorts were screened in the municipal casino, which had been hastily converted into a cinema seating eight hundred and fifty. Twenty-one nations participated, and the numbers attending were close to a thousand. Those nations selected their own films for competition (as would be standard until the 1970s), and the festival's distribution of prizes was kindly, each winning film being awarded a 'Grand Prix' of some description. The inauguration ceremony took place on 19 September in the gardens of the Grand Hotel. As fireworks illuminated the Mediterranean night sky, American opera singer Grace Moore gave a rendition of *La Marseillaise* before assembled delegates, diplomats and celebrities. The sole representative of the French government present (the absence of ministers had caused much press speculation) declared the opening of 'the first festival . . . of agriculture!' Which seems somehow apt – for 1946 wasn't really the first Cannes at all, but, rather, a resumption of proceedings after a rude interruption.

The Festival of the Free World

The project for Le Festival International du Film (or FIF, which was the official title up to 2002) dates back to the late 1930s when it was conceived as a counter-initiative to the Venice Film Festival, then under the aegis of Mussolini and fast becoming a prestige showcase for fascist propaganda. The Mostra Internazionale d'Arte Cinematografico began in 1932, making it the oldest European film festival, and was established within the Venice Biennale of Arts that had existed since 1885. The Treaty of Friendship signed between Italy and Germany in 1936, and the declaration of a 'Rome–Berlin Axis', increasingly estranged France from the two fascist powers. Meanwhile, the course of proceedings at the Venice Festival encouraged the French of the need to develop a cultural alternative of their own.

The construction in 1937 of a purpose-built Palazzo del Cinema on the Venice Lido was an art deco declaration of intent by the Italians. That same year, Jean Renoir's anti-war masterpiece *La Grande Illusion* won the Jury Prize at Venice, and went on to enjoy great commercial success. But the award displeased Hitler, and the film was banned in Germany and Italy (as it would be in France during the Occupation). The following year's Venice proved decisive. The jury wished to award an American film but pressure was brought to bear from Berlin, and the distribution of prizes was changed at the last minute. *Olympiad*, Leni Riefenstahl's documentary on the 1936 Berlin Olympmics, and Goffredo Alessandrini's *Lucciano Serra: Pilote*, shared the highest prize, the 'Mussolini Cup'. Both movies were fascist propaganda – and Riefenstahl's documentary was not even eligible for consideration, according to festival regulations that stipulated only fiction films could compete. Mussolini summarily dispensed with this impediment. This combination of blatant rigging and fascist cheerleading saw the American and British delegates resign before the prizes were even announced. Among the French contingent was a civil servant and historian named Philippe Erlanger, who returned to France convinced that a counter-festival – a festival of 'the free world' – was sorely needed. The idea began to circulate, and the official wording it found was unambiguous:

The major American, English and French film companies would be happy not to return to Venice where politics has clearly supplanted art. Need one add that recent racist measures have frightened away some of the leading figures in American cinema? If, therefore, the

Venice Festival should no longer have the same success and be replaced by a similar organisation in another country, it would be desirable that France be called on to take advantage of this.

While the notion found high-level political support, it required more than the tumult of international relations for its reason to exist. There was concern that Franco-Italian relations, already strained, could further suffer if Venice was challenged by the creation of another festival. Therefore, a sense of the potential benefits both for tourism and for the French film industry was brought, shrewdly, into play.

By October 1938, the proposal for the FIF was doing the rounds within political circles, and among possible locations mooted were Biarritz, Algiers, Vichy, Deauville, Aix-les-Bains and Le Touquet. The favourite, though, was the Mediterranean resort of Cannes, owing to powerful and insistent lobbying by local hoteliers. The head of the Grand Hotel in Cannes, Henri Gendre, was especially supportive, and had a political ally in Paris councillor Georges Prade, who promoted the idea to the minister of education in terms that were clear about its principal advantage: namely 'to significantly prolong the summer season'. (The scheduling of Venice between late August and early September had similar aims.) The intention was to put the *estival* in film festival. In retrospect, Prade's proposal reads less like overheated fantasising than prophecy, pure and simple:

> If the festival is a success, and how can it not be, it will become a fixture. Which is not to betray a secret but to reveal a beguiling plan. An ultramodern cinema will be built, a masterpiece of technology and a true French conservatory of film. And so the first step will be complete in a cycle that should make the Côte d'Azur into the centre of one of the most important industries of modern times. The Côte d'Azur must become the Florida and the California of Europe.

On 17 July 1939, it was officially announced that Le Festival International du Film would open in Cannes on 1 September. The definite

TO SERVE THE CINEMA

article spoke volumes, perhaps undercutting the official line that the festival had not been created 'to combat other such events that already exist, even less to copy them'. With the vital support of the US and Britain and with Louis Lumière, inventor of the *cinématographe*, named as honorary president, the project was under way. Invitations were issued (and duly declined by Axis powers), pre-festival events planned. MGM chartered a 'steamship of stars' to transport celebrity cargo to the Côte d'Azur, including the likes of Tyrone Power, Gary Cooper, Douglas Fairbanks, George Raft, Norma Shearer, and Mae West. The beach at Cannes was adorned with a pasteboard model of Notre-Dame Cathedral to promote William Dieterle's adaptation of the Victor Hugo classic *The Hunchback of Notre Dame*, starring Charles Laughton as Quasimodo. Fifty thousand posters were printed up – and yet Jean-Gabriel Domergue's design, depicting an impeccably elegant man and woman applauding, is full of retrospective portents and significant omissions. The salmon ruffs of the woman's dress resemble flames licking the sophisticated vignette. The couple are shown not facing a cinema screen but, rather, saluting a void. Indeed the 1939 festival was over as soon as it began. On 1 September Germany took Poland by blitzkrieg. Two days later England and France declared war.

Peacetime Remake

Conceived with a clear political and diplomatic agenda, aborted by war, Cannes' declared intention was, above all, 'to serve the cinema'. It would get its first proper chance to do so in 1946. Remarkably, the project remained on the table throughout the early pre-Occupation period of the *drôle de guerre* ('phoney war'). The combined vested interests of Cannes hoteliers and the French film industry buoyed Erlanger in keeping the idea alive, and the festival was rescheduled, first for Christmas 1939, then for the following February, and finally for Easter 1940. With the invasion of France in May 1940 and the subsequent occupation, the idea for a film festival was then enter-tained by Marshal Pétain's puppet administration in Vichy (under whose purview Cannes itself fell). The Vichy version was conceived for May 1942, not as a festival – 'the term being currently unsuitable' – but as an 'Exposition International du Film'. How truly 'internation-al' such an event might have been doesn't bear thinking about, and thankfully the idea never materialised.

Following the Liberation in 1944, the project for the festival was again picked up. At the April 1945 meeting of the organisation commit-tee (including Jean Painlevé, Georges Sadoul, Philippe Erlanger and Marcel L'Herbier, among others), September 1945 was proposed as a new start date. Additional mention was made of the fact that the princi-pality of Monaco had a project under way for a similar event. The festi-val was described as needing to be 'a grand demonstration of friendship between nations, and particularly between France and the United States who were at the project's origin . . .' These laudable sentiments, howev-er, ran up against certain logistical and material difficulties.

Principal among these was the fact that the hotels that would house the festival's guests were currently full. The American Army was lodg-ing at the Carlton, while the Grand entertained troops from the Afri-ka Korps on leave, and the Majestic was in use as a military hospital. It became clear that the earliest date at which the festival might be resumed was in 1946; and the old rival Venice was still deemed to be a 'dangerous competitor'. Thus it was decreed – start on 20 September 1946, run for fifteen days. In another vital decision, Erlanger proposed Robert Favre Le Bret as the Secretary General of the festival, and the appointment was unanimously approved. Favre Le Bret had worked as a journalist through the 1930s, and subsequently for the govern-ment. He would combine his Cannes duties with the directorship of the Paris Opera (just as the current Artistic Director of Cannes, Thierry Frémaux, also holds down the job of Director of the Institut Lumière in Lyon). And he was to remain head of the festival for twenty-five years, until 1971.

TO SERVE THE CINEMA

What then ensued was a certain amount of competitive jockeying for prime position in the summer season. Venice announced that its festival would take place from 31 August 1946. 'It appears', an official observed laconically, 'that the decision of the Italian government was taken after the announcement of the date for the Cannes Film Festival.' Erlanger was duly despatched to hammer out a deal, and it was proposed that in exchange for Venice pulling out of its 1946 slot the two festivals would, in future, run in alternate years. It was also made clear that, should Cannes find itself competing with Venice in 1946, then diplomatic representations would be made to competitor countries to favour the French festival over the Italian. Italy acquiesced. Cannes had the summer season to itself.

And yet, everything about the 1946 festival ran nail-bitingly close to the wire. It almost didn't happen, due to the refusal of the Ministry of Finance to release the necessary monies. Insistent lobbying by the film industry (plus the embarrassing fact that the government had already issued invitations) saved the day. Even then, funds were not released until the end of April. Erlanger and his team therefore had less than five months in which to organise an international film festival the like of which the world had not seen, one that would be to the glory of France. Erlanger's request to buy more time by setting back the date was rejected out of hand. By August only seven countries had responded to the invitation to compete at Cannes, and these did not include 'the principal countries' (for which, read the USA and UK). It was not until the beginning of September that responses began to arrive in earnest, a development met 'as much with terror as pride and joy' by those running the festival. As many as twenty-one nations did not declare their intention to compete until virtually the day before opening. Not surprisingly then, delegations turned up at Cannes in numbers three or four times larger than anticipated – 175 journalists were expected, 360 showed up. The hacks were well taken care of, though, the festival offering them half-price accommodation and twenty per cent off their restaurant bills. Close to a thousand

18

CANNES

people travelled to the festival, taxing the capacity of the two dedicated trains between Paris and Cannes. The problem thus revealed would be resolved to the festival's advantage through the institution of the famous *trains bleus* that would shuttle guests between the French capital and the Côte d'Azur throughout the 1950s, adding greatly to festival mythology.

Most problematically, though, for a festival devoted to projecting celluloid on to screens, very few of the competing countries observed the regulation stipulating that they submit prints of their films at least two weeks before opening. Compounding matters, a strike by customs officials backed up those prints that had just arrived. Checking print quality – always a key concern for projectionists – was made yet more difficult, and in some cases impossible, while some of those that were inspected were found to be in 'disastrous condition' (partly because in almost every country in the world the quality of celluloid, an oil-based medium, had declined greatly due to wartime restrictions). The projectionists had their work cut out, and any mistakes during screenings furnished grounds for diplomatic scandal. The festival team of projectionists had to be reinforced with extra hands recruited from among the municipal gardeners. One such later recalled how he projected two reels in the wrong order during a screening of the Soviet film *The Turning Point* by Fridrikh Ermler. Apologising to the Russian delegation, he proposed an extra screening. So appeased were they by his offer, they awarded him the Gold Medal for Services to Arts and Peace. But then, all those who received Russian hospitality that year were made to wear a red-flag insignia bearing the legend 'Art in the service of Peace'. Quite apart from the complimentary baubles, Soviet receptions proved popular for their unlimited supply of vodka and caviar. One American official was so overcome with the spirit of détente that he fell out of a first-floor window.

The festival spared itself further technical headaches by insisting that all films be shown in their original versions without subtitles. Dilys Powell of the *Sunday Times* found this 'on the whole a salutary

TO SERVE THE CINEMA

rule, forcing the spectator to judge each piece on its handling of pictorial narration and sound'. But the rule proved flexible in the case of some less common languages, including Russian. At screenings of Soviet films attended by Powell, she found it not uncommon for 'an invisible translator to industriously interject bits of French into the silent spaces of the soundtrack'. She also noted how the Cannes audience 'may applaud a single sequence or a single shot'. An early mark of connoisseurial appreciation perhaps, though in years to come the notoriously passionate Cannes crowds would add bravura displays of hostility to their repertoire of responses.

Of course, the festival was not just about watching films. Special events, gala evenings and excursions were laid on for guests. A British correspondent found herself among three hundred dignitaries and delegates invited to the Victorine Studios in Nice where the first French colour film was being shot. In her account of the lunch that followed, she gives an insight into the festival's already eye-watering extravagance. Horded en masse into the Palais de la Méditerranée – 'surely a set from the Babylonian sequence in D.W. Griffith's *Intolerance*' – she helpfully totted up the bill: 'Lunch cost the French Government £2.8s a head. Aperitifs cost £27. Champagne for the company £72; coffee £18; liqueurs £36; the flower bill was £30. Add transport and drinks served at the studio and the total for the day was £1000.' In today's money, that would be something like £27,600. Laconically the British correspondent noted that 'the evening papers told of the reopening of the Paris schools for the autumn term. Nearly two-thirds of the children are reported suffering from malnutrition . . .'

Behind the bonhomie of the VIPs, there were, of course, the stirrings of a Cold War, evidenced by certain Soviet–American wrangles that set another precedent for future festivals. The opening night screening of *Berlin*, a Soviet war documentary by Yuli Raizman, was plagued by technical problems and interrupted several times, leading the delegation to cry sabotage and threaten to withdraw from the festival. When reel projection order went awry during Alfred Hitchcock's *Notorious*,

American representatives threatened to go home. Tender ministrations from the organisers enabled sense to prevail. The ideologically charged banter between the great powers is nevertheless revealing. Director Mikhail Kalatozov, a luminary of the Soviet delegation, demanded of the French: 'Why do you open wide your gates to American films and so risk the demoralisation of your national production?' The American representative retorted that when Kalatozov had recently visited America he had been heard to declare that 'after the Russian films, the only films that count are American'. Still, the Soviet accusation touched a raw French nerve.

When she was not busy calculating the cost of lunch, our British correspondent was keenly noting the political machinations barely concealed by lavish hospitality and the somewhat strained *entente*. Observing that *Notorious* was the only new film Hollywood had in competition, she was approached by a journalist from the *New York Herald Tribune* who asked why there was no formal American delegation when almost every other country had sent one.

> I gave it as my opinion that Hollywood did not want these festivals; did not want anything which promoted the growth of any film movement in any country but its own. That, by definition, it regarded 'a film' as a motion picture made in the US. United Artists and Universal had no entries. RKO Pictures had two films screened at Cannes, *Make Mine Music* and *Wonderman*. I asked the view of Harold Smith, European representative of the Johnston (ex-Hays Censors) Office. He denied that there was any attempt by Hollywood to boycott the festival. 'It is only a few months since Hollywood was able to re-establish its offices in France.' Informed journalists were quick to point out that Hollywood's participation in the festival was out of all proportion to its predominating position in the film world; that not one American star was present, except Maria Montez, as the wife of a French star; and that other nations had no more time to prepare.

The fact was that Hollywood had its eyes on a prize bigger than anything Cannes could offer. Until as recently as mid-August, the French government had been hammering out the terms of a deal with the Americans that would provide post-war economic assistance to France. One of the most tortuous and controversial details in the negotiations was the American demand that France increase the level of quotas for the distribution of Hollywood films. During the Occupation American films had been banned, so there was four years' worth of backed-up Hollywood product capable of turning a profit on French screens. The Americans had made it clear that without an agreement on screen quotas the package of financial agreements would be held up. In mid-August, terms were finally agreed in the Blum–Byrnes Accord that set the quota reserved for the exhibition of French films as 'no more than four weeks per quarter'.

Consequently America was accused of 'dumping', and the terms caused such an outcry that they had to be renegotiated two years later. Then-ambassador and several times president of France, the socialist Léon Blum had stated, 'If I had to sacrifice the interests of the film corporations for the general good I would not hesitate to do so.' But during negotiations, the Americans held off declaring whether they would participate in Cannes until a little over a week before the agreement was secured. Interestingly, the official report on the first Cannes festival makes no mention of this when describing how late many countries left their announcements that they would participate.

Hard realities of trade and politics aside, the spectacle of Hollywood films at Cannes provoked wonder tempered by frustration: wonder at their technical perfection and frustration over the infantile avoidance of anything that spoke directly to the European experience of life during wartime. Writing in *Le Monde*, Henry Magnan singled out for praise the 'perfection' of the *mise en scène* in George Cukor's *Gaslight*, the audacity of Rudolph Maté's cinematography for *Gilda* and, in *Notorious*, Hitchcock's confirmation as 'one of the most virtuoso of Hollywood artisans'. The great critic André Bazin also enthused over 'the formidable machinery of Hollywood which seems at last to have attained the degree of perfection whereby the artist is liberated from technology'. But both commentators bitterly lamented that such sophistication served only to represent a world in which, as Magnan put it, 'nothing should be taken seriously enough to trouble the spectator's confidence'. While both scribes made a qualified exception for Billy Wilder's *The Lost Weekend*, Bazin observed of the American films that they seemed 'suspended in a stratosphere where the problems of individual or collective life, of politics or morality, are no longer addressed but as imaginary, like death in a detective novel'. He added that those privileged enough to attend the festival would have seen fewer good films than a discerning viewer was able to see in Paris over the last six months – such as *Citizen Kane*, *The Little Foxes* and *How Green Was My Valley*.

The revelation at Cannes of the state of American cinema would continue throughout France as the country saw the films it had been denied during the Occupation. Despite the political ructions caused by the Blum–Byrnes Accord, this exposure to American cinema would have colossal impact upon younger film fans, in particular for the *nouvelle vague* directors-to-be who would write for magazines like *Cahiers du cinéma* (co-founded by Bazin) and *Positif* in the 1950s. There, they would elevate Hitchcock from 'talented artisan' to 'genius *auteur*'. They would develop an approach to film criticism that was, by and large, uninterested in the perceived worth or otherwise of a film's subject matter, and concentrate primarily on a film-maker's skill with cinematic language. They would refuse the 'form versus content' debate central to all criticism and look to style as everything. And later still they would transform cinema in France and around the world in a succession of New Waves throughout the 1960s and 1970s. Hollywood was their motherlode, Bazin one of their mentors.

Another was Roberto Rossellini, whose *Rome, Open City* won Cannes' Grand Prize for Italy in 1946, so easing international acceptance

TO SERVE THE CINEMA

of the rough-hewn documentary immediacy of Italian neo-realism. Bazin observed that Rossellini's was but one of a number of films, including René Clément's *La Bataille du Rail*, that addressed a theme common to many of the European entries from countries that had suffered occupation – namely, the 'common mythology' of resistance. As for Cannes' part in the less exalted business of cinema, one American festivalgoer recalls, 'Rossellini had sold the American rights to the film a few hours before it was screened, for several hundred dollars.' Rossellini, though, was by all accounts stoic in the wake of his varying achievements. 'At noon I was a bum', he is said to have mused, 'and by two I was an international artist . . .'

The lesson most clearly drawn from the festival of 1946, reiterated the following year, was the need for Cannes to construct a purpose-built cinema. Technical hitches were simply too numerous and made screenings into sites of needless confrontation. Even if Cannes no longer looked to replace Venice it still needed to be taken seriously as a rival – and for that, it needed a Palais. There were obstacles to realising the project, however. The French had made a deal with Venice to take turns in alternate years, and construction of a new Palais no longer seemed so urgent given the time-lag. Furthermore, parliament refused funding for the festival. François Mitterrand, then acting Minister at the Department of Arts and Letters, stated that such a festival could not be an annual event. Indeed there was little continuity in the early years, with no Cannes in either 1948 or 1950. In 1949, however-er, the festival finally inaugurated its new showcase cinema. Despite official obstruction, the communist mayor of Cannes had decided to push ahead with the project of building a new Palais. Local militants from the main French union worked on the construction for free and construction went on right up to the wire of opening at 9.30 p.m. on Friday 12 September 1949. The trade paper *Le Film Français* reported that 'a few hours before the opening we were still walking through debris and gravel. But at the allotted hour, after days and nights when the construction teams had only taken a few hours' sleep (during ninety days of work), the cinema was officially opened.' The structure was imperfect, with only 1000 seats as opposed to the intended 1800, and on the closing night a strong wind carried the roof away. Thus the prize-giving ceremony had to happen at the municipal casino. Nevertheless, with the inauguration of the Palais – which would remain the much-loved epicentre of the festival until replaced in 1983 by a new behemoth of a *blockhaus* immediately dubbed *le bunker* – Cannes declared that it was here to stay.

II

Avoiding Offence

'The French are too damned independent!' The French *are* independent. They are proud. They are individualists. So are we. That's one reason there is friction between us.

From '112 Gripes About the French', published by the Information
and Education Division of Occupying US Forces in
Paris, 1945

One might say that the two great antagonists of the Cold War each knew where they stood in respect of cinema. 'For us', Lenin legendarily declared, 'cinema is the most important of all the arts.' The United States, too, was well aware what was at stake when it came to the medium's tremendous power. 'Trade follows film', asserted Will Hays, Republican, namesake of the infamous Hays Code, and first president of the Motion Pictures and Producers Association of America (MPAA). It was inevitable that communists and capitalists would find in cinema one more terrain on which to trumpet their respective achievements and declare the absolute superiority of their favoured ideology. Cannes became another conspicuous battleground upon which this competition played itself out, and it would derive a portion of its identity from the same.

The laborious birth of Cannes had occurred in the early stages of Cold War hostility in Europe, its first edition unveiling only six months after Churchill's declaration in March 1946 that 'an iron curtain has descended across the continent'. The festival aspired to make of itself the film world's pre-eminent 'trade fair', one from which Hollywood could not afford to be absent. Cannes was also conceived as a forum of

French cinematic prestige, and while it was cinematic achievement that was ostensibly being celebrated, the glory sought was also national. Such nationalism was characteristic of the 1940s and 1950s, and made for all manner of political and diplomatic pressures.

Under de Gaulle's Fourth Republic, established in 1947, France was part of the Western alliance and a de facto ally of America, with whom she had signed significant economic agreements. Principal among these, as we have seen, was the Blum–Byrnes Accord, which settled French war debt as well as opening up French markets to US films. In such a context, talk of American 'cultural imperialism' was not without justification. Indeed, cinema has since remained a principal focus of the enduring 'battle' between the two countries – between commerce and culture, between the French 'cultural exception' (in which cultural products are exempt from international trade agreements) and the American anti-quota, anti-tariff 'free-market' dogma. But with France economically dependent on America, US influence would extend to the Cannes Festival.

What has been described as 'an incessant diplomatic ballet' between the French organisers and the representatives of the White House was a feature of the festival's early years. The emphasis was politico-diplomatic first, cultural second. In the decisions over which countries were invited to participate and those deemed *persona non grata*, the role of the French Minister of Foreign Affairs was central, and the United States was assiduously courted. After all, this was the world's dominant film producer, whose participation was not only crucial to the festival actually taking place but was, moreover, highly favoured by rules that based volume of film selection upon the quantity of a nation's annual output: the more films you made, the more you could show at Cannes. A US pledge to show up did not come without conditions, however. America did all it could to bolster its presence at the festival, threatening boycotts when the mood took it and imposing conditions on selection criteria, as well as capitalising on the commercial presence of its films in Europe. Much to the chagrin of the locals, it also would occasionally moor battleships of the Sixth Fleet off the Riviera coast during the festival.

Given Cannes' uncomfortable intimacy with Hollywood, and its explicitly pro-Western identification as 'the festival of the free world', there were bound to be problems with the Soviet Union. Nevertheless, in a display of international unity crucial for the success of the inaugural Cannes, the USSR presented six feature films and four shorts; and the Eastern bloc states of Romania, Poland and Czechoslovakia were also present. The Soviets also knew how to throw a lively party, somewhat to the irritation of American representatives. However, while the festival struggled to establish continuity in its early years, the USSR was only intermittently represented there. With international relations extremely chilly come the second Cannes in 1947, Hungary was alone of the Eastern bloc countries to be present. Precisely none were on display at the next edition in 1949, the USSR having taken umbrage at the festival rules and chosen to compete at Venice instead. The Soviet complaint here was not without basis: they declined the invitation to present a single film (as against twelve American films) by arguing that a more equitable set of regulations would allow for a more representative international selection, and suggested that each competing nation should be represented by the same number of films.

The festivals of 1951 and 1958 proved particularly significant for the Soviets – 1951, indeed, marked something of a new start for Cannes. For the first time it took place in April, was happily ensconced in a new Palais with a showcase cinema, and could boast for the first time the participation of Japan, while also welcoming the return of the Soviet Union to the fray. However, the banner of art was not able to conceal or ward off ideological confrontations and diplomatic imbroglios. The collected titles of the short films presented by the Russians offered a pulse-slowing shorthand for their particular dignities and self-image: *Soviet Azerbaijan, Soviet Estonia, Soviet Lithuania*, and – touchingly – *Ukraine in Bloom*. A further factor made the 1951 festival decidedly different from the previous three: since the recent absence of Eastern bloc countries had hurt Cannes' claim to be truly international, so rules were changed enabling the countries with the largest film production to present three films, while others were entitled to one. In the backdrop of this decision – a not uncalculated blow to US expansionism – were deteriorating relations between the French and Americans since the immediate post-war period, owing to America's differences with France over their colonial adventure in Indo-China. With American privilege partly receded, the Eastern bloc considered participation at Cannes to be permissible once more. But if it began in a spirit of compromise, this festival was quickly mired in stand-offs and touchy displays of political sensitivity.

As festival historian Loredana Latil describes, quoting from a diplomatic report of the time, 'a few days before the opening of the festival of 1951, the secretariat of the Festival International du Film had to choose the opening film. Copies of only two films had arrived, one from America, the other from Switzerland. Diplomatically, it opted to give "preference to the Swiss film in order not to appear to favour one of the great powers".'

The Swiss film in question was Leopold Lindtberg's *Four in a Jeep*, a story of four Military Policemen, each a representative of the occupying powers in Vienna. The selection committee's assessment of the film was ambiguous, to say the least. The Russian characters were presented in a 'less than flattering light, being referred to as "Bloody Russians"', an American Military Policeman was depicted as disobeying his superiors for the love of a woman, a French gendarme and his wife were portrayed as 'perfectly ridiculous if full of good intentions'. While such character traits and flaws could be considered needful to an involving drama, from the vantage of Cannes in 1951 they offered something to offend everybody equally. To skirt any such problems, the festival authorities drafted in a last-minute replacement, George Stevens's *A Place in the Sun* starring Elizabeth Taylor and Montgomery Clift. At a press conference, Lindtberg explained that a preview of his film had upset the Soviets, who argued that 'the Soviet soldier (in the film) was presented as a morally inferior character compared to the allied soldiers' . . .

This was by no means an end to hurt feelings. On 17 April the French Ministry of Foreign Affairs demanded that Cannes should not present *Liberated China*, a Soviet documentary by Sergei Guerasimov, about a country with whom France was then engaged in combat in Korea. The Soviet delegation offered considerately to amend the title to 'New China' . . . but this was not deemed adequate, and the film was withdrawn from the official selection, receiving only press screenings. Filing for *Sight and Sound*, the British writer Gavin Lambert noted that: 'Art and Mammon are usually fighting for first place at film festivals, but at Cannes this year – with the Russians participating for the first time – each had a rival in politics.' The Soviet entries he considered 'austerity products not art, not commerce, but propaganda'. But his wider conclusions regarding the state of cinema were no more positive:

> Nobody at Cannes commented on the irony of the fact that the chief awards of a luxurious festival went to the humanely pessimistic De Sica [*Miracle in Milan*], to the savage Buñuel [*Los Olvidados*], and to a Swedish adaptation of Strindberg's cruel and bitter *Miss Julie* [directed by Alf Sjoberg] . . . The Soviet delegation's dismissal of the entire function as an outbreak of western decadence has its point – though it was made the wrong way. But then, [the Russian entries] offer for many an even more depressing alternative, and the same is true of the incongruous materialist optimism of *The Next Voice You Hear*, America's religious fable about a small-town family that hears, and is comforted by, the voice of God. As an art, the cinema is on its way to becoming the most powerful medium of disillusion in the present age; as an industry, of course, it continues to serve as an opiate for millions.

As the 1950s progressed, the presence of the Soviet Union and its satellites at the festival was initially sporadic. Refusing to participate in

1952 and 1953, they nevertheless settled down to regular appearances from 1954. Moreover, their films started to win significant prizes – in 1955, Sergei Vassiliev's *Heroes of Chipka*; in 1956, Sergei Yutkevich's *Othello*; in 1957 Grigori Chukhrai's *The Forty-First*. The wider political context was that of a perceived 'thaw' in Cold War relations, following the death of Stalin in March of 1953. The conditions of the 'thaw' were most evident in details leaked to the international press of the seminal 'secret speech' given to the twentieth Communist Party Congress in 1956 by new premier Nikita Khrushchev, in which he did the unthinkable and condemned Stalin's legacy and 'the cult of personality' that had attended the old tyrant. The effect was so electrifying that by legend some die-hard apparatchiks are said to have keeled over from heart attacks, while others went home to put bullets in their brains. Khrushchev also rejected the Leninist idea of the inevitability of war with the West and called for a doctrine of 'peaceful coexistence' between capitalist and communist countries.

Cultural intercourse was central to this new relationship. The most illustrious example of Soviet film-making during the 'thaw' was Mikhail Kalatozov's *The Cranes Are Flying*, screened at Cannes in 1958. After twenty years of state-decreed socialist realism, Kalatozov's tale of a love affair between a young couple, Boris (Alexei Batalov) and Veronika (Tatyana Samojlova) during the Second World War, caused a sensation and became the only Soviet film ever to win the Palme d'Or. In its technical virtuosity and extravagant formal experimentation, the film was seen as revitalising the magnificence of Soviet cinema of the 1920s. David Robinson of *Sight and Sound* was among those to admire the film's bold undercutting of the clichés of Soviet patriotism, its readiness 'to show, for example, that there were whores and racketeers and evaders of military service in Russia during the war, alongside the heroes'. Nor did Robinson fail to note the presence at the festival of 'exotic, withdrawn beauty' Tatyana Samojlova, the improbable belle of that year's starlet contingent, this in spite of competition from the seasoned likes of Gina Lollobrigida and Jayne

AVOIDING OFFENCE   31

Mansfield. The beauty-pageant element of Cannes – another international battleground of sorts – is one to which we will return.

The Insider

Inseparable from the nascent eminence of Cannes was the illustrious figure of avant-garde Jacques-of-all-trades Jean Cocteau (1889–1963). Poet, painter, playwright and film-maker, Cocteau also bequeathed us some fascinating insights into the festival's formative years: three times president of the jury – in 1953, 1954 and as honorary president in 1957 – his diaries and letters supply revealing commentaries. The twelve members of the 1953 jury, nine of whom were French, included the pioneering French director Abel Gance; the very founder of the festival, Philippe Erlanger; and American actor Edward G. Robinson, making a second visit to the festival. The star of *Little Caesar*, a keen private collector of fine art, endeared himself to Cocteau by admitting to a certain discomfort in his latest role, telling him, 'I've always played thieves and criminals and now I'm a judge . . .'

The difficulty of adjudicating upon the creative endeavour of others is a recurring refrain in Cocteau's commentaries – 'No question about it, I belong on the side of the accused, not of the judges,' he confided to his diary – and the inherent complications of the activity were made more difficult by the political tenor of the times. Twenty years after Cocteau's death, Robert Favre Le Bret, then administrator-general, described the poet's presidency in glowing terms: 'He had a kind word for everyone, after each screening he would compliment the delegation of the relevant country so much that each would tell themselves, "We're going to get the Grand Prix." He was well above the backroom quibbling and rumour-mongering that one sometimes sees at Cannes. He rose above everything with the lordly elegance that was his prerogative.' The impression of imperturbable style and good humour was doubtless the public face that Cocteau wished to give his presidency. But his diaries and letters attest to the day-to-day travails of the festival, as well as to

CANNES

the more serious problems arising from political interference.

Among the thirty-five films in competition that year were works by some of the world's leading film-makers, including John Ford's *The Sun Shines Bright*, Alfred Hitchcock's *I Confess*, Vittorio de Sica's *Stazione Termini*, Luis Buñuel's *El*, Walt Disney's *Peter Pan*, and Jacques Tati's *Les Vacances de M. Hulot*, as well as films from Sweden, Spain, Great Britain, Japan, Mexico and Brazil. One of the most controversial proved to be the French competition entry *La Vie Passionnée de Clemenceau* by Gilbert Prouteau, a documentary portrait of the right-wing nationalist Georges Clemenceau (1841–1929). Twice prime minister of France, Clemenceau represented France's victory in the First World War and asserted that Germany had been too leniently treated by the terms of the Versailles peace. Following complaints by the German delegation that the film was gravely offensive to their country and ought to be withdrawn from the festival, it was finally screened with certain strategic re-cuts, the inflammatory anti-German term '*boches*' replaced by 'these gentlemen', 'German barbarism' by '*Kulturkampf*'. Cocteau told his diary on 12 April that the picture was altogether lamentable: 'Incredible nerve of the government, which imposes on us, for an international festival, a film speaking only of "*boches*" and "the German hordes". I asked Erlanger to find out who wanted to have this film shown and why we were compelled to take these extra-cinematic detours.' The next day, Cocteau wrote: 'Answer given to Erlanger . . . "The ministers." "And why was that?" "It's none of your business to psychoanalyse our feelings."'

American sensitivities also manifested themselves both within the jury and beyond, eminently in the case of Henri-Georges Clouzot's competition film *Le Salaire de la peur* (*The Wages of Fear*). An extremely tense and fatalistic thriller set in Venezuela, it follows the exploits of an international group of roughnecks (Yves Montand, Charles Vanel, Peter Van Eyck and Antonio Centa) hired by an American oil company for the suicidal job of transporting highly sensitive explosives to extinguish a fire at an oil well. Several times in his diary entries Cocteau declares himself a supporter of the film, describing it as 'a thousand miles above all the others in the race'. He also admits, 'I had agreed to the presidency in order to obtain prizes for Clouzot (and Vanel). Otherwise he would never have had it. Any other president would have been scared of the Americans.' But Cocteau became conscious of the jury's own initial resistance to his enthusiasm. 'They will take the opposite tack', he feared, 'systematically.'

Cocteau likely weakened his position by making his regard for Clouzot public knowledge, as he readily admits in a pre-festival diary entry: 'A newspaper has repeated that I found Clouzot's film splendid. Whence the ill humour of the Americans, who claimed we had made up our minds in advance. Favre Le Bret has had to go to Hollywood to persuade them to take part in the festival.' At least the film's screening on the opening night had the desired effect on the jury, one Cocteau described as 'like a battering ram which knocks down the wall and opens a breach'. But the following day Cocteau reports: 'An American trick: *The Herald Tribune* publishes an article accusing *The Wages of Fear* of being a communist film and insulting to America. This was neither the American delegation's attitude nor Edward G. Robinson's. I can see Robinson is afraid of something – which is natural. Myself, I shall never admit that extra-cinematic considerations can influence our votes.'

Le Monde reported that the American delegation was vexed by the film's depiction of the oil business as gangster capitalism, 'seeing in the character of the Yankee oil company proprietor a caricature of the American businessman that Communists would be pleased with'. On 18 April Clouzot had lunch with the American delegation, at which, Cocteau surmised in his diary, the reasons for the *Tribune* article became clear; they were a combination of linguistic misunderstanding and political prejudice. At one point in the film, a character named O'Brien says '*Merde à vous*', a line to which the Americans had taken exception. 'They thought O'Brien's "shit to you" was an insult not knowing it was our French formula for good luck,' Cocteau commented, also observing, 'Actually it's the choice of Yves Montand which makes the film suspect in their eyes.' Montand and his wife, Simone Signoret, were well-known as active leftists. The *Hollywood Reporter*, describing the film as anti-American, dubbed Montand a 'communist actor'. But ultimately Clouzot's film prevailed just as Cocteau had wished.

Edward G. Robinson was ultimately supportive of Clouzot but less favourably disposed towards the Spanish title *Bienvenido, Monsieur Marshall* directed by Luis García Berlanga, a comedy set in a Castilian village whose inhabitants enthusiastically await the arrival of the Americans with Marshall Plan aid. However, the Americans don't stop at the village and the villagers express their anger by dragging the Stars and Stripes through the mud. Cocteau described the film's festival projection as 'charming. Each time America is made fun of, the audience applauds . . .' There is no mention in his diaries of Robinson's threat to resign from the jury if the film, which he accused of ridiculing America, was not withdrawn from the selection. It was decided that the film's last shot, the sullying of Old Glory, be cut so as to placate American sensitivities. The film remained in the selection, even winning the oddly named 'Prix international du film de la Bonne Humeur' (presumably a Cocteauesque designation for 'Comedy Film'), which only goes to show that one nation's ridicule is another's good humour. But there was no laughter among French communist film-makers and technicians who saw the re-editing as censorship in the guise of diplomacy, and organised protests around the Palais which lasted until the end of the festival. Tracts were distributed denouncing Robinson as 'an informer for HUAC' – this, the mark of another rumbling and rebarbative political controversy, to which we shall turn shortly.

All Must Have Prizes

Several times during the 1953 festival Cocteau expressed bemusement over the business of prize-giving in tones that ranged from the sarcastic to the despairing. During the preparatory run-up to opening night he wrote, 'If I were the only judge I would give the prize for best actor

AVOIDING OFFENCE

to Walt Disney for Captain Hook . . .' By 14 April he was suggesting 'an ideal prize, taking into account everything I've heard everybody else say. I'll ask for a discussion on this basis. Erlanger suggests a Cocteau Prize, to be given to America, which has come off rather badly.' No further mention is made of the 'Prix Cocteau', but the categories of awards that eventually materialised were a combination of the pragmatic and the suitably idiosyncratic. Alongside categories for 'Adventure', 'Good Humour', 'Entertainment' and 'Drama' were 'Best Legendary Film', 'Best Exploratory Film' and 'Film Best Narrated by Images'. On the penultimate day of the festival Cocteau unburdened himself of his overall opinion of the proceedings, bemoaning in his diary that 'the exhaustion of a festival necessarily leads to an atmosphere of embarrassment and uneasiness and bad humour. I deplore it. I wish festivals didn't hand out prizes and were just a place for exchange and encounter. To preside over the Cannes jury is an experience I won't repeat.' But, of course, he returned the following year, and again in 1957. Cocteau's presence was clearly important in the fledgeling years of Cannes, lending a patina of artistic credibility to the 'free-for-all', as he described it in letters to his lover, the actor Jean Marais. In 1955, Cocteau would be associated with the creation of the award now as integral to the aura of Cannes as those red-carpeted steps up to the Palais des Festivals – the Palme d'Or.

On the occasion of the festival's fiftieth anniversary in 1997, Cannes was witness to one of the most prestigious photo-calls in the history of cinema, as every past winner of the Golden Palm (or, in the case of the deceased or indisposed, their representatives) lined up for the cameras. In celebrating its own history, Cannes was also paying tribute to cinema itself, for which other festival could gather such luminaries? Reviewing the photographs, one can spot a greying Francis Ford Coppola at the far end of the front row, Tim Burton in shades and rat's nest hairdo lurking in the back, and Emir Kusturica (one of only five double-winners) towering over his neighbour, the diminutive Mike Leigh, who does a passable impersonation of the British cat who got the French cream. And at front-and-centre of the gathering – one arm linked with that of a tanned, semi-paralysed Michelangelo Antonioni, another round the lithe shoulder of a beaming Gong Li – is another master showboat, the man the French call 'Chameleon Bonaparte': Jacques Chirac, president of the Republic. Later, with thirty of the honorees fanned out across the stage of the Palais like a row of dignified penguins, Jeanne Moreau presented the 'Palme of Palmes' to Ingmar Bergman (accepted, in the great Swede's absence, by his daughter Linn Ullmann). The spectacle begged the question: what is the collective noun for a gathering of Palme d'Or winners? A 'palais', perhaps? Another answer might be found in what they stood and absorbed for several minutes: an ovation.

While those present (excepting, of course, Chirac) could be said to represent the crème de la crème of fifty years of world cinema – the filmic canon incarnated in a once-in-a-lifetime team photo – not all of them, strictly, had won the Palme d'Or, for the simple reason that the prize existed in name only as of 1975. The idea for the creation of an award by which Cannes could differentiate itself from other festivals and promote itself internationally first arose in 1955. Hollywood had its Oscar, Berlin its Golden Lion, and, from 1947, the Venice Festival began to award a 'Grand Prix International' to replace the 'Mussolini Cup' of the pre-war years. At Cannes it was the somewhat uniform designation of the 'Grand Prix' that was offered to the top film, for which the winners were presented with sculptures or canvases by artists such as Chagall and Utrillo, trophies later replaced by simple diplomas. In 1952, the American authorities suggested to the French Minister of Foreign Affairs that the festival distribute 'Gold and Silver Laurel Awards' but Favre Le Bret would have none of it. In response, the festival in 1955 decided to award a prize for the official competition, resembling the coat of arms of the city of Cannes. Several local jewellers were requested to submit designs, and the winning entry took the form of a jewel in the shape of a palm. The shape evolved over the years, from a jewel in gold plate accompanied by a diploma, to the elegant, solid gold frond that we know today. However, between 1964 and 1974 the denomination 'Palme d'Or' was not used. In 1962, Favre Le Bret had formed the view that it was simply too tacky: 'awards with the word "gold" in them are automatically tarnished', he decided. Hence the 'Grand Prix', represented by a golden palm. It has been suggested that Jean Cocteau was involved in the creation of the prize (the jewel being placed on a pedestal designed by Cocteau). But Cocteau's contribution was a myth, albeit of a strategic kind, combining his artistic style with his involvement in the festival – and the rumour of his involvement did no harm to the prize's artistic value. In the intervening years, the Palme d'Or would become the festival's logo, a globally recognised guarantee of cinematic quality.

Reverse Angle

While Cocteau bequeathed an insider's take on the machinations of the 1953 festival, the celebrated critic André Bazin delivered a different sort of assessment from the outside, one that prefigures decades of jaundice and general disappointment among those accredited press who come to Cannes to write about the films they have just seen. 'One of the most boring festivals we've known,' Bazin remarked acidly of 1953 in *Cahiers du cinéma*. 'Day after day we awaited the promised revelations. Night after night we went to bed more or less disappointed.' The relatively low quality of the films selected was probably an inescapable consequence of the overall mediocrity of the year's cinematic output. Bazin, though, had bones to pick with the selection committee, and argued that the choosing should in fact be done by 'a small number of people with an indisputable knowledge of the history and art of film'. Of the composition of this imagined elite he argued that 'it shouldn't be necessary to be over thirty years old in order to participate'. In arguing for his panel of philosopher-kings Bazin was, surely, gesturing toward the critical upstarts then cutting their teeth on *Cahiers*.

Bazin was not happy that press conferences were dominated by stars rather than directors: 'At the end of the day the opinion of William Wyler about his work has more importance than that of Leslie Caron . . . a few words from De Sica in the hubbub of a cocktail reception can hardly be taken for a substantial declaration. The Cannes Festival will not survive for very long, despite the multiplication of stars, with a lack of grey matter.' Along with this cerebral deficit, Bazin identified 'a rather puerile' emphasis on 'worldly elegance' in the compulsory wearing of evening dress. If there is something a shade puritanical in the critic's abhorrence of dressing up, he offered a more salient point in the form of metaphor, arguing that the selection films themselves had been made to 'don the correct outfit: red ties were forbidden and refined language was *de rigueur*'. Bazin read the true character of Cannes as 'the festival of diplomatic censorship', with reference to what he called 'without doubt the best of the French documentaries, unanimously selected, and of which so many cuts were demanded that [director] Alain Resnais preferred to withdraw it'.

Bazin doesn't name the picture in question. Most likely it was Resnais's 1953 film *Les Statues Meurent Aussi* ('Even Statues Die'). Made in collaboration with Chris Marker, this black and white essay-film, less than half an hour long, begins as a documentary on African art but builds into an impassioned plea against colonialism. (It also featured footage of the then-*député* François Mitterrand, which might in part have explained the demand for cuts.) Despite winning the Prix Jean Vigo in 1954, the film was nevertheless banned in France for over ten years. Resnais would suffer this sort of fate at Cannes on a number of occasions in close succession, most notoriously with the withdrawal from the 1956 festival of his seminal work about the Nazi death camps *Nuit et brouillard* ('Night and Fog'). But in 1953 Bazin laid the blame for Resnais's travails firmly at the feet of a piece of 'diplomatic levelling' commonly referred to as Article Five.

If one looks hard enough during the opening credits of a French film, one will see the words *Visa d'Exploitation* ('Exhibition Visa'),

AVOIDING OFFENCE

followed by a number. But if that film was made by Jean-Luc Godard, one often sees the same simple piece of state bureaucracy given the prominence normally accorded to the name of the star. Upfront and in large type, it then assumes the status of a declaration: 'The French state has allowed this film to be screened'. The 'exhibition visa' protocol derives from the practice of film censorship in France, which became institutionalised from 1919 and was extended after 1937 to include all imported films. From 1939, films intended for export also fell under its remit. A decree passed by the Popular Front government stated that French films should not 'be likely to wound the national sentiments of foreign peoples and hence provoke diplomatic incidents'. Perhaps necessarily, and rather unhappily, this decree was incorporated into the regulations of Cannes, and extended to include all participating countries. Such a regulation appeared needful so that the festival could take place without ruffling diplomatic feathers at a time of acute international tension. However, 'Article Five' would provoke numerous problems between competing nations throughout the 1950s. The regulation permitted a film to be withdrawn from the festival if it was deemed to be 'by nature insulting to the national feeling' of a particular country. Since the nations themselves selected their representative films, such diplomatic incidents were a source of intolerable bad feeling. Mercifully, the regulation was annulled in 1957.

It should be said that André Bazin did not merely carp from the corner about the failings of Cannes as he saw them: he also rolled up his sleeves and endeavoured to show how he would do better, organising a festival that was explicitly conceived as an 'anti-Cannes' endeavour. As well as writing and lecturing widely on cinema, Bazin was involved in one of the most successful of the post-war Parisian ciné-clubs. Established in 1948, Objectif 48 showed only current films and was able to attract large audiences, present premieres and invite directors such as Welles, Bresson and Rossellini to discuss their work. In 1948, the club had a tremendous success with its 'Festival of American Film Noir' and the logical extension of this triumph was for Objectif 48 to

40   CANNES

organise its own festival. The following year, the group (having shrewdly changed its name to Objectif 49) brought off the first edition of an independent *Festival du Film Maudit* ('Festival of Accursed Films'). It aimed to celebrate the 'accursed works' that the industry had consigned to oblivion: films by Visconti, Michelangelo Antonioni's first works and Norman McLaren's experimental animations, the first time these were screened in Europe. In the post-war years, festivals had begun to proliferate: Brussels, Marianské-Laskné in Czechoslovakia (later to be named Marienbad), Knokke-le-Zout in Belgium. Yet more sprung up throughout the 1950s – Lisbon, Buenos Aires, San Sebastián, Durban, Cork, Manila . . . Bazin was not about to be left in the dust, and the Festival du Film Maudit, as was the fashion, chose an upmarket resort as its location, in this case Biarritz. The festival was presided over officially by Jean Cocteau, and Orson Welles's name adorned the Committee of Honour that also boasted the mayor of Biarritz and one Marquis d'Arcangues. It was here that many of the young critics and *cinéphiles* of what was to become the *nouvelle vague* gathered, as Bazin's biographer recounts:

> A doorman politely checked all guests and detained or turned away those who didn't belong or were improperly attired. Some of the people who clearly didn't belong were Rivette, Godard and Truffaut. All under 20, 'bohemian' and vociferous, they started a scene with the doorman until the timely arrival of Cocteau, dressed in tails. He shepherded his young friends in with a wave of his hand and, as president of the festival, succeeded in holding together, or at least at a safe distance, the aristocracy on one hand and the young Turks on the other.

If for Bazin Cannes was something of a tuxedo-wearing trade-fair (and if, to some extent, he had a point), he remained nonetheless an unequivocal supporter of the idea of a major festival and, in 1954, served on the Cannes jury whose president was Cocteau, alongside the likes of Luis Buñuel, Philippe Erlanger and the screenwriter Jean

AVOIDING OFFENCE

Aurenche. For Bazin, then, came the mixed blessing of having to face American displeasure as Japanese director Teinosuke Kinugasa was awarded the Grand Prix for *The Gate of Hell*, the honour widely interpreted as a slap in the face for the US entry *From Here to Eternity*, recent recipient of more Oscars than any film since *Gone with the Wind*. As the poacher turned gamekeeper, Bazin's mantle as Cannes nemesis-in-chief was passed on to the young François Truffaut, then making a name for himself as the *enfant terrible* of film criticism. Truffaut's broadsides in *Cahiers* and the weekly *Arts* not only took aim at Cannes but also had the entire French film establishment in their sights, and we will return to Truffaut's own Cannes trajectory in Chapter V.

Un-American Friends

During the 1950s Cannes unavoidably became another of the stages on which one of the most shameful aspects of America's Cold War politicking was played out. As of 1947, Republican politicians had begun to harry a Hollywood community they suspected of harbouring communist sympathisers. The House Un-American Activities Committee (HUAC) presided over an inquisition that began by targeting film-makers, writers and actors, then advanced to scour the nation, exposing so-called 'subversive' activities in unions, schools, orchestras, and civil rights groups. The writer Lillian Hellman memorably skewered the period as *Scoundrel Time*, and, equally memorably, took the stand at the hearings but refused to answer the committee's questions, employing the formula 'I cannot and will not cut my conscience to fit this year's fashion.' The two HUAC investigations of Hollywood radicals, in 1947 and 1951, produced the unedifying spectacle of former leftists either recanting their beliefs for career purposes or, more infamously, 'naming names' of fellow radicals. Some, however, refused to collaborate with their inquisitors. A group of writers and directors known as the 'Hollywood Ten' claimed First Amendment rights as grounds for not answering the committee's questions; the US Supreme Court slapped them down and they were sentenced to jail terms. A brief attempt to mobilise Hollywood opinion against the hearings was crushed.

HUAC had real and tangible consequences in Tinseltown, leading to the ignominy of the 'Hollywood Blacklist' whereby those tainted Red by association with radical groupings and causes found themselves unable to get a gig. Jules Dassin was one of many film-makers who left the US to seek work abroad during the period. Dassin went to Europe where, after five years of unemployment, he found refuge and commercial success first in France then later in Greece. Others, such as Joseph Losey and Cy Endfield, based themselves in the UK. Still others settled in Spain, Italy and Mexico while some stayed in Hollywood and, if they could find work, like Dalton Trumbo (screenwriter of *Spartacus* and *Exodus*), took pseudonymous credits if they got credits at all. At the eighth Cannes in 1955, various participants in the HUAC story were brought together in competition: blacklisted film-makers, exiles in the Hollywood diaspora and 'friendly witnesses'. The list of prizewinners that year contained a group whose lives had been changed by the blacklist.

Elia Kazan, who had testified to the committee, won the Prix du Film Dramatique for *East of Eden*. Jules Dassin shared the Prix de la Mise-en-Scène for *Du rififi chez les hommes*. And blacklisted actress Betsy Blair was Best Actress in Delbert Mann's *Marty*, which also took the Palme d'Or. A relatively low-key story of a romance between a butcher and a schoolteacher, *Marty* was lauded by the Cannes jury for 'its beautiful humanity', usually a synonym in such citations for films that deal with proletarian matters. That said, Lindsay Anderson, covering Cannes for the *Observer*, reported that 'to a Russian delegate, the theme of *Marty* was strange. Loneliness, personal frustration – such problems, he remarked, are not relevant in Russia . . .'

Blair arrived in Cannes with her husband, Gene Kelly, himself Hollywood royalty, with an additional reputation as one of the town's leading progressives, and the two became something of a lightning-rod for political shenanigans. In a scene straight out of Graham Greene, Blair received an intriguing summons to a covert meeting with the Chinese delegation aboard a yacht moored away from the crush of the Croisette. Blair's hosts showered her with compliments then presented her with the gift of a traditional Chinese painting. But it was not intended for her. She was to act as an unofficial envoy for the Chinese government and present the artwork to Chinese-American camera-man James Wong Howe, master of light behind *Body and Soul* and *Sweet Smell of Success*, who, the delegation earnestly hoped, might be persuaded to share his wisdom with Chinese film-makers. Blair made the delivery, and the next morning found another gift in return for her pains, deposited outside her hotel room: a small can of grocery-store pineapple, causing her to have serious thoughts about Chinese scarci-ty and US abundance.

In her memoir Blair would describe the 'glorious night' of the Cannes prize-giving as a utopian moment tinged with sorrowful retro-spection:

> We, the winners, walked along the beach, barefoot in our evening clothes; a Soviet director, a communist or two, some fellow-trav-ellers, a blacklisted director and his wife, a formerly blacklisted actress . . . Laughing, full of champagne and success, we felt the Left was invincible, that taking the prizes at the festival in Cannes was only the beginning. Most of us crashed to earth with a giant thud the very next year. The Twentieth Congress of the Supreme Soviet exposed the villainy of Stalin, and the Russian tanks rolled into Hungary . . .

For sincere leftists – driven from their home shores but laurelled upon others, and credulous to the end about Stalin – it was perhaps the best and worst of times.

The 'blacklisted director' Blair mentions was Dassin, whose gang-ster film *Du rififi chez les hommes* had been selected to represent France and went on to win a prize, much to the embarrassment of the

US. Dassin later remembered, 'Some guy from the American Embassy was assigned to come and visit and talk to me and it looked as though he wanted to give me my passport back. That would have fixed things, but you know the manner in which they wanted to fix things, so it didn't happen . . .' It was déjà vu in 1957 when another of Dassin's films, *Celui qui doit mourir* ('He Who Must Die') was once again presented at Cannes under the French flag. Dassin recalls the round of negotiations that was required in order to settle his status at the festival and the exquisite ballet of social awkwardness that ensued around him and blacklisted screenwriter Ben Barzman, as to whether they would receive invites to a reception at the American Embassy. Eventually, 'Ben and I were invited and the receiving line was peopled with functionaries and Hollywood stars. That very morning, people had ducked under tables to avoid being photographed with us – such was the fear. Now, as we proceeded down the receiving line, backs were nimbly turned, and Hollywood stars held up champagne glasses to cover their faces; the French press enjoyed this . . .'

'Article Five' in Overdrive

Recognised now as one of the major post-war French directors and a cinematic pioneer, Alain Resnais also enjoys the less auspicious reputation of being the director with the most films withdrawn from Cannes under a cloud. His film about the Spanish Civil War, *La Guerre est finie*, was axed from the 1966 edition in order not to offend the Spanish government. *Hiroshima, mon amour*, his seminal modernist examination of atomic war and love among the ruins was pulled from the 1959 festival after complaints by the USA (although it has also been claimed that the film's images of shaven-headed women during the *épuration* in post-war France were as likely to have been the reason). True, his *Je t'aime, Je t'aime* was selected without threat and would have screened, but that year was 1968, and the festival was shut down in sympathy with the May demonstrators.

The most infamous of all Resnais's controversies was that surrounding his 1955 film *Nuit et brouillard* ('Night and Fog'). The first major French film to deal with the Nazi concentration camps, this 32-minute piece was commissioned by the Committee for the History of the Second World War in order to convey the memory of the death camps and the deportations. Resnais combined mostly black-and-white archive footage of the death camps with colour material shot contemporaneously among their ruins and in the surrounding landscape. The film's impact came at least in part from its musical score by the East German composer (and former Brecht collaborator) Hans Eissler, and to the commentary written by poet Jean Cayrol who had been interned as a 'Nacht und Nebel' ('Night and Fog') category prisoner in the Gausen camp, a satellite of Mauthausen. Eissler's score included an irreverent musical vamp in which the German national anthem was treated in distorted form, and the choice was one of many about to come in for unwarranted scrutiny.

The diplomatic context of the time favoured post-war reconciliation between France and Germany – on to which notion Resnais's film fell like a bombshell, being a deeply uncomfortable reminder of Germany's shameful past and France's own collaboration. Initially, *Nuit et brouillard* was unanimously voted for inclusion in the 1956 Cannes Festival by the selection committee. 'This choice was judged not to be the best. By who?' So enquired Resnais's producer Anatole Dauman, having been asked to show the film to the German Embassy. 'About thirty showed up, led by the Cultural Attaché who, after the screening, was extremely cold towards me.' Dauman recounts how the German ambassador expressed his feelings to Cannes director of 'artistic affairs' Philippe Erlanger, who decreed that a Cannes screening risked affronting the Germans, and so invoked 'Article Five' of the festival statutes. Forty-eight hours after the news that the film had been selected, Dauman was informed that the decision was reversed. An official communiqué ruled that the rescindment was first and foremost, out of respect for the deportees, their families and their memories. Those who will see the film elsewhere – a very beautiful film assembled with all the tact one could wish for even while showing the suffering of human beings caged, threatened, tortured and consigned to death, amongst which some could recognise loved ones – will understand that it is improper to present such a document in an atmosphere of international festivity such as the annual meeting at Cannes.

A masterpiece of double-speak, disingenuously claiming moral high ground, the communiqué merely confirmed to any sane being that a profound cinematic meditation on state barbarism had been reduced to the status of an embarrassing social infraction, unfit to pass among the *beau monde* at Cannes, owing to the delicate nature of post-war relations between two former adversaries.

A vigorous defence of Resnais's film was mounted. Clearly, for many observers, at stake was not only the grave duty of historical memory but whether Cannes itself was anything more than an anodyne pageant rather than a festival showing films that were authentic responses to the times. Jean Cayrol wrote in *Le Monde*, 'The film tells us a story which did not only involve the Nazis but also our country, we must not modestly lower our eyes before a drama which has contaminated us all.' Anger at the decision was not restricted to France. Two West German newspapers also queried its sense. The *Berliner Zeitung* demanded, 'Whose feelings might it hurt? Who, therefore, took it upon themselves to protect Himmler and his henchmen?' The *Tagesspiegel* declared that the 'false political susceptibilities recently demonstrated at the Cannes festival are disastrous for the artistic climate of film festivals'. Such protests led to exchanges in the Bundestag in which the secretary of state declared that the film 'might contribute to a revival of hatred against the German people engendered by the crimes of the National Socialists'. 'On the contrary', a deputy from Bonn responded, 'the film could assist in the understanding between the two peoples.'

Yet the German government's opposition to the Cannes screening was only one aspect of the censorship to which the film was subjected – another originated within the French government. One scene in the film alluded to the collaboration of the French authorities with the Nazi occupiers. An offending image, visible onscreen for five seconds near the beginning of the film, showed a French gendarme, identifiable from his distinctive kepi, standing near one of the watchtowers of the Pithiviers concentration camp. After long discussions, Resnais consented to the offending kepi being painted over with gouache. Another troublesome aspect for French sensibilities was the film's implicit invocation of the spectre of French war crimes in Algeria, the colony then involved in an extremely bloody independence struggle. The commentary ends by addressing the spectators collectively: 'as if we were cured of the concentration camp plague, we who pretend that all that belonged to a single country at a single time and who don't think to look around us'. Resnais made it clear that Algeria was not far from his mind in the conception of the piece: 'What I feared was making a film that said "Never again"; it was the evil Germans, but now that Hitler is vanquished, it's over, it can't happen again . . .'

Among those determined that Resnais's film have its day at Cannes were former Resistance organisations, the Communist Party, and deportee associations. Resnais recalled, 'The deportees from the Nice and Cannes region said "Fine, okay, but if you don't show it we'll come in deportee costumes and occupy the Palais."' On 19 April, the French press reported a communiqué from the Secretary of State for Industry and Commerce which, while confirming the decision to withdraw the film from competition in Cannes, suggested that the film be shown during the festival on the day commemorating the deportees. One can only wonder whether this was a crafty recuperative manoeuvre doubling as a form of damage limitation. *Paris-Presse* reported the screening as a 'sensation', which according to their correspondent took place 'behind closed doors, before a public frozen in horror who applauded at the end. For my part, I would have preferred silence.'

Conveniently, the screening took place after the German delegation had left the festival. With fitting irony, their entry *Himmel Ohne Sterne* ('Sky Without Stars', directed by Helmut Kautner) had been withdrawn from competition after complaints from an Eastern bloc country – under the terms of the dread 'Article Five' . . .

III

That Riviera Touch

The evolution of the Cannes film festival could be told as the story of a tourist fair with a cinematic pretext that, bit by bit, was consumed by the god whose religion it mimicked and was finally possessed by the art in whose glory it had draped itself.

Pierre Billard

In 1955, French writer Edgar Morin described Cannes as 'a great rite', a secular equivalent of Ascension Day. In the same year, André Bazin wrote a lengthy and only partly tongue-in-cheek account of the festival as a 'holy order'. As worldly as the festival might appear to outsiders, for critics like Bazin it represented two weeks of 'pious retreat and a strictly regulated life'. Bazin's canard still contains a vestigial truth. Where one group of believers routinely treks to Lourdes in search of miracles, another makes its annual pilgrimage to the temple of Cannes. For *cinéphiles*, the festival represents a particularly intense, and intensive, communion with the art of cinema.

By the mid-1950s the festival had acquired all the attributes necessary to be considered as a ritual: the regularity of its editions, the specificity of its location, the nature of its conventions, the variety and type of its habitués. The combination of scandal, awards ceremonies and press conferences along with the congregation of paparazzi, starlets and *cinéphiles* became the template for film festivals around the world. Does a ritual simply become routine when it ceases to be unique? Hardly. The religious believer draws strength from the knowledge that ritual observance, depending on denomination, is pretty much the same all over. Ritual is debased only when the element of faith goes missing. And in the case of Cannes it is cinema that is the fount of such devotion. Having dutifully attended a four-hour, black and white Hungarian *chef d'oeuvre*, the *cinéphile* staggers out of the dark into the blazing Mediterranean sunlight, and may be confronted by some desperately grinning blonde in a bikini, surrounded by hungrily snapping paparazzi. Cannes remains both *cinéphile*-factory and starlet-incubator because these are the archetypal inhabitants of its overlapping worlds of art and commerce.

'The question asked of those returning from Cannes', wrote Morin, 'is, first, "which stars did you see?" and, then, "which films?"' The story remains the same fifty years on, only more so: more cameras, more media and an ever more voracious celebrity culture that hungers for the factory-like production of stars, starlets and stargazers. But to step back from this spectacle discloses a wider context into which the festival fits – that of its location on the French Riviera.

Lying on the crescent of the Gulf of Napoule, situated between Nice to the east and St-Tropez to the west, Cannes is synonymous with what the nineteenth-century French poet Stéphen Liégeard christened *La Côte d'Azur*, the stretch of Mediterranean coastline that is both a tourist trap (with some of the most extortionately priced property in the world) and a place of great natural beauty (with miles of beaches and coves set against the rocky hinterland of Provençal countryside). Even the French are willing to acknowledge that Cannes was the creation of an Englishman or, more precisely, the Scots-born English nobleman, Henry Brougham, Baron of Brougham and Vaux. Today, an imposing statue of him stands between a McDonald's and the Palm Square Restaurant on the 'Place Brougham' in Cannes. The forefinger of the statue's right hand points down as if to emphasise the Provençal motto: 'He who comes here once stays the rest of his life'. Which is exactly what Brougham did. 'Cannes belongs to two nations: France and England', Liégeard observed. True of the nineteenth century perhaps, but since the twentieth it has been the comparable *frère–ennemi* relationship between France and America that has most marked the

THAT RIVIERA TOUCH 51

city. Anyone taking the autoroute towards Cannes will notice that the city is twinned with Beverly Hills, and has been since 1986. Some of the city's other twins tellingly include London's Royal Borough of Kensington and Chelsea, and Gstaad in Switzerland, *noblesse* and new money making a pact comparable to that between the English and the French in the 1800s.

Brougham was a Whig, an abolitionist, co-founder of the *Edinburgh Review*, and, as he travelled south through France towards Nice in November 1834, he held the high office of Lord Chancellor. Running up against a cordon sanitaire formed to check the advance of the cholera epidemic that had decimated the north of Europe, Brougham could go no further and had to kick his heels on the coast while awaiting the visa that would allow him to continue his journey. Initially intending to stay in Antibes and rent a chateau where Bonaparte had spent time in 1815, he was deterred by the protests of locals horrified by the thought of the former emperor's residence falling into English hands. Brougham had to slum it at the only lodging house in Cannes – at the time, a small fishing port of 40,000 inhabitants. At which point in the story a distinctly French touch is evident in a detail that subscribes to what we might call the Gastronomic Theory of History, according to which the owner of the lodging house served the visiting English nobleman an unfamiliar dish of 'bouillabaisse', or fish soup. (Served with croutons it remains today a relatively affordable stomach-filler for penurious hacks at festival time.) Several spoonfuls later and, as legend has it, Brougham was smitten with not only the local cuisine but the area itself. Eight days after he arrived, he bought land on which he would build his residence. Thirty-four years later, in 1868, 'the inventor of Cannes' died there aged ninety, and was buried in the city. After Brougham, the English gentry began to frequent the Mediterranean village and build properties. German, Russian and Swiss aristocrats would follow. Many came for the perceived health benefits of the climate and in 1882 Guy de Maupassant would describe 'this warm and ravishing region' as 'society's hospital and the cemetery of Europe'. Cannes' future as a tourist destination was set.

In 1977 Philippe Erlanger, one of the founders of the Cannes Festival, published a coffee-table book about the city in which he stated: 'No other holiday resort has ever had the same publicity, for the enormous popularity of the festival has ensured that every season it is mentioned by thousands of reporters in the Press and on radio and TV.' By the time Erlanger wrote, tourism had become Cannes' principal source of revenue, as it was for many of the other small towns along the Mediterranean coast. The 'thirty glorious years' (*les trentes glorieuses*) of the post-war period had seen the growth of mass tourism in France: prosperity had increased and people took advantage of paid holidays to leave the cities and head out into the countryside or towards the seaside. By the mid-1950s, when three-quarters of French people would routinely set out on their annual vacation during July and August in what is called *les grandes vacances*, the ritual of the summer holiday was recognised as being a sufficiently widespread phenomenon to serve as the basis for films. Jean-Marc Thibault's *Vive les vacances* (1957) had a couple of car-worker pals heading down to the coast on their scooters for sun and amorous escapades. For *Les Vacances de M. Hulot* (1953), Jacques Tati set the further misadventures of his immortal comic creation in a holiday resort. And an enterprising svengali named Roger Vadim would put the small fishing village of St-Tropez firmly on the map as the location of his film *Et Dieu créa la femme* ('And God Created Woman', 1956), a vehicle for a little-known starlet named Brigitte Bardot. These were the years when the Côte d'Azur became 'The French Riviera', a globally recognised destination for international tourism where a still unsullied Eden was accessible to many, no longer the oasis of a privileged class.

Cinema had a hand in promoting this image of the region. When Jean Cocteau mused that there was 'nothing stranger than this Côte d'Azur seen in Technicolor by the Americans' he was thinking of *Lili* (1953) in which Leslie Caron cavorts around the Riviera in the role of a carnival performer. He might just as well have had other Technicolor excursions in mind, such as Danny Kaye as an entertainer working the cabaret circuit in *On the Riviera* (1951), or Cary Grant and Grace Kelly in Hitchcock's *To Catch a Thief* (1955). By the mid-1960s, even the wheezing British cinema had caught up with the trend, despatching the nation's best-loved TV comedy duo of Eric Morecambe and Ernie Wise to film their second big-screen outing, *That Riviera Touch* (1966).

That the Cannes Festival should have played a role in promoting both the town and the region is hardly surprising, but this role would contribute to a struggle over the purpose of the event. Was it merely a chic attention-grabbing platform to attract more tourists to the region, or an event at which cinema was sovereign? The battle over the identity and purpose of the festival would dominate the first twenty years of its history. One of the most vocal proponents of the idea that Cannes should place its duties towards *le cinéma* above all others was François Truffaut, who was under no illusions about the other temptations it faced. In 1957 he observed, 'the essential goal of the festival is to bring paying customers into the hotels and casinos at a time when business is poor'. It is clearer now, in retrospect, how Cannes was at the forefront of a phenomenon that has since become widespread: cultural tourism. Not that this phenomenon is new. In a study of what he calls 'the economy of prestige' (whereby the giving of cultural prizes at award ceremonies or cultural festivals is seen as indissociable from where they take place) the American scholar James F. English reminds us that prizes for artists date back to the sixth century BC when annual festivals combining music, poetry and drama were widespread in the cities of east central Greece. The most notable were the drama contests in Athens, held in honour of the god Dionysus. Such events were 'culture parties on a grand scale, orgies of cultural consumption. Such orgies are still common enough today. One thinks of the hectic eight-films-a-day pace of moviegoers at Cannes or Toronto.'

Cannes' success in joining culture to tourism was helped in no small part by it being home to an 'A-list' film festival, but it had also been

54 CANNES

able to build on the considerable cultural cachet that had accrued to the Côte d'Azur since the nineteenth century. In 1883, four years before that sky-blue term was coined, Pierre Auguste Renoir and Claude Monet had taken a two-week painting tour of the coast. Both would return many times, drawn by the landscape but also by the extraordinary quality of the light. Monet wrote of Antibes: 'It is so beautiful here, so bright, so luminous. One swims in blue air and it is frightening.' Paul Cézanne, a Provençal by birth and upbringing, was painting views of the Gulf of Marseilles in 1884. During the early mid-twentieth century a veritable pantheon of artistic heavyweights were regular visitors to the region, including Picasso, Raoul Dufy, Nicolas de Staël, Pierre Bonnard, Georges Braque, Jean Cocteau, Marc Chagall and Fernand Léger (who dubbed the region's tonic effect *médicine en azur*). Matisse, Picasso, Cocteau and Chagall all left their mark in numerous mosaics, murals and chapel decorations across the region. In 1946, Picasso would establish himself in the small town of Vallauris where, for the next twenty years, he produced a large amount of ceramics. His former *atelier* in Antibes is now the beautiful Musée Picasso. In the 1950s, one of the artists associated with the *Ecole de Nice*, Yves Klein, executed one of his first neo-Dada acts and 'signed' the luminous blue of the Riviera sky calling it his 'first and biggest monochrome'. And in 1964, the Fondation Maeght was inaugurated in St-Paul, the first museum of modern art built in France since the Musée National d'Art Moderne in Paris in 1934. By then, the most modern of art forms, cinema, had been added to Cannes' tourist-friendly combination of sun, sea and sand. And with cinema came the starlets.

The Tragedy of 'Silly Simone'

Who remembers Simone Silva now? The film career of this 1950s starlet was hardly illustrious, comprising a couple of minor, uncredited roles in French films in the early 1950s followed by a succession of British films such as *Lady Godiva Rides Again* (1951), *Third Party*

Risk (1954) and *The Gelignite Gang* (1956) in which she played gangsters' molls and nightclub chanteuses. Her opulent, exotic looks (she was born Simone de Bouillard in 1928 to Greek–French parents in Cairo) suited the vogue for the 'European woman' in fifties' British cinema but Silva was not to find the prominent roles offered to other European actress such as Hildegard Neff in *The Man Between* (1953), Simone Signoret in *Room at the Top* (1959), or even Brigitte Bardot in *Doctor at Sea* (1955). It was Silva's walk-on part at Cannes for which she is now recalled these days, if at all.

At the seventh edition of the festival Silva attempted to outdo Bardot, whose bikini-clad appearance on the beaches of Cannes at the previous year's festival had charmed Kirk Douglas and captivated all available photographers. In 1954, Silva used a seafront photo opportunity to generate publicity for herself and her career (a film in which she had a minor role, *The Weak and the Wicked*, having recently been released in Britain). After the ensuing scandal, she described her self-serving ambition in terms that seem better suited to the amoral cynicism of present-day reality TV contestants than to the still-prudish sensibilities of mid-fifties Britain: 'As long as sex is box-office and I keep my figure', Silva told the press, 'I'm out to be the sexiest thing on two legs.' The naked clarity with which she described her equation of fame and the energy with which she put it to work led to her being pilloried in the British press as 'Silly Simone', 'Sad Miss Silva' and 'Little Miss Make Believe'. What had she done to bring down such opprobrium?

In the manner of Bardot-meets-Kirk, Silva manufactured a similar cheesecake-meets-beefcake photo opportunity; the Hollywood tough-guy in this instance being Robert Mitchum who, with his wife, Dorothy, was visiting the festival for the first time. On the Ile de Lerins, one of the four small islands in an archipelago off the Cannes coast, Mitchum was posing for photographers in a cliff-top publicity session when Silva sashayed hungrily into the shot, scantily clad in a minuscule grass skirt and a transparent pink scarf-top. The couple posed together for the pack of fifty or so lens-hounds (their species was yet to be known by the Fellini-derived collective noun of *paparazzi*) and Silva threw caution – and modesty – to the wind, deciding suddenly to go topless. In the ensuing melee, several photographers tumbled off the cliffs into the water below, one of them fracturing an elbow. Mitchum, who afterwards claimed he wasn't sure what was going on, gathered Silva to his chest to preserve a little of her dignity, the photographs of the encounter making it look like he was, as he put it, 'copping a feel'. The incident provoked a publicity uproar: the photographs of the topless starlet in the arms of the Hollywood star were published around the world and the festival let Miss Silva know she was no longer welcome in town. The festival director apologised, fearing a conservative backlash. Gilles Jacob, later the director of Cannes himself, recalls that the incident required measures of damage limitation and charm offensive: 'Robert Favre Le Bret went to the US the following year in order to convince the Americans to return to the festival because the Leagues of Virtue as well as [gossip columnists] Louella Parsons and Hedda Hopper, two formidable women, were all saying: "Don't go to Cannes! It's Hell! It's Sodom! And, anyway, it's finished!" So it was necessary to convince these people that the festival was not there to fabricate erotic scandals but to defend cinema . . .'

Favre Le Bret sought to make amends the following year and – as if to dispel the lascivious image of Mitchum and Silva – began to explore ways of enticing the fragrant Grace Kelly to Cannes. Silva, however, was unrepentant. It had been assumed that the whole episode was planned by her, even before she was found the following morning, posting copies of the picture up and down the Croisette. (Mitchum remembers the police tearing them down in her wake.) As she 'explained' in a *Pictorial* feature, 'Let them say that I was bold to pose without a top to my dress with American star Robert Mitchum at Cannes. How many actresses COULD do it – even if they dared? Don't forget that Marilyn Monroe first drew attention to herself and got her lucky break after posing nude for a calendar. And it was publicity for her figure that got Jane Russell where she is today.' Flushed with her newfound notoriety, Silva took off for Hollywood for a year in which she signally failed to become the next Monroe or Russell – though she claimed to have been the guest of Howard Hughes, she was offered little more than striptease work. On her return to the UK in 1955, *Photoplay* reported that 'in America there was hostility in certain quarters, Americans are moral people. Miss Silva's antics in Cannes did not amuse them.'

Too hungry for fame, too nakedly ambitious, candid to the point of exhibitionism . . . Silva suffered only because she was ahead of her time. Her demise was sudden and tragic. The punishing equation of fame that demanded she 'keep her figure' for the sake of box-office sex appeal saw her embark on a damaging regime of dieting. She was found dead in her Mayfair flat in January 1957. Her death was reported as suicide. It is tempting, in retrospect, to see in the Simone Silva story something akin to a Cannes creation myth: Silva an exposure-hungry Eve, Mitchum an unwitting Adam, together in a suitably Edenic setting swarming with serpent-like paparazzi.

Raincoats vs. Bikinis

Cannes in February instead of May? It seems an almost inconceivable notion today, but a switch to the depths of winter was seriously considered at various junctures by the CNC (Centre National de la Cinématographie) during the festival's first fifteen years. Of course the first editions of the festival had taken place in September, moved briefly to April in 1951 and then settled on May in 1952, where it has remained ever since. But nowadays it's widely accepted that Cannes has become the pre-eminent film festival ahead of Venice and Berlin despite, rather than because of, its position in the calendar year. Late spring is not a good time for producers and studios to be unveiling their wares, the summer months being the least profitable unless you're a Hollywood blockbuster, although recent summer revenues suggest even that's no longer a certainty. Instead producers will generally wait until early autumn, which is late to try to capitalise on the publicity generated by a Cannes opening – or better still, a prize – back in May. There's no doubt that Cannes' main rivals Berlin (February) and Venice (end of August/early September) are much better positioned for subsequent rapid commercial exploitation.

The Cannes Festival committee prevaricated on this issue right into the early sixties. Important arguments weighed against moving to February, the most obvious being the income generated through large numbers of tourists attracted by the warm spring climate, the festival's glitzy reputation, and the opportunity to get up close to major international stars. Right from its inception the festival's expansion was closely tethered to its hometown's commercial fortunes – several local dignitaries and business people sat on the festival committee, and local people who stood to benefit from the festival's growth contributed to the festival's budget via taxes raised locally. The mere suggestion of – as one committee member put it – 'a festival in raincoats' was anathema to many, despite complaints from French industry bodies and regular lobbying by producers worldwide.

It's impossible to underestimate the combined impact of clement weather and the town's natural advantages – palm trees, the beach, the gently winding Croisette, expensive yachts bobbing in the harbour – in planting the festival in the popular imagination. They furnish a ready-made iconography with which Venice and particularly Berlin simply can't compete. Linked to these important geographical advantages, and perhaps most crucial of all in clinching the argument for May, was the preponderance of scantily clad starlets, who began to make their presence felt from the second festival in 1947. These fame-fixated young women – a mixture of models and bit-part actresses – rarely if ever received official invitations, which would have meant being accommodated at the festival's expense in one of the luxurious hotels along the Croisette. (Bardot was never officially invited on her early visits; one apocryphal story relates that photographers paid her hotel bills so she could stay longer at the festival in 1953.) Budgets were still very tight after the war – hence the festival's mothballing in 1948 and 1950 – but the starlets' presence was nevertheless welcomed and encouraged by the festival authorities. It gave rise to a mutually beneficial situation. Cannes could assist in catapulting a starlet towards a high-profile career and stardom, à la Bardot (although in truth this was the exception rather than the norm – some of these starlets had to settle instead for marriage to a rich and powerful man); while Cannes, still a long way from establishing itself as the behemoth we know today, would gain from the extra press exposure. Philippe Erlanger expressed it succinctly, and memorably: 'One shouldn't forget, in ensuring the success of the festival, the primordial role of starlets in bikinis.'

The primordial was just about everywhere you looked as you stepped outside the Carlton between the years 1947 and 1960, if contemporary reports are to be believed. This was the heyday of the starlet, the Croisette and beach overrun by bikini-clad young women (many accompanied by their mothers) who were, as the years passed, more than happy to divest themselves of their top half at the merest whiff of interest from a passing photographer. It may well be the case that the starlet phenomenon has been exaggerated; Peter Lennon, who attended the festival several times in that era as a journalist and filmmaker, believes that many newspapers and magazines tended to focus disproportionately on the eye-candy. Nevertheless, in most people's eyes (especially those outside this charmed world), Cannes and starlets became synonomous, fostering a powerful and lingering *idée fixe* of the festival as a site of licentious excess. Actress Rita Tushingham arrived at Cannes in 1962 with Tony Richardson's *A Taste of Honey*, and witnessed the scam in action: 'It was sort of posed; the girl would take her top off and run, and all the photographers would be falling over themselves, chasing her down the beach. A lot of them were just dirty old men with cameras . . .'

In the fifties a 'Miss Festival' competition set up by the magazine *Cinemonde* showcased about twenty candidates each year and further

60

CANNES

swelled the numbers of eye-catching beauties. With all this competition, some starlets resorted to stunts to get attention – Diana Dors sported a mink bikini, while Françoise Deldick galvanised the paparazzi by entering the Carlton Hotel bare-breasted on a white horse, trumping Bianca Jagger's famous entrance into New York's Studio 54 by nearly twenty years.

Small wonder that journalists (overwhelmingly male, it must be said) look back on this period as a golden age. Nowadays many thousands of journalists are accredited to the festival each year. Back in the forties and fifties, however, far fewer made the trip to Cannes and the festival authorities, keen to court them and increase their numbers, made sure the ones who came were invited to numerous lavish receptions and an annual champagne dinner hosted by the municipality. As the post-war expansion of the mass media began to gather pace, the number of journalists and photographers attending the festival in the fifties rose dramatically. Once the Marché (film market) had been officially installed in 1959, those numbers exploded. It was a straightforward trade-off; the festival needed publicity, while the burgeoning magazine and newspaper market pounced hungrily on the festival's reliable provision of stars and starlets, with all the attendant gossip and reader titillation. As Maurice Bessy, delegate of the FIF from 1972 to 1977, put it, the festival 'did all it could to maintain the legend of these blonde, so blonde young misses, their talented chests puffed out'. A hungry public, not long emerged from the deprivations of war, was eager to gobble up these glamorous images.

Into this febrile atmosphere a teenage Brigitte Bardot would saunter merrily in 1953. Cannes would serve as a crucial springboard to launch her phenomenal leap to international stardom, the prime mover behind which was her husband, former journalist Roger Vadim – who in hindsight seems a highly intuitive and prescient pop culture svengali figure in the Brian Epstein/Malcolm McLaren mould. In May 1953 they'd only been married for four months but Vadim had been Bardot's mentor for some three years, constantly reworking and refining her image and gradually raising her profile through his media contacts. The still only eighteen-year-old Bardot came from a background of dancing and modelling; she'd appeared on the cover of *Elle* and played small parts in a couple of films, one of which was *Act of Love*. Vadim spotted an opportunity when he learned that this American-financed film was to be shown that year in Cannes. The star of the picture, thirty-seven-year-old Kirk Douglas, would be attending, plus a galaxy of other American big names; there would inevitably be endless photo opportunities for his beautiful young wife.

Best of the lot, it turned out, and the one still endlessly recycled in the myriad books about Bardot, was the scene – let's use that word 'primordial' again to describe it, given its distinct Tarzan-meets-Jane overtones – which unfolded on the beach at Cannes, with Kirk Douglas in his trunks and Bardot in a bikini. (Douglas later claimed this was the first time he'd seen such a fetching item – touchingly innocent times.) Imagine today a big American male superstar, George Clooney, say, sitting on the beach in his swimming trunks at Cannes. Douglas was archetypal 1950s American manhood, straight out of a Charles Atlas ad, and twice Bardot's age. (Although, delightfully, Leonard Mosley of the *Daily Express* – supposedly the first journalist to have discovered Bardot – described Douglas at a Cannes party that year as looking 'madly gay'.) Douglas was sporting stubble, growing a beard for his next film role. Bardot's abundant, uncombed hair – still in its natural pre-blonde state – had already drawn much comment. Female hair, particularly on aspiring and fully fledged film stars, was supposed to be coiffed and sculpted to within an inch of its life. The assembled photographers captured Douglas using Bardot's hair as a pretend moustache, a lovely gesture bristling with all manner of intriguing subtexts – had the shade of Sigmund Freud been taking the Cannes air at that moment, he would surely have been much exercised. For Vadim, however, it couldn't get much better: a memorable photo-op with a huge US star.

There was one more iconic moment to be seized before the festival ended and those highly prized American stars departed. Vadim had heard that the crew of the American Sixth Fleet aircraft carrier *Midway*, anchored in the bay at Cannes, would be hosting an end of festival party. When the appointed hour arrived and the party was in full swing, with the likes of Gary Cooper, Edward G. Robinson, Lana Turner and Olivia de Havilland all basking in cheered encouragement from the massed ranks of sailors, Bardot slipped on board the aircraft carrier wearing – horror of horrors! – a raincoat, that symbol of doom in the minds of the Cannes organisers. Biding her time until Gary Cooper was close by, so guaranteeing maximum photographer attention, Bardot shed the raincoat to reveal a tight-fitting teenager's dress, which together with her ponytail produced an image calculated to score highly with the watching Americans. *Paris-Match* reporter Raymond Cartier witnessed what ensued. 'There was a second of silence, just enough for the electric charge to pass between the crowd of males. Then the *Midway* was engulfed in a single shot of lightning and a crash of thunder: thousands of flashbulbs and shouts of admiration that exceeded in volume all the previous acclaims put together.' We should probably take this overwrought description with a fairly generous pinch of salt, not least because Vadim (a former *Paris-Match* journalist) had done a deal with the magazine to cover the moment. Nevertheless, it was an inspired move on his part, as he slowly but surely shaped the Bardot myth without the benefit of a studio or publicity department, making the most of what was freely available at Cannes to a canny opportunist with good press contacts.

Whatever these past triumphs amounted to, Vadim and Bardot's most important trip to Cannes was in 1956, to raise extra funds to allow Vadim to shoot his directorial debut *Et Dieu Créa la Femme* ('And God Created Woman') in colour rather than black and white. Vadim successfully raised the money he needed and the film was shot later that year in striking Eastmancolor. It was a masterstroke to hold out for colour; the film would surely have had nothing like the same impact in monochrome. Bardot's face was well known in France before its release but the film would catapult her to international stardom, the culmination of Vadim's painstaking media manipulation and image construction. *And God Created Woman* appeared at a transitional moment in French culture, capturing a mood with uncanny precision; the first stirrings of youthful disenchantment with stifling conventions in mid-fifties France, still predominantly defined by conservative attitudes and Catholicism. It was not just a massive commercial success, but a genuine social phenomenon. Bardot played flirtatious child-woman Juliette, a fascinating amalgam of earthy innocence and rebellious perversity, casually throwing off conventional morality in her pursuit of sensual pleasure. Pursued by a rich widower (Curd Jürgens) but attracted to fisherman Antoine (Christian Marquand), Juliette finally succumbs to the latter's less worldly brother Michel (Jean-Louis Trintignant) whom she marries and genuinely tries hard to be happy with. But a sexual encounter on a beach with Antoine sets in train a fraternal conflict which leads directly to the famous mambo scene, where Juliette's pent-up conflicts and frustration explode all over the screen in a blur of sexual energy.

Many critics cite *And God Created Woman* as the first 'New Wave' film, not for any genuine formal ambition or audacity – it's a fairly conventional melodrama in many ways – but because of its revolutionary social impact, which was due to several elements: its depiction of a recognisably contemporary France, its natural performances, and its full-blooded acknowledgement of a young woman's emancipated – if not amoral and predatory – sexuality. For these, it drew heavily on aspects of Bardot's image which Vadim via Cannes had already helped to construct, so eliding the gap between the real and fictional Bardot into one unified persona. The choice as the film's location of St-Tropez (where Bardot would eventually live; she has been heavily associated with the Côte d'Azur throughout her life) was inspired. Just down the road from Cannes, and at that time still a poignantly unspoiled fishing village, it reinforced all the work that had already been done at the festival. Those cheesecake photographs on the beaches constituted crucial groundwork, fashioning an image of 'natural', carefree spontaneity and projecting an aura of sunburned hedonism without a trace of sexual inhibition. At the level of performance, Bardot delivered her lines in a flat monotone, again designed to seem more 'natural', a decisive break with over-refined styles of French classical acting grounded in formal elocution. 'Brigitte does not act, she exists,' Vadim famously pronounced. 'When I'm in front of the camera, I'm simply myself,' was Bardot's version. As an actress she was dismissed by partisans of *cinéma de qualité*, but for the *Cahiers* critics such as Truffaut she signalled a novel, revitalising injection of authenticity. This rhetoric of the 'new' would feed into the New Wave, the preoccupation with novelty given added impetus by the election of de Gaulle's Fifth Republic in 1958.

The film inevitably fell foul of French watchdogs. When it was finally passed for exhibition it had to be released quickly and with very little fanfare in France. But its massive success in the States (it grossed $4 million in its first run, whereupon Bardot's earlier films were swiftly snapped up for distribution) where it became something of a phenomenon, produced a rebound effect in France. 'Of course', Vadim conceded, 'some of *Et Dieu*'s success came from its sexual frankness, and that's why so many of the first New Wave films, like Malle's *Les Amants* and Godard's *A Bout de souffle*, are equally casual about nudity. It's what distributors, especially American ones, were asking for.' While sex was being sold in the Carlton suites, you only had to gaze out over the balcony to have the sales pitch nicely reinforced by all that bronzed starlet flesh on the beach and along the Croisette. *And God Created Woman* had singlehandedly revolutionised the 'foreign film' market.

From the mid-fifties onwards European art cinema – as typified by the likes of Bergman, Fellini and Resnais – was also starting to make inroads into the US market, audiences drawn to its psychological and sexual realism, as enabled by less stringent censorship codes in Europe. Bardot spearheaded European cinema's drive, an important weapon in its bid to penetrate the US market, and Cannes was the

THAT RIVIERA TOUCH 65

ideal shop window for ensnaring those important US distributors. Compared with those unattainable, manicured female stars beloved of the Hollywood studios such as Grace Kelly or Doris Day, the tomboy-ish Bardot frolicking half-naked on the beach with dishevelled hair was a breath of fresh air. Our old friend Leonard Mosley sounded the mood: 'Bardot ushered in the era of the great unmade bed.' The joyous reaction of those American sailors in the bay at Cannes prefigured the impact Bardot's sexual magnetism would exert in the States. She became the first big European rival to those legendary US stars and paved the way for the likes of Jeanne Moreau, Françoise Hardy, Sylvie Vartan, Catherine Deneuve, and Françoise Dorléac. She reputedly earned France more foreign currency through export of her films than the Renault car factory. (Interestingly Bardot always refused to work in Hollywood, worried the studios would try to turn her into one of their typically mannequin-like, overly confected studio stars, or 'Madame Pompadour' as she termed it.) A few critics have even suggested that Bardot's films were marketed as soft porn in the States – no doubt the scene in *Cinema Paradiso* (1989) depicting a row of males masturbating at a screening of *And God Created Woman* enshrines one prevalent response to the film back then.

This was a transitional moment in American culture, particularly in Hollywood, where the studios seemed out of touch and in decline. James Dean's angular brand of cool was showcased by *Rebel Without a Cause* in 1955, and Bardot's jeans-wearing, rebellious persona chimed nicely with the prevailing mood among a younger generation. Given the response to the Simone Silva incident, one might have expected the Americans would be nervous confronted with Bardot's frankly sexual allure only a couple of years later. But two years is a long time and a new generation was making its voice heard; even the longstanding Hays Code, in force since 1934, was being undermined and enfeebled by the pressure of wider social developments. And let's not forget that Bardot was very big business – where there's a market, there's usually a way. Moreover, despite Vadim's talk of nudity, in truth the presentation of Bardot tended to rely heavily on suggestion, albeit fairly blatant; you will seek in vain for topless shots of Bardot at Cannes, for example. But what had been taboo for Silva in 1954 became the norm just a year later at Cannes. By the early sixties the tease had degenerated into porn-inflected sleaze.

France in the fifties was racing headlong into modernisation faster than just about any other country in Europe, and Bardot was herself part of that drive. This process was not without its tensions and birth pangs; France was still a patriarchal, predominantly Catholic country not long emerged from war and occupation. Women only got the vote in 1945, and birth control was still heavily regulated. Bardot's liberated persona became emblematic of a new, emergent type of womanhood, but there were contradictions and controversial aspects. She was the standard, all too familiar sex-object, but with novel dimensions, a young woman in control of and comfortable with her sexuality, depicted as an instigator of sex in *And God Created Woman*. For libertarian feminist writers such as Françoise Sagan and Simone de Beauvoir, Bardot represented a powerful overthrowing of taboos and repression. For more conservative women writers and many male critics (Truffaut was a notable exception), she incited fear and even hatred. 'A monument of immorality,' thundered one commentator. She was even spat at and attacked on several occasions by members of the public.

Madonna is probably the closest recent parallel to Bardot in terms of iconic stature. Like Madonna, Bardot's influence on young women's attitudes was expressed partly through fashion, fuelling new appetites at a time of rising youth consumer power. Bardot represented a decisive rupture with prevailing norms and dress codes for women, which typically involved constricting, coordinated ensemble outfits and girdles – basically a middle-aged look. Bardot, on the contrary, favoured cheap, skimpy garments and trendy young designers, including one with an outlet in Cannes. French couture's hold on the fashion industry was in decline in the late fifties, America its upcoming rival, but

THAT RIVIERA TOUCH

Bardot's new, more casual style was quickly exploited. As both a French and an international star, Bardot was crucial in enabling the French fashion industry to maintain its grip on the American market, and her films became an important part of France's fashion export drive. The links between fashion and cinema had already been set out in Franco-US trade agreements, the Blum–Byrnes Accord of 1946–8, according to which French luxury goods were traded for American entry to the French film market.

Right from the off, the Cannes film festival became integral in consolidating France's international reputation for luxury. *French Beauty*, a documentary film directed by Pascale Lamche (2005), skilfully unravels today's close-knit links between fashion, sponsorship hype and French actresses. 'French beauties', she says, 'are caught in a two-way flow between business and cliché, and nowhere is that more apparent than at the Cannes film festival, sponsored by L'Oreal.' The red carpet and the *montée des marches* apotheosises those links between fashion and cinema and relays them to the world via TV coverage or through the sponsored photo-shoot, where several photographers will be charged with getting a shot of a star wearing her sponsor's products – Bulgari earrings, maybe, or a Louis Vuitton bag, or a couture dress. Meanwhile, all over the Croisette glossy L'Oreal perfume ads starring French actresses compete for space with ads for Hollywood blockbusters. Cannes is more than ever the epicentre of huge vested commercial interests. One outcome is the stifling dress codes at Cannes, not relinquished even after 1968; small challenges to it cause minor scandals, as when Bardot wore a raincoat (again!) over an evening dress at a Cannes soirée. Nowadays it's hard to imagine even such tiny dents in the festival's smooth functioning and corporate image. We've come a long way since Douglas and Bardot in their swimwear on the beach.

By Cannes 1957, Bardot's image was almost everywhere. She chose not to attend the festival that year but instead threw a huge party in nearby Nice, where she was shooting a film. The party just happened to be on the same night as a big reception hosted in Cannes by Robert

Favre Le Bret. It seemed like a calculated snub; her party, at which Bardot presided wearing jeans and a T-shirt, was of course where everyone went that night. 'She considered it her duty, her job to come to Cannes, to do photos and meet producers and journalists, but she couldn't care less about the social side of the event,' Vadim has said. Bardot had grown impatient with festival protocol and formality, and the constant hassles she faced there. Thereafter she shunned Cannes for a further decade – by which time her moment was long over. She was gradually displaced and ultimately eclipsed during the sixties by French actresses such as Anna Karina, Catherine Deneuve and Jeanne Moreau, stars who projected more complex, even cerebral versions of feminine allure, partly through working partnerships (and often love affairs) with French auteur directors such as Godard, Malle and Truffaut. Bardot and Vadim, though not in the same league artistically, had nevertheless augured this pronounced tendency in French cinema for director–star coupling, so profoundly influential on French cinema's erotic reputation and the way French actresses have been perceived.

Bardot's impact had been seismic, on both French cinema and the Cannes Festival, through her complete command and embodiment of the zeitgeist. She'd played a major role in enhancing the festival's aura of seduction and glamour, a fact not lost on the Cannes hierarchy, who literally begged her to return. In 1967 there were rumours of phone calls from the festival director Charles Debray to her then husband Gunther Sachs, exhorting him to try to wield some influence over her. She finally succumbed, in what was to be practically her last public appearance. The footage of her entry to the old Palais in 1967 is incredible; the hysterical crowds and frenzied jostling were unprecedented even by Cannes' standards. Bardot and her husband were completely engulfed by a broiling mob of men in dinner jackets or kepis. It's interesting to compare this scene to the generally much more carefully managed, sanitised spectacle of celebrity the festival serves up nowadays. A star may well arrive with an entourage of bodyguards and be driven the short distance from hotel to red carpet in a black

THAT RIVIERA TOUCH

limousine. The space along the Croisette and in front of the Grand Palais is much more heavily controlled and policed. It should be remembered that the appallingly perfunctory murder of John Lennon in 1980 quite clearly seared itself in the consciousness of the world's biggest movie stars as well as its rock stars: such was the emphatic end of the innocence in terms of walkabouts in city streets and easy mingling with autograph-hunters.

As of 1983 the new Palais's imposing, corporate scale and positioning appeared designed to prevent impromptu disturbances, reinforced by the ranks of crush barriers. Stars are now commodities to be admired from a distance, rather than surrounded and jostled and touched, as in the past. Should a star decide to dispense with the security protocols, frenzy can descend. In 1994 the novelist Kazuo Ishiguro was a festival juror and so keeping company with president Clint Eastwood. He quickly gathered that the crowds of Cannes stargazers

have no shame in what they do: if they see someone going by in a car they would, en masse, go into the street and try and stop the car, waving autograph books and screaming and banging on car windows. It really took Clint Eastwood aback, took him about two or three days to adjust to this. I remember the first time I was going to something in the evening that the whole jury was to attend. I was being taken in a car along the Croisette and I saw what looked like a commotion on the pavement and I realised it was Clint. He'd chosen to walk from his hotel down the Croisette. It was only two hundred yards and he thought that was okay. And, of course, immediately he'd been engulfed and he was trying to be cool, be like Clint Eastwood, smiling and not perspiring, but he was having a great deal of difficulty. When we were all together he said that he hadn't expected this, because where he lives in Carmel in California, and generally in Hollywood too, people leave stars alone. But this still didn't teach him because the next day he tried to go jogging on the beach early in the morning, with predictable results.

For a further taste of the crazed atmosphere Ishiguro evokes, one need only think back to Madonna's characteristically unquiet appearance on the Cannes red carpet in 1991, accompanying the shrill documentary/concert-film *Truth or Dare* which had received a slot in Official Selection. Covered extensively on TV, this event was undoubtedly more carefully policed and exhaustingly stage-managed than any of Bardot's appearances. What one made of Madonna's coiffure and outfit – a pink silk wrap that (briefly) hid a pointy-cupped white Gaultier bra – for the crowd on the scene she was clearly the very definition of fabulous. They screamed their heads off. That's glamour, that's movies, *plus ça change*.

Can we yet imagine the day when Madonna might forsake this spotlight as thoroughly as did Bardot? She retired from the screen in 1974, embracing first the cause of animal rights, then that of far-right French nationalism. Jacques Rozier's short documentary *Paparazzi* (1964), which followed Bardot on the set of Godard's *Le Mépris*, beautifully captures her standing on the cusp of modern celebrity culture, the point at which stardom became something else; when just about any shot of our latest celebrity obsession could dramatically increase magazine sales. Fame became a monster Bardot couldn't control and, like Garbo before her, she began to loathe the intrusion. 'I understand what it is to be a wild animal caught in the telescopic sights of the hunter,' she complained. 'The photographers didn't want to kill me but they did want to kill something in me. They steal something of your soul . . .' But then wasn't this the devil's pact Bardot signed with Vadim, and sealed on the beach at Cannes?

IV

Sacred Monsters

SULLIVAN: I want this picture to be a commentary on modern conditions, stark
   realism, the problems that confront the average man.
LEBRAND: But with a little sex.
SULLIVAN: A little, but I don't want to stress it. I want this picture to be a docu-
   ment. I want to hold a mirror up to life. I want this to be a picture of dignity –
   a true canvas of the suffering of humanity.
LEBRAND: But with a little sex.
SULLIVAN: With a little sex in it . . .
   From *Sullivan's Travels* (1941), written and directed by Preston Sturges

'ORGY FILM WINS TOP AWARD'. That blunt headline, from Britain's now-
defunct *Daily Herald*, typified the more excitable reporting of news that
Federico Fellini's eighth film, *La Dolce Vita*, had carried off the Palme
d'Or at Cannes in 1960. Small wonder that the film went on to break
box-office records pretty much everywhere it was shown – in the US
alone it grossed $8 million, surpassing the biggest previous foreign suc-
cess to date, Roger Vadim's *And God Created Woman* (and further
proving the exchange value of 'a little sex'). In France it attracted 3 million spectators. In Fellini's native Italy, where it prompted a fierce political and moral controversy, receipts were 1.5 million *lire* in just three
months, putting it comfortably ahead of past box-office records held by
Gone with the Wind, *The Ten Commandments*, and *Ben Hur*. Italians
flocked to see what all the fuss was about, tickets changing hands at
extortionate prices. There were even reports of people bussing out to
small towns because *La Dolce Vita* had sold out in the big cities.

Thrilling rumours about the movie had been in circulation long
before it arrived in Italy's theatres. It was common knowledge, then,

that *La Dolce Vita* would prominently feature the infamous Via Veneto in Rome, preferred site for partying celebrities, their fawning retinues, and the paparazzi who preyed on them. Much of the film was shot in Cinecittà studios, but scenes filmed on location in Rome – particularly Anita Ekberg's iconic cavorting in the Trevi fountain – had drawn hundreds of spectators and photographers. Such local gossip – added to the film's huge cast and long, difficult gestation – made rich pickings for Roman media, and a strong anticipatory buzz. Despite all of which, nobody would have predicted the ensuing thunderstorm.

Nearly three hours long, Fellini's ambitious, prophetic film filters its vision of spiritual aridity and moral decline through the exploits of jaded playboy journalist Marcello (Marcello Mastroianni), whose pursuit of sensational stories and Anita Ekberg's coquettish, distractible starlet propels him through a Roman demi-monde that both attracts and disgusts him – a milieu steeped in hedonistic vice and populated by vain celebrities, decadent aristocrats and others newly enriched by the Italian economic miracle. Fellini's tour de force delivered a salvo of screen taboos and shock-tactics – prostitutes, strippers, homosexuals, a so-called orgy, promiscuous sex (in one instance, in the bed of a prostitute), Anita Ekberg's ample bust in conjunction with an ecclesiastical habit, and a faked sighting of the Virgin. Even the city itself becomes a potent symbol of current decline; Rome's former glories now seem firmly buried away in the past, and the redundancy of Christian mythology is signalled in the flamboyant opening spectacle of Christ's statue being airlifted away by helicopter over the city's rooftops. From that point onwards, the film's narrative comprises an eerie, episodic drift through locations in and around the city, conveying Marcello's disconnected sensibility. Marcello is one of the earliest examples of what would become a common figure in European art-house films of the sixties and seventies – the alienated, conflicted protagonist undergoing a profound spiritual crisis from which Fellini, in this instance, permits no escape or redemption, another element that startled the film's contemporary audiences.

SACRED MONSTERS

Just prior to release *La Dolce Vita* was previewed in Rome, where Anita Ekberg attracted all the press attention. This was swiftly followed by another preview screening in Milan in early February, now entered into the realm of legend, for it was dogged by a raucous cacophony of boos and shouts, and afterwards an angry crowd jostled and spat on Fellini in the foyer – this, perhaps, the rage of a Milanese *haute bourgeoisie* seeing its face in the glass. Despite the notoriety, *La Dolce Vita*'s export licence was duly granted, which meant it could be entered in competition at Cannes in May – then as now, the festival's regulations permitted films to be shown in their own country before Cannes. Unsurprisingly Fellini was not selected to represent Italy, an honour that fell to Antonioni's *L'Avventura*. But it was the festival's wise custom to invite other films alongside those nominated by individual countries, so as to ensure a high standard of entries in the competition, and Cannes could hardly resist the picture that had debauched all Italy.

Fellini would show ten of his films at Cannes across his career, what Pierre Billard calls a 'veritable love affair with the festival'. But *La Dolce Vita* was only the second of these, following *Nights of Cabiria* in 1957. Fellini's longstanding relationship with Cannes came about partly because his earlier film *Il Bidone* was horribly mauled by the critics at Venice in 1955, despite the acclaim previously given to his *La Strada*. This was such a traumatic experience that Fellini refused to return to Venice until 1969, and only then outside of competition. Venice's loss proved to be Cannes' gain. In May 1960 *La Dolce Vita* had a robust claim to be the most eagerly anticipated film in Cannes' history. Critic John Gillett wrote, 'The first week was dominated by the one film that everyone had come to see. Fellini drew a packed house, waiting to be scandalised.' As in Italy, Fellini split the Cannes viewing public right down the middle, producing a typically rowdy screening.

It is worth pausing here to consider the composition of the average Cannes audience at that time, described by the critic Richard Roud in his festival report that year:

There are about ten rows reserved for the press, and about ten for directors and actors. The rest of the seats are given out to producers, distributors, and important exhibitors. If there are any seats left over, they are sold to the public at a guinea per show. Any seats that the producers cannot use they give away to shopkeepers, hotel personnel, and others in return for rebates, reductions, small favours and so on. So the Palais du Festival is not crowded with lovers of the cinema, as one might imagine, but rather with those who have come to see the stars, to be seen, and above all to say they have been. And it has long been a Cannes tradition that the audience shall express its delight or displeasure in the most audible manner possible.

French critics were on the whole dismissive of *La Dolce Vita*, but jury president Georges Simenon, the Belgian detective novelist who enjoyed a massive following in France, had liked what he had seen. Simenon was a strong-minded, opinionated personality, who had already clashed several times with the festival authorities. He was also a stickler for protocol, who had taken time to familiarise himself with festival regulations before heading down to Cannes. Consequently he had already expressed displeasure when high-handed festival director Robert Favre Le Bret declared Simenon president, despite the rules stating that a president should be elected by the jurors. At the very first jury meeting, the festival director took up his customary position in the jury room until he was spied by Simenon, who unceremoniously kicked him out, a humiliating first for the polished and politically astute Favre Le Bret. On the day the awards were due to be dispensed Favre Le Bret took Simenon aside and told him it was imperative the Americans were given at least one major prize. Simenon by this stage had other ideas. His admiration for *La Dolce Vita* was compounded by an acquaintance with Fellini and his wife struck up in the course of the festival. There was resistance to *La Dolce Vita* from several jury members but Simenon had an ace up his sleeve. He had developed a close rapport with fellow novelist and juror Henry Miller, who'd spent much of the festival indulging his passion for table tennis and hadn't even managed to see all the competition films. The indifferent Miller volunteered to vote as directed by Simenon which, together with the jury president's casting vote, sufficed to get *La Dolce Vita* the Palme d'Or. Several years later, learning about the Simenon jury shenanigans for the first time, Fellini declared that it was to Simenon that he owed his career.

Fellini was booed when he went to collect his prize, yet by comparison with the rough ride endured by his compatriot Michelangelo Antonioni, he escaped lightly: *L'Avventura* had already been met with jeers when shown a week earlier. On the final night in the Palais those scenes were replayed with even greater ferocity when *L'Avventura* and *La Dolce Vita* received their prizes. Peter Baker of *Films and Filming* described the ceremony as 'a scene I have never before witnessed at Cannes; a fantastic melee of formally-dressed critics, film-makers and delegates booing and cheering, hissing and foot-stamping. [Simenon] turned pale under the onslaught.' Evidently the critics who had disliked Fellini's film now believed the jury had made a 'box-office decision', while their own favourite, Grigori Chukhrai's *Ballad of a Soldier*, left empty-handed. To make matters far, far worse, Simenon announced that works by Bergman (*The Virgin Spring*) and Buñuel (*The Young One*) had not even been considered for awards, since their makers were already acknowledged masters of cinema. Simenon was under the impression that this verbal homage would suffice, but as one audience member pointed out, homage is hard to hang on a marquee. *La Dolce Vita*'s US distribution rights, meanwhile, were suddenly set at $1 million. Bergman's producer threatened never to bring another of his films to Cannes.

Holding Back the Sixties

Those attending the festival in 1960 seemed to sense a new mood, one of uncertainty about the kind of festival Cannes was becoming. There were no Hollywood stars on show, and a dearth of the customary attention-grabbing press agent antics. Such starlet incidents as

76 CANNES

occurred were met with palpable embarrassment. Critic Thomas L. Rowe wrote: 'What is most destructive to festival prestige and public morals alike is the dishonest use by the tabloid press to blow up isolated incidents, such as the nude starlet in the pool at the *La Dolce Vita* party, to make Cannes out to be the unbridled orgy it was not.' The political backdrop to the festival was doomy, a 'superpower summit' set for Paris having been cancelled after the Soviets brought down a CIA U-2 spy plane east of Moscow. The presence of the US Sixth Fleet squadron anchored as usual in the bay, a source of cheesy photo-ops for the likes of Brigitte Bardot just a few years earlier, instantly acquired more ominous overtones. But the seriousness of Cannes in 1960 had as much if not more to do with aesthetic considerations. 'Cannes this year, at its best, managed to look like a festival of maturity which had not abandoned exploration', wrote the critic Penelope Houston.

There had not been much maturity on display as the closing night gala had revealed, and a tightening of competition standards and an overhaul of the jury system were now deemed essential if the festival was to retain the full participation of the major producing countries, particularly America. Juries had been too often swayed either by the jury president's personal whim or by external political and economic pressures, or both. The criteria governing awards needed to be properly regulated as well; the incompetence and amateurishness at the closing gala sent out all the wrong signals to the Hollywood majors and their representative body the MPAA, already wary of sending big-budget American films to Cannes for fear of damaging their commercial prospects in important European markets. The absence of Hollywood stars was hardly unexpected, as there had been but one US film in competition, Vincente Minnelli's *Home From the Hill*, which found no favour with the jury – the first year in the festival's history that the US hadn't won a major award.

After 1960, slowly but surely, Cannes became a little less of a place to be seen, a little more of a place to see films. The era of high-profile international auteurs was now in full swing and film could legitimately be regarded as a serious endeavour to rank alongside the other arts. The market too had expanded; buyers and sellers had replaced the starlets on the Croisette, giving the festival the feel of a trade fair. Critics who grumbled about the quality of films in competition could retreat to the numerous little market cinemas on the rue d'Antibes (their numbers vastly reduced since the opening of the new Palais complex in 1983, which houses lots of little cinemas to serve the market's needs), to discover what one French critic called 'clandestine pearls'. In 1960 the market was bulging with *nouvelle vague* films, including a first feature by the firebrand critic Jean-Luc Godard. The French, after some toing and froing, had decided not to put Godard's quirky little picture forward to represent France in competition. *A Bout de souffle*, thankfully, found its own way into the world. The market was the place where the new era of international co-productions was being plotted and fuelled, and keen eyes could spot new trends.

One such trend was the increased levels of nudity and sexual explicitness in the arthouse scene. The sixties were young, church- and state-sponsored censorship prevailed, and we were still some years shy of the art-porn tropes purveyed by Catherine Breillat, Michael Winterbottom and Carlos Reygadas's *Battle in Heaven*. But *La Dolce Vita* proved to be one of the earliest in a lineage of 'shocking', morally scandalous works. That said, its notoriety in Italy wasn't reproduced elsewhere, other than Catholic Spain. The Office Catholique Français du Cinéma took the thoroughly Christian view that 'Fellini loves his characters and regards each of their lives in turn tinged with this love'. For the US *La Dolce Vita* was passed uncut with the Production Code seal.

The Palme d'Or catapulted Fellini to international recognition, so much so he became the first foreign film-maker to be nominated as Best Director by the American Academy. He was not the first Euro-'director-superstar' – Bergman's Cannes prize for *The Seventh Seal* in 1957 meant he got there first – but Fellini was now among a blue-chip band of directors whose films could be sold on the strength of their name, their careers avidly monitored by a newly evolved, highly committed, international *cinéphile* audience fired up by the auteur theory of *Cahiers du cinéma*. Italian cinema was positioned right at the cutting-edge of this arthouse scene, thanks also to Pasolini, Antonioni, Bertolucci, Visconti. *La Dolce Vita*'s phenomenal box-office success prompted an increased investment in 'quality films', particularly in Italy, where previously reluctant producers now saw the point. Cinecittà studios in Rome became a centre of technical excellence which benefited the Italian industry at all levels. One Italian critic coined the phrase *superspettacolo d'autore* or auteurist blockbuster, which the Italians became renowned for producing in the sixties. There would be another Italian double at Cannes in 1963 – the Jury Prize for Antonioni's *L'Eclisse* and the Palme d'Or for Visconti's *The Leopard*.

Italian stars such as Sophia Loren, Claudia Cardinale, Monica Vitti and Marcello Mastroianni were beautiful and charismatic too, of course, as well as earthy, natural and less remote than their US counterparts. Together with Venice, Cannes was both a beneficiary and a facilitator of Italian cinema's newfound glamour. In the absence of anything resembling Hollywood's publicity machinery for grooming its stars, Cannes' annual sprinkle of glitter and aura provided that vital iconic push, enabled by the plethora of publicists newly arrived on the scene in Europe. Mastroianni is reckoned to have attended Cannes on more occasions than any other star in its sixty-year history. Loren was probably the only personage other than Bardot who could bring the festival to an absolute standstill. She was the competition jury president in 1966, the first woman ever to hold the position singlehandedly (Olivia de Havilland had shared presidency duties a year earlier with André Maurois).

This Italian golden era lasted till the eighties, when Italian cinema sank into a doldrums from which it has yet to fully recover. A Cannes award to Giuseppe Tornatore's nostalgic *Cinema Paradiso* in 1989, and the film's subsequent global success, was thought at the time to herald a revival. In retrospect it would be simpler to say that *Paradiso* signalled a whole new strain of subtitled but audience-friendly 'crossover' films, heavily associated with Miramax in the US, which displayed very modest ambitions set next to their arthouse forebears of the sixties and seventies. Cannes still awaits the cinematic *Risorgimento*.

A Spaniard in the Works

No other film director has drawn down the wrath of the Church and other self-styled guardians of civic morality with such metronomic frequency as the masterly Spanish surrealist Luis Buñuel. The opening salvo in this protracted, career-long skirmish was *Un Chien Andalou* (1929), an iconoclastic *jeu d'esprit* fashioned in collaboration with Salvador Dali, which opened with an assault upon an eyeball with a cut-throat razor, nestled amongst other imagery of equally shocking and incendiary power. The virulently anti-Church *L'Age d'Or* in 1930 provoked one of the most violent reactions ever directed against any film. Groups of thugs urged on by the French right-wing press attacked the Parisian theatre where the film was showing, smashing chairs and defacing the surrealist paintings in the foyer. The film was immediately banned and, incredibly, not shown again in Paris until 1981.

Scandal and provocation were, of course, favoured tactics for the surrealist movement from its outset, their aim to dislodge a staid public from their more comfortable, everyday habits of mind. As Buñuel's career developed, he began to leaven his own blatant shock-tactics with larger doses of subtle irony, paradox, ambiguity, and, above all, dark humour. Nevertheless, controversies remained his meat and drink (or, we might say in light of his famous preferences, his Martini and Gauloises). In 1955 surrealist spokesman André Breton advised Buñuel that 'it's no longer possible to scandalise anyone'. Buñuel disagreed, and would prove Breton wrong on several further occasions. In 1960 Buñuel wrote and directed *Viridiana*, a sort of scabrous parable about religious faith and its often perversely distorting effects on human desire. The convulsions occasioned by the picture at Cannes in 1961 were astonishing, even in a career dedicated, like Buñuel's, to skewering hypocrisy in all its manifestations. To fully savour the nuances of this volatile moment, it's worth taking a brief detour back through his earlier career.

Buñuel remained committed to the aims of surrealism throughout his productive life (although he formally parted company with the group in the mid-1930s, somewhat disillusioned). But the atheism he was bound to profess as a card-carrying surrealist was complicated. 'An atheist, thank God', was how Bunuel described himself, a delightful and teasing paradox. Catholicism dominated and shaped Buñuel's life during his formative years, breeding an enduring fascination with ritual and iconography. Buñuel, though, reserved particular contempt for tyranny imposed in the name of the faith, especially for those repressive political regimes legitimised and supported by the Vatican, and his films are full of characters whose lives are damaged by irrational belief and religious dogma. Of his boyhood experience of Catholicism he remarked, 'Ironically, its implacable prohibition [of sex] inspired a feeling for sin which for me was positively voluptuous.' Evidently his youthful imagination was already set on a course that the Church might not condone.

Buñuel departed Spain in 1925 and settled in Paris, where he thrived amid a germane cultural ferment. He was thus a distraught onlooker when the Spanish Civil War broke out in 1936. Franco's Falangist forces eventually defeated the Republicans in 1939, inaugurating a thirty-six-year reign during which Spain became an isolated Catholic theocracy; political parties were banned, the media was censored and basic freedoms were heavily curtailed. (Buñuel was actually forbidden from returning to Spain until the 1950s.) He moved to New York and ultimately settled in Mexico in 1946, embarking on a twenty-year period of startling creative fecundity, during which he took up Mexican nationality in 1949. The first of Mexico's so-called cinematic golden ages was then on the wane. Throughout the forties a particular strain

SACRED MONSTERS

of epic melodrama, glorifying the revolution, had enjoyed success at Cannes and so claimed the world's attention – prizes were awarded to Emilio Fernández's *María Candelaria* and *Flor Silvestre* in 1946 and 1947. But the interloper Buñuel exhibited a different sensibility and a harder vision, beginning with *Los Olvidados* (1950), a bleak realist portrait of crime and poverty in Mexico's slums, the first of eight times Buñuel was called into the Official Selection at Cannes, and the winner then of the Prix de la Mise en Scène. *Nazarin* (1959) also won him a Prix, and Cannes succeeded almost singlehandedly in keeping Buñuel's reputation alive in Europe during his difficult and often painful exile in Mexico.

In 1960 Buñuel decided to shoot *Viridiana* in Spain, where Franco, in an attempt to lessen Spain's isolation, had announced an amnesty for all Spanish artists. Buñuel's exiled Spanish Republican friends in Mexico were deeply shocked. 'Until now', they protested, 'we have had three citadels, three rocks: Pablo Casals, Picasso and Buñuel. And now the citadel of Buñuel has fallen.' But Buñuel had accompanied *The Young One* to Cannes in 1960, and there encountered a younger generation of Spanish critics, producers and directors. It was their enthusiasm which swayed his decision to return to Spain, but only on condition that *Viridiana* would be produced by a company with a history of anti-Francoism. Still, even Buñuel's closest friends found it difficult to comprehend his motives; why endorse Franco's supposed liberalisation, and at the same time submit his new film to the most rigorous censorship anywhere in the world? Was he planning to put the amnesty to some kind of test? The truth was probably more simple. Buñuel missed his native land, and had never fully settled in Mexico. 'I am fatally attracted to Spain,' he told a close friend. His Cannes experience had also opened his eyes to the newer currents and riches in European cinema, fuelling an eagerness to reestablish his own cinematic practice in his home continent.

Buñuel and his collaborator Julio Alejandro duly produced a script for *Viridiana* and submitted it to the notorious Spanish censor, who

82

CANNES

demanded several changes. The censor was especially horrified by Buñuel's proposed ending, with its overt suggestions of a male character's sexual congress with two women successively (outside of wedlock, and one of those a novice nun). Paradoxically, Buñuel confided later, the censor's interventions actually helped him to overcome difficulties he had been having with the script; but the changes he made as a result in fact nudged the film into potentially more blasphemous and explosive terrain. His altered ending, for example, now hinted fairly robustly at an impending *ménage à trois*.

The story in fact bore some superficial similarities to his *Nazarin* of two years previously. Here, too, a Christian protagonist discovers that her virtue is redundant in the contemporary world. Viridiana is a novice nun whose attempts to practise charity only serve to hasten her spiritual degradation. An uncle consumed by fetishised lust and grief confuses Viridiana with his dead wife, and tries to seduce her. When he later commits suicide, Viridiana's guilt propels her to lavish charity on a gang of beggars and outcasts, who abuse her generosity at every turn. Humiliated, Viridiana renounces her faith and finally takes up with her cousin and his mistress. The film is laden with erotic and blasphemous symbolism – a flick-knife in the shape of a cross, and a Last Supper parody comprised of drunken, lecherous beggars at an orgy. It's a scathing, bitter, unequivocal denunciation of a morally bankrupt Spain languishing in the darkness under Franco. In its anguished view of a society dominated by Catholicism, it shared a certain kinship with *La Dolce Vita*, as several critics noted.

Shooting of the film was completed in Madrid in April 1961, and its producers, despite Buñuel's reticence, were keen to show the film at Cannes in May. The official Spanish commission which normally passed films to be shown at festivals (not the same office as the censor, but closely linked to it) requested to see the film. They were given an incomplete version without sound or music. Meanwhile a duplicate negative had been sent by boat to Paris so that post-production work could be completed by Buñuel in better equipped Parisian facilities.

SACRED MONSTERS 83

Five days before the opening of Cannes, the picture was ready, but there was inadequate time to get the film to and from Madrid for approval by the commission. To everyone's surprise, *Viridiana*'s producers were granted exceptional and unprecedented authorisation for the film to be shown without such approval.

No other Spanish film was selected to show at Cannes that year. And there was no ambiguity about the film's status – despite it being a Spanish/Mexican co-production, José Munoz Fontán, the director-general of Spanish cinema and theatre, arrived in Cannes and let it be known on several occasions to various organs of the press that *Viridiana* was officially representing Spain. It was originally scheduled to screen mid-festival, but the delays in 'post' and in subtitling meant that a print didn't arrive in Cannes until the penultimate day, to the consternation of festival officials. Yet director Robert Favre Le Bret was determined to show it, repeatedly altering the schedule to accommodate its impending arrival. *Viridiana* finally played on the afternoon of 17 May, and again that evening, the last of the competition screenings in what had, by all accounts, been a fairly uninspiring year. Mexican actress Silvia Piñal, the film's blonde and thrillingly husky heroine, later recalled the aftermath of that first afternoon. 'The spectators emerged from the Palais like mad people, declaring: "A bomb, Buñuel has detonated a bomb . . ."' Its distributor François Gergely remembers similar consternation. 'From the moment the afternoon screening finished, the rumours up and down the Croisette were all about *Viridiana*.'

Buñuel didn't particularly enjoy attending film festivals, and had decided to remain in Paris with his wife. He had not enjoyed himself at Cannes as a juror in 1954, feeling so frustrated with the noise, the crowds and his fellow jurors that he stormed out of the closing ceremony and threw his dinner jacket into the sea. In 1961 it was probably a wise decision of his to stay away. The atmosphere was tense. Police were swarming everywhere, fearful of an attack by Algerian terrorist groups. A French minister was due to preside over the closing ceremony in the Palais, which meant security, tight throughout the festival, was stepped up even further in the final two days.

The jury had been, by all accounts, very uncertain about the choice of laureate up until that late stage. The evening screening of *Viridiana*, however, clarified matters. Buñuel's biographer John Baxter claims that Robert Favre Le Bret pulled strings to ensure Buñuel won the Palme d'Or, although this is now impossible to verify. (The next year, according to the same source, Favre Le Bret diverted his patronage from Buñuel's *Exterminating Angel* to Sidney Lumet's *Long Day's Journey Into Night*, so as to placate Hollywood.) What is certainly true is that Favre Le Bret had gone to some lengths to ensure *Viridiana*'s presence at the festival; and that, in general, the Palme d'Or tended not to go to a film appearing so late.

Viridiana was awarded the top prize ex aequo [equally] with the French film *Une Aussi Longue Absence*, directed by Alain Resnais's collaborator Henri Colpi, scripted by Marguerite Duras. At the closing ceremony, jury president Jean Giono was vigorously applauded for his announcements, most especially for *Viridiana*, which a beaming Señor Fontán went up on stage to accept. Some people may view this film as scandalous, Fontán told the assembled throng, but for Spain this was an important moment, the first time it had ever won a big prize in an international film festival. (It remains to date Spain's only Palme d'Or, despite the strenuous efforts and claims of Pedro Almodóvar.) 'There is no record of a Cannes award being more unanimously approved,' wrote film critic David Robinson for the *Financial Times*. Public and critics were for once united, a marked contrast with the previous year's furore over Italy's double-whammy. The delighted Spanish and Mexican contingents partied long and hard that night. Back in Paris, a messenger brought Buñuel the news of his triumph. 'You're drunk,' he retorted incredulously.

The next day, the storm broke. *L'Osservatore Romano* published an article condemning *Viridiana* for its blasphemy and the Vatican immediately made representations to the Spanish government. The Italian press, in particular, went into overdrive – no doubt with the *La Dolce*

SACRED MONSTERS

Vita rumpus fresh in their minds – pronouncing *Viridiana* abject, disrespectful to the Church and evidence of the moral bankruptcy of Spanish cinema. The film was banned by the Procurator General in Milan, and the Italian government, following directives issued by the Vatican, condemned Buñuel to a year's imprisonment should he ever step on Italian soil. Copies were seized and destroyed in Belgium (but not before it had picked up an important critics' prize there).

The responses of different authoritarian regimes to a Cannes prize are always revealing, particularly towards a film they haven't sanctioned, or one made by a difficult 'dissident' auteur. A Cannes prize can sometimes create confusion, place a government on the back foot. Not so in this case. The Spanish government struck back fast, immediately declaring the film 'sacrilegious and impious', sacking the unfortunate Fontán and replacing him with a Falangist, Monsignor Jésus Sueros. The rest of the Spanish delegation in Cannes were also summarily dismissed. Spanish newspapers were forbidden to refer to either the film, the award, or Buñuel; one, *Pueblo*, managed a single mention before the veil of silence came down. An attempt was made to drive the Spanish production company that had co-funded the film out of business – the Spanish pre-censor repeatedly turned down their subsequent projects at script stage. There was even talk of sacking the Minister of Information. When Franco himself finally demanded to view the film, he was apparently unable to see what all the fuss was about. 'But how', Buñuel wondered, 'can you shock a man who's committed so many atrocities?'

The fallout continued for around ten months afterwards, and dealt a near-fatal blow to *Viridiana*'s commercial prospects. Under normal circumstances producers will want to release a Cannes prizewinner into French theatres as quickly as possible after the festival, to capitalise on the publicity generated. For a foreign film to do so at that time necessitated authorisation from the Commission de Contrôle Française, who in turn required various documents from the country of production. But as the Spanish government now refused to even

86

CANNES

acknowledge the film's existence, the necessary documents were not forthcoming. It transpired the original negative had been seized in Madrid, and all Buñuel's films were henceforth banned in Spain. Fortunately a duplicate negative remained in Paris, from which copies could be struck and circulated to various sales territories. But there was yet another problem. According to the Spanish authorities *Viridiana* had been smuggled illegally into France, and they now forbade all commercial exploitation of the film and circulation of copies. Pressure was applied to the French CNC (Centre National de la Cinématographie), who even sent a telegram to the French laboratory holding the negative, forbidding them to make copies. The matter dragged, and the deadlock was only broken thanks to some adroit legal work capitalising upon the Mexican stake in the film's co-production, whereby Spanish consent was rendered no longer a legal requirement. The scandal, at least, had generated massive interest that survived the film's delayed arrival in cinemas. A private screening set up before the official French release was attended by Sartre and de Beauvoir, among other Parisian notables. In New York and London too, *Viridiana* enjoyed a belated warm welcome.

Cannes, as so often before and since, had provided a stage for the unfolding of an explosive drama with myriad political repercussions. The publicity generated by a major Cannes award had, in turn, pushed important issues to the forefront of world attention, such as the perenially overweening power of the Church to intervene in artistic matters, and the iniquities of Franco's Spain (as underlined by the constant influx of Spanish immigrants into France at this time). Judged against its 'free festival' mission statement, Cannes appeared to have emerged from this debacle with its integrity and reputation intact, if not enhanced – whereas the Vatican had merely gratified rock-bottom expectations. Had the slippery Favre Le Bret predicted and to some extent instigated all this? Certainly Buñuel had a reputation for exciting scandal – alongside glamour, the life-blood of any festival with an international profile to maintain.

SACRED MONSTERS 87

Viridiana proved to be a turning point in Buñuel's career. The film critic Andrew Sarris wrote back from Cannes, 'Many of us had to readjust to a new conception of Buñuel as a master instead of a martyr.' The Palme d'Or served to position him quite rightly at the forefront of the band of great European auteurs who proceeded to revolutionise cinema throughout the sixties and seventies. *Viridiana* was also a spur to a new generation of Spanish film-makers trying to function in difficult circumstances. Franco's moribund regime would limp on until the dictator's demise in 1975, and Buñuel wouldn't make another film in Spain for ten years. But despite his intractable character, the Spanish authorities couldn't ignore Buñuel's artistic stature and occasionally made half-hearted or hastily withdrawn overtures. In Mexico, meanwhile, where a *cinema novo* was in the works, radical young directors had felt the benefit of Buñuel's anarchic presence amid the staidness of their previously genre-based national cinema.

Viridiana didn't play to the Spanish public until 1977. That same year, on the set of what would be his final feature, *That Obscure Object of Desire*, Buñuel was approached by a Dominican who claimed to have written the piece which initiated the *Viridiana* furore. When he asked for forgiveness, Buñuel threw him off the set. Buñuel died on 29 July 1983, the same year that the new Palais complex opened in Cannes, housing a screening room named in his honour. The master's spirit would live on in many an impious artwork, perhaps nowhere more raucously than in the Monty Python team, wherein it had migrated from a high to a pop-culture register. Terry Jones and company were certainly no strangers to surrealist mischief-making and Church-baiting – think only of the outcry that greeted *Monty Python's Life of Brian* in 1979. In 1983 the team's subsequent feature *The Meaning of Life* competed at Cannes, shoulder-to-shoulder with the likes of Bresson and Tarkovsky, and walked off with the Jury Prize. 'The money is in a bag behind the sink,' Jones told the black-tie gathering as he accepted the prize. One immediately seminal scene in the Python film made tremendous comedy of a horde of grubby-faced

88

period urchins born to the same working-class dad in a Northern industrial town. This father, played by Michael Palin, insists that his religion proscribes birth control, whatever the consequences for household space, then leads his clan in a musical number entitled, 'Every Sperm is Sacred'. One suspects Don Luis would have enjoyed that spectacle, especially had he been sat in the Palais with an illicit shaker of dry Martini and a supply of good black tobacco.

'They've arrested Suzanne!'

The most troublesome presence at Cannes in 1966 was a two-hundred-year-old nun named Suzanne Simonin. The titular character of Denis Diderot's novel of 1760, *La Religieuse*, she found herself reincarnated by Jacques Rivette in the shape of Godard's ex-muse Anna Karina. A former editor of *Cahiers du cinéma*, Rivette was one of the core group of ex-critics who, along with Godard, Truffaut, and Chabrol, had refashioned French cinema as the *nouvelle vague*. What was odd about Rivette's presence at Cannes was not that he had made the leap into film-making (albeit with less speed and immediate impact than Godard or Truffaut) but that his film had been selected in the first place: this, for the simple reason that it had been banned in France. Nevertheless, the Minister of Culture André Malraux consented to its inclusion as a French competition title. The anomaly – the absurdity, even – of a film banned by the state representing France at Cannes was unique in the festival's history. But it was only an episode in the remarkable and instructive story of the controversy that surrounded the film.

La Religieuse had been dogged by the threat of censorship even before it was made. As Rivette observed of France in the 1960s, 'it was a time when censorship existed for real. Any film that looked potentially risky had to go before a pre-censorship board.' More than once, Rivette had presented the script to the board, the president of which was a right-winger and fervent Catholic. 'I told him that we weren't looking to make a scandal, that we had no intention of "doing a

SACRED MONSTERS

Vadim"'. In other words, Rivette would not give Diderot the same titillating, meretricious treatment as Bardot's svengali inflicted on Laclos's *Les Liaisons dangereuses* in 1959. The film-makers were asked to make a few changes and so received the go-ahead. However, during filming in the winter of 1965, a number of Catholic organisations had begun to mobilise opinion against the film, calling on the Minister of Information, Alain Peyrefitte, to take action against a work which the president of the Union of Mothers Superior described, sight unseen, as being 'blasphemous and degrading to holy sisters'.

Two centuries after his death, Denis Diderot was, it seemed, still an incendiary figure. Critic, essayist and *encyclopédiste*, Diderot (1713–1784) was one of the towering figures of the Enlightenment who, along with his contemporaries Rousseau and Voltaire, armed himself with scientific reason the better to target the medieval obscurantism of Church dogma and the tyrannical structures of a corrupt political system. The fate of certain of his works in his lifetime came to define the intolerance of an absolutist monarchy. In 1746, his *Pensées philosophiques* was burned by the Parliament of Paris and, in 1749, he was imprisoned for his *Lettre sur les aveugles*. *La Religieuse* was Diderot's notorious satire of convent life in which Suzanne, a young woman of illegitimate birth, is forced into a convent where she submits to the attentions, variously sapphic and sadistic, of three Mothers Superior. The salacious possibilities inherent in the story are obvious and, combined with Diderot's name, were reasons enough for the faithful to fear the worst.

As the incoming Minister of Information Yvon Bourges had inherited from his predecessor a desk groaning under the weight of petitions against Rivette's film, some of which had been sent to the wife of the president, Yvonne de Gaulle, who passed them on to the minister concerned. In response to the anxieties expressed by the film's adversaries Rivette modified the title of his sober, slightly theatrical and utterly non-salacious film to *Suzanne Simonin, la Religieuse de Diderot*. Despite the Censorship Commission, having seen the film twice, advising that it be seen only by audiences of eighteen years and above, Bourges single-handedly endorsed the most punitive of political options: a complete ban, necessary, he argued, because 'this film is deeply offensive to the sensibility and conscience of a very large part of the population'. Reactions against the tough decision of de Gaulle's minister were correspondingly vociferous. In its April 1966 issue, *Cahiers du cinéma* put Rivette's film on its cover and headlined its extensive treatment of the scandal with a call to arms: 'WAR IS DECLARED.'

Elsewhere, inhabitants of a town that shared the same name as the censorious minister Bourges declared their solidarity with the forbidden film by proposing to change its name to either 'Diderot' or 'Rivette'. Daily features in *Le Monde* updated readers on 'The Affair of *La Religieuse*'. But all attested to a lively and concerned interest in freedom of expression as a right that was not be compromised by the arbitrary interference of state or church. And most were aimed squarely at the government rather than the agitating religious organisations.

The film's subsequent selection for Cannes revealed the absurdity of the ban, and hardened attitudes towards what was increasingly being seen as the authoritarianism of de Gaulle's regime. In retrospect, the actions of Malraux, the Minister of Culture, can be seen as a desire to defend Rivette's film, and by extension Diderot's novel, in the name of freedom of expression, but without becoming mired in the religious debates. The minister could not directly oppose his opposite number in the Ministry of Information but was able to demonstrate his disagreement by authorising the film's participation at Cannes. Malraux's justification was that the controversy around the film was a strictly domestic affair – in other words, not a problem at an international festival. The screening passed off without incident and the film won no prize.

Unsurprisingly Jean-Luc Godard was among the most vitriolic voices heard during the *La Religieuse* affair, most prominently in two texts published during April 1966. The first appeared in *Le Monde* the day after the ban, in which Godard spoke, acerbically, for his generation:

SACRED MONSTERS

I only knew Fascism from books. 'They've taken Danielle. They've arrested Pierre. They're going to shoot Etienne.' All these phrases typical of the Resistance and the Gestapo struck me more and more deeply but never in my flesh and blood since I'd had the luck of being born too late. Yesterday, suddenly, everything changed: 'They've arrested Suzanne'. Yes. The police have gone to Georges' [de Beauregard] and the laboratory. They've seized the copies. Thank-you, Yvon Bourges, for having made me confront the true face of current intolerance.

The second, published four days later in the current affairs magazine *Le Nouvel Observateur*, was an open letter addressed to the Minister of 'Kultur'. A masterpiece of invective, Godard's letter to André Malraux was informed not only by the director's righteous anger at the State's heavy-handed treatment of his colleague Rivette but also by his own experience of censorship. Godard knew whereof he spoke – he was already the director of ten features, three of which had suffered some kind of state interference. His second, *Le Petit soldat*, shot in 1960, was banned for two years. *Une femme mariée* (1964) had to lose the definitive article from its title so as not to defame French womanhood. *Pierrot le fou* (1965) was unavailable to audiences under eighteen on account of its 'political and moral anarchism'. By way of introduction, Godard wrote: 'I am not very sure in any case, my dear André Malraux, that you will understand a word of this letter. But since you are the only Gaullist I know, you must be the target for my anger.' And he went on to vent to his anger thus:

Being a film-maker as others are Jews or Blacks, I was beginning to get fed up having to go to see you to beg you to intercede with your friends Roger Frey and Georges Pompidou for mercy every time a film was condemned to death by that Gestapo of the spirit, censorship. But God in Heaven! I never imagined for a moment that I might have to do this for your brother Diderot, a journalist and writer like you, and for his *Religieuse*, my sister, a French citizen who humbly begs our Father to protect her independence . . .

This time, happily, your refusal to see me or to answer the telephone opened my eyes. What I took to be your courage or intelligence when you saved my *Femme mariée* from Peyrefitte's axe . . . I see now that it was simply cowardice. [. . .] Were it not so profoundly sinister, it would be profoundly moving and heartening to see a UNR [the Gaullist political party Union pour la Nouvelle République] minister in 1966 so afraid of the encyclopaedist spirit of 1789 [. . .] It is hardly surprising that you do not recognise my voice when I talk to you of assassination in connection with the banning of *Suzanne Simonin, la Religieuse de Diderot*. No. Hardly anything surprises in such extreme cowardice. You have buried yourself like an ostrich in your inner memories. How then could you hear me, André Malraux, who telephones you from outside, from a far country, from Free France?

As is often the case with Godard, the letter is a tissue of allusions and puns held together by its rhetorical tone of furious incomprehension. How could Malraux, of all people, consent to this act of censorship? The very incarnation of the politically engaged intellectual, he had been a committed anti-fascist before the Second World War having fought for the Republican cause in Spain in the 1930s as well as having written one of the definitive novels about the anti-Franco struggle, *L'Espoir* ('Hope', 1937). As well as being a prizewinning novelist, he wrote major works of art history, including the seminal *Le musée imaginaire* ('The Imaginary Museum', 1952–4). He was involved in the Resistance movement throughout the Second World War and when de Gaulle came to form his Fifth Republic government in 1958 he called on Malraux to be the first Minister of Culture. Malraux thus inaugurated a Gaullist republican 'cultural politics' which remains, to this day, a key characteristic of the relationship between the state and the French nation and which has served, not without controversy, to

SACRED MONSTERS

exalt and promote what de Gaulle called 'a certain idea of France'. Many on the left had deep misgivings about Malraux serving in the Gaullist administration. Godard, in his inimitable manner, spoke for them.

Some commentators have cast the *La Religieuse* scandal as a remarkable re-enactment of an ideological battle, worthy of the Enlightenment. Others see it less in terms of an organised conspiracy between church and state against freedom of expression than as an episode fuelled by Catholic traditionalists who considered the Church as a citadel besieged on one hand by the Revolution – in the still provocative figure of Diderot – and by modernism – in the power of cinema – at the moment when they were outraged by the reforms of Vatican II council and when right-wing politicians were assiduous in courting Catholic voters. The historian Antoine de Baecque has interpreted the affair as marking a transition among the *nouvelle vague* generation away from its all-consuming *cinéphilia* towards the discovery of political consciousness: 'the cinéphiles now knew that they should fear the Gaullist state, after having been the beneficiaries of its largesse and subsidies (notably in the form of the nouvelle vague and the Cinémathèque Française)'. This newly provoked political consciousness – noticeably absent throughout the 1950s at the time of France's colonial war in Algeria – would be further sharpened in February 1968 by Malraux's arbitrary dismissal of Henri Langlois as head of the Cinémathèque, which he had founded over thirty years before. In de Baecque's account, the events of May 1968 had been fomented among the *cinéphile* generation since 1966. The 'war' that *Cahiers du cinéma* saw the Gaullist state as having declared over Rivette's film was far from over. In 1968, it would claim all of France, the Cannes Festival included.

V

'Our mere presence here makes them die': *enfants terribles* and provoc*auteurs*

These hardened old men must die! We will no longer be satisfied with 'well-meaning films with a humanist message', we want more – of the real thing, fascination, experience – childish and pure, like all real art. We want to get back to the time when love between film-maker and film was young, when you could see the joy of creation in every frame of a film.

Lars von Trier, Manifesto for *The Element of Crime*, 1984

The phrase *épater les bourgeois* has proved so useful and enduring that it has passed comfortably into English. Literally meaning 'to flabbergast the middle class' or 'to stagger the conventionally-minded', it carries connotations that Anglo-Saxonisms like 'satirise' or 'take the piss' simply cannot – connotations of shock, scandal and controversy. The phrase is attributed both to Victor Hugo and Charles Baudelaire, nineteenth-century 'moderns' to a man. From Manet's *Olympia* and Flaubert's *Madame Bovary* to Baudelaire's *Les Fleurs du mal* and Stravinsky's *The Rite of Spring*, the chronology of modern art is a list of conventions controversially overturned and audiences suitably scandalised. In 1830, Hugo's opera *Hernani* provoked a lively public controversy that gave rise to another meaningful French phrase, *Bataille d'Hernani*, still used to describe aesthetic scandals that signify major divisions in taste and sensibilities. This is the nineteenth-century narrative in which the idea of modern art as a ritual of transgression becomes established, which is partly why the term *épater les bourgeois* has a historical ring.

In the age of film and mass media the 'art scandal' has become a widely experienced and much-mediated ritual. François Truffaut once described the classic career trajectory of an *enfant terrible* as tracing an absolutely predictable arc: from scandal and controversy to 'a house in the country and the Légion d'honneur'. Truffaut knew what he was talking about. In the late 1950s he had the reputation of being a vituperative young critic who took no prisoners among those he considered to be cinema's Old Guard. The activities of this Young Turk saw him banned from the Cannes Festival as a journalist in 1958 only to return the following year to win Best Director Prize for his first feature film *Les Quatre cents coups*. For some the route from obloquy to ovation was especially direct. For others it was less so.

The festival's early history includes an encounter that would prove highly significant for the history of twentieth-century art, though few who gathered on the morning of 20 April 1951 in the Vox Cinema on the rue d'Antibes could have sensed as much. There, in the margins of the fourth Cannes Film Festival, those present awaited the screening of *Traité de bave et d'éternité*, translated as either 'Venom and Eternity' or, more piquantly literal, 'Treatise on Slobber and Eternity'. The film was the work of a twenty-six-year-old Romanian-born poet, Jean-Isidore Golstein, who was attending the festival as the leading light of a group of Parisian avant-garde artists called the Lettrists, albeit under his *nom de guerre* Isidore Isou. The Lettrists arrived in Cannes trailing the perfume of scandal. In April 1950, four members disrupted the Easter Mass at Paris's Notre-Dame Cathedral. One of their number, disguised as a Dominican monk, read a sermon that described the Catholic Church as 'the running sore on the decomposed body of the West' and declared (or reiterated) 'the death of God'. The group then set their sights on another form of public ritual, the cinema, and yet another powerful institution, the Cannes Festival.

In true avant-garde style Isou issued a bracing polemic declaring: 'Cinema is too rich. It is obese. Suffering from a case of congestion, this pig stuffed with fat will rip apart into a thousand pieces. I

ENFANTS TERRIBLES AND PROVOCAUTEURS

announce the destruction of cinema.' In his own film-making Isou was as good as his word. *Traité* was as extreme as experimental 'anti-cinema' got in the early 1950s: it ran at four hours, large sections of which were image-free and consisted of 'an aural collage of guttural sound poetry and random noise'. Having arrived uninvited in Cannes the Lettrists proceeded to harass enough people to secure a slot for Isou's film. It was shown 'hors festival' to an audience comprised largely of members of the press and an *ad hoc* jury, though Isou interrupted the screening before the end. The desired effects of shocked incomprehension and scandalised rejection were nonetheless forthcoming. It was reported that a 'mini-riot' ensued among the journalists present with a specialist of children's films, the evocatively named Sonica Bo, slapping Isou's face. Notwithstanding – or, perhaps, precisely because of – the outraged reactions, Isou was awarded two prizes, the 'Prix des Spectateurs d'Avant Garde' and 'Prix en Marge de Festival de Cannes' by the renegade jury.

Also among the audience was a nineteen-year-old *lycée* graduate by the name of Guy-Ernest Debord, and he was much taken by the Lettrists' provocations. By the year's end he would move to Paris and throw in his lot with this most extreme faction of art agitators. Six years later, he would found the Situationist International, one of the most influential avant-garde movements of the twentieth century. But as an immediate result of his epiphany at Cannes, Debord would return the following year as part of a 'Lettrist commando team' tasked with undertaking a 'systematic sabotage' of the festival. In 1952 the Lettrists brought three films, all uninvited. And their express wish? 'We want to go beyond these derisory competitions of sub-products between little businessmen who are either already illiterate or destined to soon become so. Our mere presence here makes them die.'

But this time there was a more specific motive behind the Lettrists' militant rhetoric, to do with censorship. One of their three films, Gil Wolman's *L'Anticoncept* had been banned in France, so putting it in the company of Italian-made fascist propaganda, American pornography and Todd Browning's infamous *Freaks*. At the festival, though, they were met with relative indifference, their provocations dismissed as indistinguishable from the activities of 'autograph hunters', as the French daily *Le Figaro* put it. The festival organisation, not born yesterday, had seen them coming and erected suitable obstacles, restricting accreditation for some of their number and refusing entry to others. This led to a rather undignified 'commando operation' in which Debord participated. On the orders of one of the principal Lettrists, who went under the name Marc'O, they attacked the festival office. Marc'O's diminutive wife, known as 'Poucette' ('Hop o' my thumb') hurled herself at the press attaché who was handling accreditations, a noisy struggle ensued, the police were called and eleven Lettrists were arrested. More than twenty-five years later, Debord observed with a certain *amour propre*: 'It is sometimes surprising to discover the atmosphere of hate and malediction that has constantly surrounded me, and as much as possible, kept me hidden. Some think it is because of the grave responsibility that has often been attributed to me for the origins of the May 1968 revolt. I think rather that it is what I did in 1952 that has been disliked for so long.' Which might account for why there is no mention in the Cannes online archives of the 1951 awards given to Isou's film; and why, in 2001, when Debord's own cinematic oeuvre was given a new, restored lease of life in a complete retrospective, it screened at Venice.

Truffaut the Thug

A small group of highly motivated young Turks with a taste for issuing provocative manifestos and incendiary calls-to-arms. A collection of *enfants terribles* who, throughout the 1950s, set about revolutionising what they saw as the moribund state of French cinema. A strategy of attacking esteemed elders and assaulting the citadel of the Cannes Film Festival. Sounds familiar? The parallels between the Lettrists and the New Wave are striking yet they are rarely remarked

ENFANTS TERRIBLES AND PROVOCAUTEURS

upon. Admittedly, there are differing degrees of extremism in their respective declarations: the Lettrists (and, later, the Situationist International) sought an 'anti-cinema' as part of their overarching assault on 'the Society of the Spectacle'; whereas the New Wave wanted to explode the sclerotic structures of French film-making from within, in order to reinvigorate it with a youthful spirit. The former group desired the complete destruction of cinema as it was; the latter its revitalisation. But they pursued these goals in the same city at the same time and in the same milieux. And Cannes was frequently the focus of their radicalism.

While its directors-to-be were still scribbling polemics and hustling their first short films into production, the most effective of the New Wave shock-troops was 'that young thug of journalism' François Truffaut. The respected director Claude Autant-Lara (respected by people other than Truffaut and his ilk, at least) dubbed Truffaut thus after having been on the receiving end of one too many critical assaults by the young writer who regarded him as representative of all that was rotten in French 'quality' cinema. Still in his twenties, Truffaut was the most visible of the generation of young *cinéphiles* who were intent on redefining French cinema, and he gained a reputation as a journalist and critic set on confronting the establishment. As his French biographers put it, 'The *auteur* theory, as conceived by Truffaut, entails a strategy of continually harassing the enemy.' This he did via the pages of the monthly *Cahiers du cinéma* and in the wide-circulation weekly *Arts*. It was in *Arts*, though, that the Cannes Festival came in for a particular kicking.

Between 1955 and 1958, Truffaut attended Cannes as a journalist and criticised it from every possible angle, his articles becoming longer and more polemical the more well known he became. Film festivals were 'trade fairs and nothing else'. If smaller countries sent their best film to Cannes this was not true of the US, France and Italy. 'The forty films of all nationalities serve only to give a very imprecise idea of what is most interesting in world cinema,' he observed in 1955, relating the poverty of the selection to the cowardice of the jury. The following year, Truffaut's polemic was more trenchant. In an article entitled 'These Ridiculous Awards', he attacked the jury's perceived favouritism: 'When a jury with a French majority awards the three major prizes to French films there is chauvinism in the air.' He also claimed that the festival would become meaningless unless the selection was entirely rethought and unless 'official personages' no longer had the power to exclude from competition films like Alain Resnais's *Nuit et brouillard* and Orson Welles's *Mr Arkadin*.

From 1957, Truffaut stepped up his assault, launching ad hominem attacks on those he held responsible for what, in the festival's tenth year, he berated as 'a failure dominated by compromises, schemes and *faux pas*'. Dismissing William Wyler's *Friendly Persuasion*, which had won the Palme d'Or, as 'one of the worst films screened' at the festival, he claimed that his opinion of the festival as a wash-out was shared by the majority of his fellow critics who would not say so in print for fear of being 'struck off the list for next year'. Why was the festival 'a failure'? Because, Truffaut asserted, it was organised and run by people who, quite simply, 'didn't love cinema'. Chief among them was the festival's leading light, Robert Favre Le Bret, whom Truffaut held personally responsible:

> It's he who, directly or indirectly, attempted to oust [Bresson's] *Un condamné à mort s'est échappé* from competition by programming it in the afternoon; it's he who emptied the Croisette forty-eight hours before the end of festivities by imposing a screening of 'Sissi' of no interest to anyone, and it was yet again he who prevented Henri Langlois from screening all the films in the *Hommage to Kurosawa*; it's he who is responsible for an especially incompetent jury; and finally, it is he who caused the mass desertion of stars by clumsily handing over the festival to the Americans.

Quite a charge sheet. Small wonder that Truffaut was soon to find himself *persona non grata* at the festival. The accusation of a flight of

ENFANTS TERRIBLES AND PROVOCAUTEURS

stars is particularly intriguing and Truffaut develops the point in terms of the festival's perceived dependence on Hollywood. 'In order to get Hollywood stars to come to Cannes', he fulminated, 'and thereby holding the "one film per country" regulation in complete contempt, last year four American films were screened *all in the evening* . . . Now, it is well known that the more one flatters the Americans the more they despise you and, to get the upper hand, the following year Hollywood sent not a single star . . . One photographic agency which last year thanks to Kim Novak, Brigitte Bardot, etc, spent 600,000 francs on photographic telexes this year spent less than 100,000 . . .'

The festival regulation that dictated 'one film per country' was, Truffaut pointed out, an eminently poor one, dooming Cannes to a quota of 'official films, academic or sometimes straightforwardly propagandist'. But such constructive criticism was of no avail while the festival was being organised by 'virtuoso hand-kissers who do not love cinema', men who would condemn Robert Bresson to an afternoon slot. Truffaut proposed five 'radical solutions' without which the festival's future would be 'deeply compromised'. These included: to invite several 'ambitious' films from each country, with the right to refuse works deemed 'artistically insufficient'; to insist that producers invite the directors and performers of films to participate in the festival; to place the emphasis on film-makers attending the festival rather than on local businessmen; to integrate and hence respect the retrospective programmes put together by the Cinémathèque Française; and to designate a jury with some knowledge of cinema and 'leave them to deliberate *honestly*'. None of these solutions appears especially radical today, as each has more or less become a staple not only of Cannes but of film festivals generally. However, it would take a few more years of insistent criticism for the administration of the festival to learn to put cinema first.

Truffaut was *persona non grata* at Cannes in 1958, a fact that *Arts* boasted of in its pages which carried a further assault by 'the only critic not invited to Cannes'. Of course, Truffaut attended, and filed perhaps his most outspoken pieces under the unambiguous headline: 'Without radical changes: THE NEXT FESTIVAL IS CONDEMNED'. It went on: 'Ignored by the profession, despised by the critics, this competition has lost all artistic and commercial significance.' With an air of apocalyptic finality, he declared: 'I am convinced that we have just taken part in the last Cannes Festival because the event cannot be countenanced in its present form. If radical changes don't take place, the twelfth festival next year will take place to empty cinemas.' Radical change indeed followed but not of the kind Truffaut anticipated. His debut feature film *Les Quatre cents coups* was not only selected to represent France in 1959 but was awarded the prize for Best Director. In light of his reputation, based more on passionate *cinéphilia* and fervent polemic than on film-making (up to then he had only made the charming 1957 short *Les Mistons*), one might wonder about the motivations behind the award. Did it represent true recognition of the New Wave by the establishment? Or was it a means of recuperating its most vociferous young critic? Possibly a bit of both.

It's also interesting to note that Truffaut's polemic about the 1958 festival included mention of an earlier New Wave feature, Claude Chabrol's *Le Beau Serge*, which he described as having been unanimously received as the best film shown out of competition. In contrast, Truffaut offered an unflattering definition of a particular genre of cinematic production, the 'festival film':

> Those films produced by small countries where the director knows as he's shooting that his work will be projected at Cannes. Hence fifty or so redundant shots destined to be applauded by a tuxedo-clad public, sunsets over landscapes, interminable shots at the end of each scene, false endings, nods and winks to the audience.

Bertrand Tavernier, who attended Cannes in the late 1950s as a young press attaché, similarly recalls audiences 'applauding shots of landscapes, the sea and the sky like an audience at a jazz concert would applaud a solo'. The style of 'festival film' that Truffaut described, a kind of *de luxe* 'official' film-making, would be displaced and eventually supplanted by directors such as himself and Chabrol. The change in the style of the 'festival film', from 'academic' cinema to 'art cinema', would be the product of changes in the character and purpose of film festivals themselves.

'A slightly intestinal festival'

In the annals of Cannes scandal, 1973 remains an unforgettable year. And while it has become a kind of Cannes custom to present at least one 'film de choc' with each year, the law of diminishing returns inevitably applies the more that such controversy becomes a predictable part of the festival experience. In 1973, such controversy might not only have been predicted but appears quite simply to have been programmed, with the selection of two films by directors who had reputations as *provocateurs*. But while Marco Ferreri's *La Grande Bouffe* and Jean Eustache's *La Maman et la Putain* did indeed unleash the expected uproar and hostility, in part because both won major prizes, their status as exemplary cases of *succès de scandale* remains illuminating, giving an idea of the shifting nature of what constitutes cinematic scandal – as well as prefiguring other transformations of taboos that were just around the corner.

In terms of subject matter, more than a few films at the twenty-sixth Cannes added a new element to the timeless artistic pairing of sex and death: namely, shit. As American critic Molly Haskell put it, it was 'a slightly intestinal festival'. Thus armed, Ferreri and Eustache were well equipped to undertake the principal duty of any cinematic *provocateur* worth his salt: *épater les bourgeois*. And where better to do this than at Cannes? Ferreri, an Italian, was the veteran of the pair both in terms of his pedigree as a cinematic bad boy and as a festival invitee, having had three previous films in competition. With his roly-poly figure, chinstrap Dutch beard and maliciously distended grin, Ferreri fitted the bill of jester at the Cannes court as well as that of the assassin

CANNES

of bourgeois mores. *La Grande Bouffe* was his fifteenth feature in a career that had begun in the late 1950s and which revealed him to be a connoisseur of the bizarre and grotesque, his dominant mode black comedy in which social conventions were inverted and rendered absurd, often with a degree of freakishness or violence that could rarely be accused of subtlety.

Throughout his career, Ferreri was able to attract well-known European actors to his self-scripted productions and for *La Grande Bouffe*, Marcello Mastroianni, Michel Piccoli and Ugo Tognazzi were joined by respected French actor Philippe Noiret and the little-known French theatre actress Andréa Ferréol, in a star-powered orgy of sex, gluttony and self-destruction. Today, one can see in *La Grande Bouffe* (whose English title, 'Blow Out', one wag suggested would have been better served up as 'The Big Eat') the prototype for later gastronomic shockers such as Peter Greenaway's *The Cook, the Thief, his Wife and her Lover*, and the Monty Python team's literally gut-busting satire of extravagant *gourmandisme* in the shape of Mr Creosote from their 1983 Cannes prizewinner *The Meaning of Life*. Ferreri's film has a blackly comic dynamic in its story of four middle-aged male professionals who, repairing with the same nonchalance that they might to a ski-lodge, eat and screw themselves to death in the fastness of a suburban mansion.

'At Cannes, the scandal stank of cash,' Michel Piccoli observed of the controversy surrounding Ferreri's film. The cast and crew, especially producer Jean-Pierre Rassam, were taxed with having cynically sought to make money from a supremely scandalous piece of cinema. While the film went on to be a major international success, Piccoli made the point that before *La Grande Bouffe*, 'nobody wanted to gamble a *centime* on Ferreri, above all because of the failure of [his previous French-produced film] *Liza*.' The Cannes screenings provoked suitably outraged reactions, including a punch-up in the evening and the cry of 'To the scaffold!' being hurled at Ferreri, who defended himself vigorously at the press conference. For him, *La*

ENFANTS TERRIBLES AND PROVOCAUTEURS

Grande Bouffe was not simply a film that attacked 'consumer society' but the 'physiological portrait' of an entire nation. Rassam (whose colleague, Pierre Cottrell, was the producer of *La Maman et la Putain*) deepened the controversy when, in a newspaper interview, he accused jury president Ingrid Bergman of a conflict of interest, in her backing of a film distributed by a Hollywood studio and her relationship with an executive. Small wonder then that Bergman would make no secret of her lack of appetite for *La Grande Bouffe*.

With its small cast of characters confined to the mansion and its grounds, the film has a somewhat hermetic, theatrical feel. This atmosphere of enclosure, almost of imprisonment, is shared with *La Maman et la Putain* and with Bernardo Bertolucci's similarly infamous *Last Tango in Paris* of the previous year. The sense of restricted space makes the experience of watching these films akin to a cinematic endurance test in which we, the spectators, are shut up with a group of characters locked into terminal or self-destructive dramatic trajectories. Each film draws a great deal of its strength from its restrictive *mise en scène*. But whereas Ferreri subjects characters and spectators alike to a spectacle of indulgence – trucks deliver marbled flanks of meat, entire pigs' heads and other such delicacies – Eustache subjects his viewers to the spectacle of sex. Or, rather, the spectacle of sex-*talk* delivered in what was, for the time, scandalously explicit detail. Both films hit French *amour propre* where it hurt most: Ferreri making the legendary national attention to the pleasures of the table the source of cinematic disgust, Eustache turning the renowned French capacity for talk, discourse and discussion into a self-punishing and emotionally harrowing three-and-a-half-hour, black and white tour de force.

'Provocation was his creed': thus did actress Bernadette Lafont describe Jean Eustache, for whom she performed in *La Maman et la Putain*, winner of the Cannes Grand Prix and the FIPRESCI Prize (shared with *La Grande Bouffe*). Moreover she read him as something of an unknown quantity in French auteur cinema: 'the new wave was a middle-class revolution, we had to wait for Eustache for the prole-

106 CANNES

tariat to enter cinema'. A dandy, a Jack Daniels drinker, and a passionate *cinéphile* of working-class extraction, Eustache was the Keith Richards of the *Cahiers du cinéma* crowd. The narrative of *La Maman et la Putain* is slim: Alexandre (Jean-Pierre Léaud) is a feckless young Parisian living with an older woman, Marie (Lafont), a dress-shop owner and 'the mother' of the film's title. Having split up with a girlfriend, Gilberte (Isabelle Weingarten), Alexandre picks up a promiscuous young nurse, Veronika (Françoise Lebrun), the 'whore'. A *ménage à trois* gradually evolves, but with none of the bittersweet romanticism of Truffaut's *Jules et Jim*, a clear model for Eustache. The film is heavy with talk but to a coruscating, hypnotic degree. The characters' monologues alternate between sentimentality and savagery, poeticism and profanity; the trio's exchanges pile up the 'fucks' while at all times observing the 'vouvoiement' of formal speech. Small wonder that critics reached for Baudelaire, Bataille and Céline as literary references for the brilliant verbosity of Eustache's script. Jeanne Moreau, meanwhile, reportedly attended the festival to protest the presence of the 'abomination' that was *La Maman et la Putain*.

Molly Haskell described Eustache's film, shown midway through the festival, as 'overwhelming, it cast a shadow on all the films that followed it'. For some, that shadow was darker than others. The filthy rag-and-bone shop of the heart that the film eviscerates so mercilessly was one on loan from real people. As Eustache admitted, this was autobiography in the form of punishing psychodrama. By the time the film reached Cannes it was already mired in tragedy. The model for Lafont's character, Marie, was Eustache's partner of the time, Catherine Garnier: she did the costumes and make-up for the film, which was shot in her apartment and the boutique where she worked. Already devastated by the death of her father, Garnier committed suicide after seeing the character based on her at the film's first projection. Eustache was said to have never fully recovered from Garnier's death, committing himself to a psychiatric hospital shortly afterwards. In 1981, at the age of forty-two, with seven films to his name, he shot himself.

ENFANTS TERRIBLES AND PROVOCAUTEURS 107

At Cannes, like Ferreri and team, Eustache and company were subjected to an ordeal-by-press conference which Lafont likened to 'a *corrida . . .* like a confessional, a tribunal, an exam room, a prison visiting-room, a public square and a classroom. With all of us, the prey, docilely lined up.' One of the interlocutors informed Eustache that he'd seen his film twice, had calculated that the word *baiser* ('fuck') was used 128 times and asked whether the director was obsessed with sex. To which Eustache replied: 'If you've gone to all that trouble, it's you who's obsessed.' In the middle of one particularly long-winded question, Eustache did something that startled everyone present. According to Lafont, 'he raised his arms and started to talk. Stupefaction and terror overcame the conference assistants who were already close to a breakdown. "Grandmother, can you hear me? Listen. I'm telling you, *La Maman et la Putain is* France. Help me, come quick."' Understandably the conference terminated swiftly thereafter.

It was an inevitable outrider to the scandal of the films by Ferreri and Eustache that they had been chosen to represent France at Cannes. Given Ferreri's nationality, some of the outrage levelled at the decision was xenophobic in tone. Post-festival, questions were asked and statements made on the floor of the Assemblée Nationale, one senator demanding that the Minister of Cultural Affairs 'guarantee that the films presented in the name of France should be worthy of the taste and spirit of the French'. The minister responded that 'a Festival should be a place for the confrontation of freedom of creation and expression. It's in this context that one can consider *La Grande Bouffe* had its place in the French selection for the Cannes Festival which, this year, showed a great deal of audacity and vitality.'

But there was another dimension to the choice: the critic René Prédal points out that, in 1972, the Cannes selection committee had nakedly preferred films that would showcase French acting talent, with an eye on the prize for Best Actress. But who now remembers Jeanne Moreau in

Philippe de Broca's *Chère Louise*, or Annie Girardot in Serge Korber's *Les Feux de la chandeleur*? The strategy made for a woeful selection, and Britain's Susannah York took the prize, for Robert Altman's *Images*. The 1973 selection therefore reflected a complete volte-face by the committee, a turning away from 'professional' mainstream commercial cinema in favour of original auteur works. It was also seen as marking what Prédal calls 'the beginning of the harvest of 1968'; the generation of *les évènements de Mai* were beginning to make sense of those extraordinary, utopian moments of five years before. This was particularly the case with Eustache's film, shot through with vivid memories of the time. In one sequence, Alexandre waxes poetically on a defining vision:

> One day during May '68 I saw something really beautiful. It was the middle of the afternoon. There were loads of people and everyone was crying. An entire café in tears . . . A tear-gas grenade had landed. If I hadn't have gone there regularly every morning I wouldn't have seen any of it. While I was there, before my very eyes, a gap opened up in reality.

Eustache's characters are shown as still trying to live in the 'gap' opened up by May '68, a gap that had since narrowed to the shape of a bed in which the promises of sexual liberation slowly turned sorrowful and sour. The film's anatomisation of the generation of '68 is utterly pitiless: its regret for a lost utopian moment only serves to make the film's claustrophobic focus all the more charged with tragedy. Yet, because of this fatalistic honesty, Eustache was charged with being a 'reactionary'.

Meanwhile, another line of critical analysis, beyond the familiar left–right oppositions, was slowly taking shape. 'The bourgeoisie', noted Molly Haskell, 'was getting harder and harder to *épater* or enjoying it more.' A few perceptive critics, casting their nets beyond the films in competition, pointed to other elements in the festival that indicated changes under way in the crumbling of certain cinematic

ENFANTS TERRIBLES AND PROVOCAUTEURS 109

taboos. In her keen-eyed reporting for *The Village Voice*, Haskell coined the neat phrase 'stunt sex' for one of the predominant features of the films at that year's festival. 'Practically every film on and off the Croisette has the obligatory sex scene,' she noted. 'I suddenly felt surfeited with sex on the screen and I realised the surfeit came not from films like *La Grande Bouffe* or *La Maman et la Putain* which are *about* sex and are inundated with it, but from films that use it casually, incidentally, in a way that is not an extension but a violation of heterosexual intimacy.'

During the festivals of 1972 and 1973, it was at market screenings that American and Scandinavian film professionals revealed that the future was hardcore. Cinemas along the rue d'Antibes were screening the very latest in boundary-breaking, American 'X'-rated features including *Deep Throat*, *The Devil in Miss Jones* and *Behind the Green Door*. Haskell put her finger on the fact that, beyond the scandals generated by a pair of 'transgressive' prizewinning films, there was a wave of sexually explicit cinema waiting to break: 'the porno films in the *marché* attract turnaway crowds (it's the only chance the French have to see hardcore movies)'. This state of affairs was soon to change. Neither Ferreri nor Eustache had made 'pornographic' films in any strict sense, but it is clear in retrospect that a cinematic climate and audience was developing, ripe for and responsive to greater levels of sexual explicitness. The market had spoken. The French government was soon to listen.

1973 was a transitional moment in what got screened at Cannes, but film historian Alan Williams rates the year of lesser significance than that which followed, and which saw the death of President Georges Pompidou followed by the election of Valéry Giscard d'Estaing. This changing of the guard had real repercussions on French cinema, Giscard's administration all but abolishing censorship in 1975, and film producers spotting a sudden commercial opportunity through which to exploit the new taste for hardcore pornography. The huge commercial successes in 1974 of the soft-core feature

Emmanuelle and the candidly libertarian road-movie romp *Les Valseuses* (by Bertrand Blier) were indicative of the changes under way, astonishing if short-lived. Of the 207 films released in the 1976–7 season, 89 (43 per cent) were X-rated. By the first twenty weeks of the 1978–9 season 55 per cent of all French cinema releases were hardcore pornography. One jaundiced political observer of the business-oriented and technocratic Giscard claimed: 'This liberal wants to makes of France a more "American" society, porous and permissive. A society in which extremes are tolerated – pornography along with the Leagues of Virtue, the Fascist right along with the extreme left – in the belief that their very proliferation means that one neutralises the other.' One might also say that the famous sexual libertarianism of the May '68 generation had proved tremendously germane to Giscard's model of liberal consumer democracy. The utopian project of free love was, it appeared, good for business too, if your business was hardcore pornography. The distance from the romantic radicalism of 1968 to the market triumphalism of the mid-1970s was not so great, and Cannes in 1973 was the litmus of this transformation.

Playing the Game

Into the Cannes competition of 1985 Jean-Luc Godard brought his film *Détective*, featuring the French celebrity couple *du jour*, Johnny Hallyday and Nathalie Baye. Making his way to the press conference, tracked by a camera crew, Godard hurried through the labyrinthine corridors of the new Palais des Festivals. Suddenly, a figure emerged from the sidelines and planted a large custard pie squarely in the auteur's face. Licking cream off his cigar, Godard's reaction was reliably witty: 'It's silent cinema's revenge on the talkies.' Later, in an interview for TV, a cleaned up Godard was yet more reflective: 'We are no longer human beings but just moments in a prefabricated media-event. It can make you a bit frightened, though you can get by with humour or irony. But there can be times and places when humour is in

ENFANTS TERRIBLES AND PROVOCAUTEURS

short supply.' Cinema's *père-provocateur* was on to something. His involuntary 'silent cinema' cameo had made the news – '*Godard entarté!*' – but to what extent had the assault been conceived for TV? When do the media stop reporting events and start creating them? By the middle of the decade, the festival was infested with TV crews and cinema was being usurped by the artless arriviste. The festival was both zealous in guarding its status as the most widely covered event after the Olympic Games, and equally aware that any accommodation reached with TV's rapacious appetite was a dangerous deal. The effects of TV on Cannes – and on cinema itself – were very evident by the 1980s. Such a climate posed an obvious challenge to those *cinéastes* with provocation in mind. How to avoid the strategy being reduced to just another piece of easily digested and instantly forgotten slapstick?

The man with the flan, the self-described 'entarteur' who had creamed Godard, was Belgian prankster Noel Godin. This genial left-over from the events of May '68, author of an autobiography predictably entitled *Cream and Punishment*, was also an exponent of an entertainingly irreverent form of *cinéphilia*. In the 1960s and 1970s, he wrote for a tiny Belgian publication called *Les Amis du film* where he merrily fabricated any number of unlikely filmic creations. Among these was Elliott Gould's 'tooth-camera' ('The only drawback with this extraordinary bit of kit is that I have to open my mouth to use it. I don't have to tell you that I'm being taken for the most exhausted actor in Hollywood as I'm always seen yawning') and Marcello Mastroianni in 'his first 100 per cent vegetable role' playing a leek in the film *The Vegetables of Goodwill* (also featuring Monica Vitti as a red beetroot and Bernardo Bertolucci as a runner bean). In 1969, *Les Amis* featured the first appearance of 'Georges Le Gloupier'. This 'most harebrained of high-minded Parisians', having left a screening of Bresson's *Une Femme douce* which had particularly irritated him 'for reasons, it seems, of a purely chromatic order', immediately went round to Bresson's place where he delivered 'a superb custard pie in

CANNES

the style of Mack Sennett which the director of *Au Hasard, Balthazar* took full in the face'. Years later, Le Gloupier would become Godin's *nom de guerre*. 'I flan people in the spirit of the abusive letters the Dadaists sent to worthless celebrities,' Godin explained. The difference between the days of Dada and now is that celebrity has become a devalued currency, a condition whose worthlessness is so parodically self-evident it risks putting Godin out of business. No matter. He has bravely continued his *patisserie*-assisted crusade to make the self-important appear ludicrous and can claim an illustrious list of celebrity victims which includes Bill Gates, Nicolas Sarkozy, Bernard-Henri Lévy, Marguerite Duras and Marco Ferreri.

Godin's flanning of Godard may be seen to have contained a form of backhanded homage and Godard played along with the gag's cinematic lineage. The great French film critic Serge Daney described Godard as being 'one of the few who still puts a smile on the faces of those festivalgoers exhausted by showbiz cant'. Godard, said Daney, 'plays the game'. The 'game' in question is that of licensed jester in the kingdom of cinema who routinely pops up at the court of Cannes to inform us that the king is naked. But which king? Cinema? The festival and its attendant circus? Or is it the media, particularly TV, which requires the ritual going-over that Godard-the-jester provides? Far from being angered, TV *adores* being chastised so. To such an extent that there's even an entertaining compilation film made up of forty years' worth of Godard's TV appearances called *Godard à la télé* (Michel Royer, 1999). So, Godard plays the holy fool in interviews, on television and at film festival press conferences, a task that he routinely approaches both as a kind of Platonic dialogue (he can depend on most of the questions being idiotic, and shine accordingly) and a bully pulpit from which he can ironise, fulminate and cogitate. Daney nailed it thus: 'Godard's privilege at the press conference is that of a man alone who has the right to dream out loud.'

It's fair to say that the Godard press conference has become a rite in itself, so much so that when Gilles Jacob put together a special DVD

ENFANTS TERRIBLES AND PROVOCAUTEURS

featuring some of the most famous moments of Cannes' history in 2005 he dedicated it to Godard (who once complained that he had dedicated a film to Clint Eastwood but no one had ever dedicated a film to him). Press conferences at film festivals are rarely exciting affairs. The film-maker and his cohort of actors, producer and moderator face rarely probing questions put by the international press and entailing a fair amount of translation. They are events of such surpassing tedium one yearns for a little élan or some unexpected departure from proceedings. And that's where Godard comes in. He's not so much a *provocateur* (in the sense that he can be relied upon to do something outrageous or say something scandalous), more that his mere presence puts the whole depressing rigmarole up for grabs. Actor Claude Brasseur, whom Godard directed in *Bande à part* (1964) and *Détective*, speaks for many when he says, 'I don't think much of his films but I'm a great fan of his press conferences.' At one such in 1998, Godard declared 'it is impossible at Cannes today to have the kinds of battles there were for *L'Avventura*'. The hostile reaction to Antonioni's film in 1960 remains a benchmark in the festival's history and has passed into film legend as a moment when an indisputably original film caused uproar among the audience and galvanised critics and film-makers to its defence. However, Gilles Jacob begs to differ with Godard, albeit subtly: 'There is a sort of general weakening in the way a film is received now which doesn't have the same vivacity, the same howls of outrage, booing and hissing. There are no longer "Battles of Hernani". But since *L'Avventura* there's been *La Grande Bouffe* in the 1970s, there was Pialat in the 1980s, there was *Irréversible* in the 1990s which was very badly received.'

Jeremy Thomas would also beg to differ with Godard on the strength of the clamour that greeted the competition bow of his production of David Cronenberg's *Crash* in 1996. Thomas asserts:

If you say that Cannes is the main cathedral of film in the world then the screen is the sacrificial altar. You put your films up to be sacrificed. It's a bit like the Forum in Rome, too – it has that gladiatorial aspect. Films have lived or died out of Cannes. You get very strong reactions, people leaving in droves, seats banging, shouting. I've been in Cannes screenings when people in the audience have shouted, 'This is a piece of shit.' So it's the toughest audience, and the film can get great reviews elsewhere, country by country, but it's killed in one day at Cannes. I've had some of the best experiences of my life in the Palais, because I've been there with some pretty good movies. Even with *Crash*, where we got a very mixed response, we were still thrilled with that. You knew not everyone was going to like that movie . . .

The panoptic Godard, of course, was making his point as part of a larger concern with cinematic form, innovation and the state of the art. For him, the controversy over *L'Avventura* was provoked by form, not content: the 'shock of the new' rather than the 'shock of the nudes', a break in cinematic language for which the Cannes audience was unprepared. The question remains whether it is still possible for a Cannes audience to be provoked not so much by *what* a film shows but by *how* it shows. Jacob's reference to Maurice Pialat provides an instructive example. In 1987, Pialat won the Palme d'Or for *Sous le soleil de Satan*. A dark, intense adaptation of a novel by the French Catholic author Georges Bernanos (also adapted by Bresson in *Le Journal d'un Curé de Campagne* and *Mouchette*), starring Gérard Depardieu and Sandrine Bonnaire, it was far from an aesthetic quantum leap but, rather, a refinement of Pialat's painterly naturalism. And it was an extremely controversial choice for the top prize. As soon as Catherine Deneuve announced the award a surprisingly vehement chorus of booing and hissing broke out which increased as Pialat made his way to the stage. (It may well have been Pialat's rather odd sartorial combination of cardigan and dicky bow that provoked some of the outrage.) Then regarded by some as the greatest living French director, the true heir to Renoir, Pialat (1925–2003) was the son of a

ENFANTS TERRIBLES AND PROVOCAUTEURS 115

railway worker and had trained as a painter. Famous for his truculent bare-knuckle personality, he responded in his inimitable style telling the audience, by now in a rapture of catcalls, 'All your boos and hisses make me happy. And if you don't like me, I don't like you either.' For good measure, he left them with an enthusiastic gesture, what the French call *le bras d'honneur*, or a 'Fuck you' sign.

Pialat's defiance remains a famous – some have even called it a 'historic' – moment not just because it summed up a well-known aspect of the man's choleric personality but also because it signalled a major split within the ritual of Cannes. Pialat's diagnosis? 'The French don't like winning. I won. That's all there is to it.' For some, this incident signified that the festival's rituals were no longer able to produce an audience worthy of its directors, and hence violated a certain pact. It certainly made for good TV, which may go a long way to explain the lingering repercussions. But clearly the boos and hisses were different in nature to those that *L'Avventura* received, as Serge Daney observed. 'The audience adopts the role of the villain in a play that takes place only once a year in front of the TV cameras at Cannes and in which Pialat knew his role and the critics theirs (which was to defend the artist out of principle).'

We could dub those film-makers who thrive on cultivating controversy 'provoc*auteurs*', because provocation is part and parcel of their directorial signatures. Abel Ferrara, Gaspar Noé and Catherine Breillat would be key defendants. But the principal repeat offender in this regard is the Danish imp, Lars von Trier. Von Trier has revealingly admitted a youthful fascination with David Bowie, because 'he managed to construct a complete mythology around himself. It was as important as his music.' As constantly self-inventing media icons go, Bowie is the pop ideal of the performer who incorporates their persona into their work to such an extent it becomes hard to judge where one ends and the other begins. One might see von Trier as one part Bowie to one part Godard (with a dash of Carl Theodor Dreyer: a definitively postmodern cocktail of influences). Von Trier combines self-conscious showmanship and a taste for manifestos and polemics with a zestful cinematic imagination, and he has adroitly exploited Cannes as the ideal forum for reinventing the persona of the director as superstar provoc*auteur*.

The scene was set upon his first invitation to Cannes in 1984 with his feature debut *The Element of Crime* in 1984, which was included in competition but went away with what was usually dismissed as the token award of a technical prize. Von Trier disdained the award, making it clear that he considered the film worthy of nothing less than the Palme d'Or and suspecting that president Dirk Bogarde had been instrumental in keeping the award out of his hands. According to the director, his suspicions were confirmed when he contacted Bogarde a few years later to see if the actor would consider a role in his film *Europa* (1991). Bogarde had loathed *The Element of Crime*, and was not in the least tempted to work with the Dane having threatened to walk off the jury if it had followed the will of the majority, which had been to award the film the top prize. In the year of *Paris, Texas* and Angelopoulos's *Voyage to Cythera*, one doubts von Trier's version very much.

But Cannes was simply the most high-profile stage on which von Trier could demonstrate the knack for self-promotion he had been polishing (all in the name of his art, of course) since his film school days in the 1970s when the aristocratic 'von' first began to feature in his surname. Or, as he recalls it, 'No one really cared how my films looked or how well they did. But this "von" business, on the other hand, really upset people': a valuable lesson learned early (but since he accepted a knighthood in 1997 perhaps the 'von' is now redundant). An already familiar episode took place at Cannes in 1991 where von Trier had *Europa* in competition and again came away with what he regarded as minor baubles, the technical prize (again) and the Jury Prize, shared with Maroun Bagdadi's *Hors la vie*. Von Trier made known his gratitude by throwing away the certificate he was awarded during the ceremony (he, like all the other recipients, was instructed not to open their beribboned scrolls during the ceremony lest it be

ENFANTS TERRIBLES AND PROVOCAUTEURS 117

made obvious that they were blank). He then topped this performance with a remark during the press conference where he referred to jury president Roman Polanski as 'a midget'. The throwaway line made headlines. Von Trier's rather lame alibi was that Polanski had called himself a midget in *Chinatown* (1974), though he also issued written and verbal apologies to Polanski (who took the wisecrack in good part) and festival head Gilles Jacob.

The next time von Trier had a film in competition was in 1996, with *Breaking the Waves* and this time he stayed away. As a man who lays claim to a veritable smorgasbord of phobias, including a fear of flying and a dislike of travel in general, he refused to take the train to the Riviera. Representatives from Zentropa, his production company, told him that his no-show jeopardised the film's competition chances, which were strong following a very positive reception. Von Trier still wouldn't budge and sat it out at home taking a phone call from his producer who, after the gala projection of *Breaking the Waves*, relayed the audience's ovation to him via her mobile. It still wasn't enough of an inducement to hit the road, even when the Zentropa team learned that the film was a favourite for the top prize and had gathered that *some* prize at least was theirs. During the televised awards ceremony, while his press agent watched the coverage at von Trier's home, the director played a computer game in the next room. The news came through that the top prize had once again eluded him, the film taking the Grand Prix.

All of which would just be so much show-biz mood music were it not for the fact that von Trier's persona so closely resembled his films, in which cinema is seen as a sparring partner, a medium to be taken on, challenged and reinvented. To be a provoc*auteur* can provide an image or persona that brings work and director together in a fusion that lends a clearly defined identity to both. 'A film by Lars von Trier' provokes an immediate set of expectations. And while this has proved to be a neat way of standing out from the crowd, as it has become harder to be truly provocative the risk attached to laying claim to the

CANNES

mantle of provocation becomes greater, the returns fewer. Von Trier has carried on with some integrity by making the 'shock' aspect reside in the work's styles and forms – which, when all is said and done, is where it matters most. *Dancer in the Dark* finally won von Trier his Palme d'Or in 2000, while his female lead Björk got the Best Actress award. The film's reception was beset by media stories of a colossal falling-out between director and actress, Björk accusing von Trier of 'emotional pornography', reports of the director 'terrorising' his star. The film is an 'anti-musical' that dances all the way to the gallows and, in Björk's Selma, features another incarnation of von Trier's Sadean fascination with a figure of female innocence being submitted to all manner of punishing indignities (think also of Bess in *Breaking the Waves* and Grace in *Dogville* [2003]). But it was *The Idiots* (1998) that remains the exemplar of von Trieresque provoc*auteurism*.

This film was a Dogme 95 production, made according to the self-imposed restrictions set out in another of von Trier's beloved manifestos of the sort he had been issuing since *The Element of Crime*, and which he and his co-conspirator Thomas Vinterberg were said to have composed during an inebriated spree. Dogme's 'vow of chastity' bound its 'brethren' to a bracing regime of location-based shooting with handheld cameras; recourse to genre convention and other such luxuries were strictly forbidden. Dogme 95 was playing the game of provocation on every level. For a start, it was historically provocative, with von Trier explicitly aligning the outfit with the sixties 'new wave'. It was obviously a provocation in terms of filmic style, given the 'vow of chastity' each director was compelled to observe. (Though for budgetary reasons Dogme directors immediately violated one aspect of their vows by shooting on digital video.) But crucially Dogme was *instrumentally* provocative. In other words, it proved a brilliant publicity stunt that attracted the attention of the world's media to the sort of film-making that had grown used to existing under the radar. Low budget, European, arthouse cinema was suddenly 'sexy' again for the first time in years.

ENFANTS TERRIBLES AND PROVOCAUTEURS   119

The sweetest touch, the one that really rankled with literal-minded film traditionalists, was Dogme's anti-auteur animus. It was, of course, utterly fraudulent and hypocritical yet somehow spot-on for the 'brethren' to proclaim that 'the auteur concept was bourgeois romanticism from the very start and thereby false'. That they were able, in 1998, to showcase the first Dogme productions at Cannes, that haven of auteur cinema, says everything about the nature of the modern provoc*auteur*. Nor did it harm the Dogme profile when Vinterberg's *Festen* came away with the Jury Prize ex aequo. This time, von Trier graced the Croisette with his presence, having made the journey from Denmark in his camper van. *The Idiots* tells of a collective of young Danes led by the malcontent Stoffer (Jens Albinus), who live in an abandoned villa from which they conduct an experiment in separating themselves from society. They do this by attempting to find their 'inner idiots' and by 'spazzing', or pretending to be retarded, a facade they maintain both among themselves as well as in public. Von Trier had been partly inspired by Ferreri's *La Grande Bouffe* and had adapted some of the film's elements such as the claustrophobic communal setting and the atmosphere of tight-knit metastasising mania.

The queasy see-sawing between voyeurism and alienation that *The Idiots* induces in the viewer is superbly evoked by an actor's description of the shoot: 'I felt like I was in a porno film for *adult babies*.' The film cannot help but be read as simultaneously an act and an allegory of upping the ante, a demanding filmic wind-up of its cast, audience and director alike. For its use of genuinely handicapped people in one scene, as well as a dose of hardcore sex, *The Idiots* attracted accusations of being 'tasteless', 'fascistic' and of 'kicking the audience in the face', as well as challenging the censorship laws in many of the countries where it was released. Godard was reportedly very taken with the film, writing von Trier an appreciative letter and describing *The Idiots* as 'going all the way'. Until, of course, the next provoc*auteur* goes further. From Truffaut to von Trier, Cannes has consistently been the test-bed for strategies of cinematic provocation. And while the festival was slow off the mark to spot the New Wave the first time round, the new wavers would proceed to transform it from within. Cannes demonstrates the push-and-pull of provocation and, as an institution, exists in dialectical rapport with it. After all, it's better to be provocative than predictable; even if, now and then, the act of provocation itself risks predictability – not cries of outrage, but rather knowing and avuncular smiles.

VI

'Beneath the paving stones . . . the beach'

The cinema had taught us how to live; but life was to take its revenge.
Jean-Luc Godard, foreword to François Truffaut's 'Letters'

May '68. The date is iconic, a signpost of the moment when the day-glo optimism of the sixties turned black and white and bloody. May resides in memory now, endowing the image repertoire of that decade with striking poster art whose stark graphics declaimed utopian slogans: 'All power to the imagination', 'Take your dreams for reality'. 'Beneath the paving stones . . . the beach'. The images that come to mind are *vérité* stills of street fights: the raised fist, the arm frozen in the arc of hurling missiles, crowds scattering before baton charges, cars ablaze, barricades. There is a paradox in the collective memory of May '68. On one hand, we have grown accustomed to the generalised image of 'sixties radicalism' as a gallery of famous faces – Fidel, Che, Jane Fonda with the Vietcong, Jean-Luc Godard with the Stones – because the sixties was the decade when the mediascape that we now inhabit started to take shape in earnest, when Vietnam as the first 'TV war' played itself out in the world's living rooms and when politics and celebrity began to merge until one became indistinguishable from the other.

On the other hand, it is worth remembering that the images of May '68 were mostly generated from within the uprising. The state-controlled French media did its utmost to avoid reporting the events, so

CANNES

the striking newsreel cameramen, film-makers and artists produced their own images and militant films, known as *ciné-tracts* and *films tableaux noirs* ('blackboard films'). As film historian Jean-Pierre Jeancolas observes: 'May '68 had been one of the first historical events in which the cinema intervened in order to record scattered moments of that unlikely month, but also as an agent of militant action.'

In retrospect, 1968 reads like a chronology of dashed hopes. January's 'Prague Spring', when Czech President Alexander Dubcek attempted a liberal 'reformist' programme within the sphere of Soviet influence, would be crushed beneath the Warsaw Pact tanks that rolled in during August. The scope and savagery of the Vietnam War increased with the launch of the Tet Offensive in January. In April, Martin Luther King was gunned down in Memphis. Robert Kennedy would suffer the same fate in August. And in March, student protests at the new university of Nanterre on the outskirts of Paris lit the fuse for two incendiary months of social upheaval. Factories and faculties were occupied, students and police fought in the streets of Paris and the entire country came to a standstill. At one point, France seemed on the verge of civil war, with President de Gaulle leaving the country to consult his generals in secret. Revolution appeared to be in the offing and France's film-makers were in the thick of things. Taking place in the midst of the May uprising, Cannes might seem like a provincial sideshow to the main events, but there were direct consequences for the festival both during May and beyond. For only the third time in its history the festival did not take place, at least not completely. It was called to a halt because of the vociferous intervention of a group of film-makers. The previous occasions when the festival had not happened, 1948 and 1950, were during its earliest years when budgetary and organisational constraints made the fledgeling event vulnerable. 1968 was different.

Where the British say 'champagne socialist', the French reach for the equally derisive *gauche caviar*, and in 1968 Cannes served up generous helpings of both (though to do justice to the period's delirious political schisms one would have to extend the epithet ad infinitum:

'Mercedes Maoist', 'Yves Saint Laurent anarchist', et cetera). Director Claude Miller describes the festival as 'having the atmosphere of Cuba in the time of Batista', adding that it was the bad conscience of the film-makers present that prevented them from sipping champagne while the rest of the country was on strike. Bad consciences or no, the events of May succeeded in penetrating what film-maker Gérard Mordillat called 'the extremely thick wall separating the cinema in France from politics in the larger sense' – the most glaring example of which had been the silence over the Algerian War. In the years since, it has become conventional to talk of the Cannes Festival before and after 1968, for reasons that will be explored later but that have to do with acknowledging that cinema could be an unerringly accurate weathervane of political and social changes.

Scheduled for 10–24 May the twenty-first festival had a jury in place that included Roman Polanski, Louis Malle, Antonioni's muse Monica Vitti, and Terence Young, the British director of the early James Bond films. Among the twenty-six films selected for competition were Alain Resnais's *Je t'aime, Je t'aime*, Milos Forman's *The Firemen's Ball*, Jan Nemec's *A Report on the Party and the Guests*, Richard Lester's *Petulia* and Carlos Saura's *Peppermint Frappé*. But despite being over five hundred miles away from Paris, despite the television news blackout regarding events there, Cannes was not beyond the reach of what was unfolding in the capital. The most auspicious event of the festival's opening night was not the gala screening of a 70 mm version of *Gone with the Wind* in homage to Vivien Leigh who had died the year before. Nor was it the absence of Olivia de Havilland who had demanded a purse of 125,000 francs to attend. That event did not even take place in Cannes, but on the streets of the Latin Quarter in Paris where, through the night of 10 May, students and police were involved in savage and protracted street fights in which hundreds were injured and much damage was done. 'The Night of the Barricades', as these clashes were called, would result in the major labour unions joining with the students in a mass demonstration on 13 May.

Earlier in the month Louis Malle, who had recently returned to Paris after six months in India shooting a documentary, had gone out for dinner with his brother one evening when the pair were assaulted by gendarmes; an experience which, as Malle recounts, 'put me on the side of the students straightaway'. The opening night of Cannes was overshadowed by the upheavals, as the critic Jean-Louis Bory observed: 'the funereal boredom of the dusty commemorative gala seemed to chime with the baton blows and teargas grenades raining down on the students'. What had started off as a student protest was looking increasingly like a mass insurrection combined with a general strike whose effects were starting to be felt throughout France. By 18 May, public transport was at a standstill, post offices were shut and Cannes was heading uncertainly into its second week. But before dealing with all that was wrought upon Cannes, let us flashback briefly to a cinematic argument generally agreed to be a crucial prelude to the great May.

'Long Live Langlois'

Bernardo Bertolucci's 2003 film *The Dreamers*, a fond piece of *cinéphile* revisionism, opens with a reconstruction of a demonstration on the steps of the Cinémathèque Française in February 1968. As Eva Green lashes herself becomingly to the entrance to prevent anyone from getting in, and before riot police bear down on the crowd, the actors Jean-Pierre Léaud and Jean-Pierre Kalfon – both of whom had been on the spot in 1968 – demand the reinstatement of the Cinémathèque's founder Henri Langlois, who had recently been dismissed by Minister of Culture André Malraux. The Cinémathèque Française had started life in a bathtub in Paris (one of the earliest places where its collection of film reels was stored) and would become one of the most prestigious institutions in the French *état culturel*. Since its inauguration in 1935 up to its recently opened purpose-built location in Bercy in the east of Paris, the Cinémathèque has had a huge influence on film culture in France. It

BENEATH THE PAVING STONES . . . THE BEACH

was the work, passion and jealously guarded province of one man, Henri Langlois, who Cocteau described as 'the old dragon who guards our treasures'.

Along with his stalwart colleagues Mary Meerson and Lotte Eisner, Langlois would create what Jean Renoir called 'the church for movies'. By any measure a maverick whose idiosyncratic working methods seemed designed to drive state functionaries mad, Langlois was a difficult man, secretive to the point of paranoia. Truffaut commented that 'one felt great sympathy for his paranoid volubility until that moment in February 1968 when it became clear that it all had a foundation in fact'. Crucially, Langlois's Cinémathèque was not only a place where films were preserved (all and any films Langlois could get his hands on: he made a point of collecting without discrimination) but also where they were screened in a famously eclectic repertory programme. Jacques Rivette explained the particular appeal of Langlois's programming style: 'One could see there successively at 6.30 p.m. Griffith's *Broken Blossoms* and at 8.30 Andy Warhol's *Chelsea Girls*. And it was fabulous because one could see Griffith and Warhol together on the same night. Because it was then that one realised that there are not two or three kinds of cinema, there is only one cinema.'

In early February it had been proposed that Langlois be replaced as artistic and technical director of the Cinémathèque by Pierre Barbin, head of the Tours and Annecy film festivals. Langlois found himself in the undignified position of having the locks on the building changed, and Mary Meerson was summarily dismissed. The decision to dismiss Langlois and the contemptuous, heavy-handed treatment of staff was widely condemned in the French press and resulted in an immediate mobilisation of protest, with *Cahiers du cinéma* playing a leading role. Forty film-makers – including Abel Gance, Georges Franju, Robert Bresson and Jean Renoir, as well as Truffaut, Resnais, Godard, Chris Marker, Chabrol, Rohmer and Jean Rouch – protested against the Ministry of Culture's decision and announced that they would not allow their films to be projected by what they dubbed the

126

CANNES

'Barbinothèque'. The ministerial response was that the Cinémathèque had become such an important institution that it could no longer be run in the same amateurish way that had been Langlois's style for the past twenty years.

In the press, Truffaut blamed Malraux directly. The CGT (the national federation of trades unions) also took a stand, maintaining that the dismissal of Langlois was further evidence of the government's increasing authoritarianism. There were several demonstrations in February with Truffaut calling in the press for mobilisation. On 14 February three thousand people gathered in the gardens of the Trocadero near the Cinémathèque's Palais de Chaillot screening rooms. They had company – phalanxes of riot police baton-charged the protestors, nothing of which appeared on French TV, barred from reporting the event. It was hardly surprising that the New Wave directors rallied round Langlois: the Cinémathèque was their alma mater after all. It was the roll call of legendary cinematic figures who signed up to Langlois's defence that broadened the campaign, including Charlie Chaplin, Orson Welles, Nicholas Ray, Roberto Rossellini and Joseph Losey. Eventually, the major Hollywood studios would weigh in with support, a decisive step that broke the French government's resistance to reinstating Langlois. The confrontation dragged on until late April when Langlois was finally restored to his post. But while the government grudgingly gave back with one hand, with the other it snatched away a million francs' worth of subsidy.

While it may not be strictly correct to claim that the 'Langlois Affair' precipitated the events of May, the establishment of the Committee for the Defence of the Cinémathèque and its successful protests had elements in common with the coming events: anger and frustration at the autocratic and out-of-touch way the government responded to legitimate grievances, as well as a dogged and unexpectedly successful militancy. The French film world had become increasingly politicised throughout the 1960s, whether protesting censorship or defending the Cinémathèque, and its effectiveness in mobilising support meant that they could react swiftly to keep the momentum of protest rolling. As Bertolucci's film shows (likewise, *Les Amants réguliers* [2005] by Philippe Garrel, another film-maker forged in the crucible of sixties Parisian *cinéphilia*), cinema was central to the moment itself and remains an animating part of its mythology. Film-maker Pierre Kast, one of the older generation of *Cahiers* writers, commented presciently in the magazine's April 1968 edition which was dedicated to Langlois: 'I realise that though it's impossible to shout "Long Live Castro" without shouting "Long Live Langlois", it's perfectly possible to shout "Long Live Langlois" without thinking "Long Live Castro". But still, these scuffles, these tracts, these committee rooms, these discussions reach way beyond the Cinémathèque Affair . . . And defending the existence of the Cinémathèque française is a political act, oddly enough.' In the 1980s Truffaut would sum it up more succinctly: 'With the passing of time, it seems obvious that the demonstrations for Langlois were to the events of May '68 what the trailer is to the feature film coming soon.'

Curtains

'It looks as if this is going to be a nice festival, interesting, calm and not terribly exciting,' Richard Roud reported in the *Guardian*, clearly having left his usual keen critical sense at the beach. A few days later, he observed 'there was definitely an air of 1917 over the whole proceedings'. The festivals' selection committee had taken certain precautions prior to the festival but for reasons other than the events of May. Two films about Vietnam had been turned down, Peter Brook's *Tell Me Lies* (UK) and Eugene S. Jones's *A Face of War* (USA), because negotiations were taking place in Paris between the Americans and the North Vietnamese at the same time as the festival. Events in Paris were starting to cause ripples on the Croisette, however. On 13 May, the French Critics Association issued a statement calling on those present

128

CANNES

to join a demonstration in support of the students 'to protest against the violent police repression which is an assault on the nation's cultural liberty, the secular traditions of its universities and its democratic principles'. They demanded that the festival be suspended. Favre Le Bret refused, emphasising that the foreign participants could not be mixed up in what were specifically French affairs. However, he called off parties, cocktails and dinners.

Emboldened by the success of the campaign to defend the Cinémathèque, François Truffaut now had the specific goal of shutting down the festival. The call to close Cannes came in the form of a motion passed by a new organisation that had emerged during the events bearing the somewhat portentous name 'Estates General of French Cinema'. This was a reference to the *Etats Généraux* of 1789 which, in 1968, had twin connotations. On one hand, the *soixante-huitards* were placing themselves in a revolutionary lineage of historical progressives. On the other, it was a less than direct acknowledgement of their model's bourgeois character. The Estates General of Cinema was made up of over a thousand film students and members of the film technicians union, as well as directors, critics and actors, who held regular meetings for over two weeks at the site of the French National Film School in the rue de Vaugirard. Their aim was a root-and-branch transformation of the institutions of French cinema and the motions called for a total strike of workers in the film and audiovisual industries, a call widely heeded. Moreover, they desired the stoppage of the Cannes Festival. It fell to Truffaut and his *camarades* on the Côte d'Azur to bring this about.

On the morning of Saturday 18 May in Cannes, Truffaut took to the stage in the Salle Jean Cocteau for a press conference organised by the Committee for the Defence of the Cinémathèque. Flanked by Godard, Claude Lelouch (who, in true *gauche caviar* style, had arrived at the festival in his private yacht), Malle and Milos Forman, he read out the communiqué he had received from the Estates General of French Cinema and called on the critics and film-makers to shut the festival down.

BENEATH THE PAVING STONES . . . THE BEACH

Forman announced to applause that he had withdrawn *The Firemen's Ball* from competition. 'Films roll like heads', wrote the *Evening Standard*. Warming to the revolutionary theme, it further observed 'such is the guillotine atmosphere that some of the women's eager faces look as if they were expecting the free distribution of knitting needles'. Forman left the stage to be replaced by Roman Polanski who, at one point in the proceedings, leaned over to Godard and said, 'Everything you say reminds me hugely of the time I was in Poland under Stalinism.' In *Variety*, Polanski was reported as calling Truffaut, Lelouch and Godard 'little kids playing at being revolutionaries' adding 'I pulled out as a gesture of solidarity with the students whose actions I wholeheartedly support. I never intended it be seen as an anti-Cannes gesture.'

The next day and a half would play itself out in an hour-by-hour sequence of debates and confrontations shifting from the Salle Jean Cocteau to the Grand Salle and back again, alternating between good-humoured rallying cries and invective-laden brawls. Even in the early stages, it was clear there were tactical differences between those leading the call to close down the festival. Some favoured complete closure, others called for 'modification' which would allow screenings to continue. The difference between 'radicals' and 'reformists' would generate the most heated altercations. Meanwhile, jury member Louis Malle had been busy behind the scenes:

> My role was to encourage the festival jury to resign. The Committee thought that if the jury resigned the festival couldn't continue. During a jury meeting Terence Young announced that he'd had a phone call from the French union and as he was a member he had to follow their advice. I'd convinced Monica Vitti. Truffaut went to see Roman Polanski who said he'd withdraw but immediately regretted it.

If this was not a majority, nevertheless the jury was rendered impotent and Malle took the news to his colleagues who had decamped to the Grande Salle, now packed with camera crews and people overflowing into the aisles.

Following Malle's announcement, Robert Favre Le Bret proclaimed the festival non-competitive but insisted that it would continue nevertheless. David Robinson noted in the *Financial Times* that 'the directors of the Berlin and Venice festivals had gleefully gone around all the participants, competitively snapping up all the withdrawn films for their own festivals in July and August'. The battle, half-won, became bitter. Malle would later claim that he was held responsible for the festival's closure. 'I became *persona non grata* at Cannes,' he said. 'The businessmen were furious and the rumour went round that it was all my fault . . . When I went to the Café Bleu next door to the Palais they refused to serve me.' Nevertheless, the documentary he had been shooting in India earlier that year, *Calcutta*, would be selected to screen out of competition at the following year's festival. Young American producer Sandy Lieberson, then preparing for his first job on Nic Roeg and Donald Cammell's *Performance*, was at the festival in 1968 and well remembers the reaction in the trade:

> They were shocked by it – maybe not the French, but people who had come to Cannes because of that sense of 'This is our business. We're here to see movies, sell movies, buy movies, make deals.' It did catch us off-guard. But then you got caught up in it. I loved it. You couldn't be left-wing in the United States any more – communism, are you kidding? 'Socialist' was already a dirty word, this before 'liberal' got to be a dirty word. So in 1968 it was like, 'Fuck, *yeah*! The French are doing it! They've got the guts to stand up to the government.'

Even some of the producers got into the mood, albeit counter-revolutionary, and, on Sunday 19 May, staged a sit-in on the steps of the Palais in favour of continuing projections which, in the case of market screenings in the Cannes backstreets, did go on for a few days more. In spite of strikes and petrol shortage, the festival found the means for the producers and distributors who gather every year at Cannes to continue their deal-making in Rome, the nearest capital city. *Variety* reported that Elizabeth Taylor and Richard Burton had despatched a private plane from London to get the stranded Universal Studio contingent out of town.

One of the most striking features of newsreel footage of the festival is the onstage dynamic between the leading protestors, especially between Truffaut and Godard. Truffaut does a good job of communicating clearly, informing those assembled why Cannes should be closed down, even if he appears to entertain the possibility of continued screenings. Godard, on the other hand, comes across as grim-faced, hectoring and abusive, his legendary sardonic wit clearly having left the building. It was almost as if the duo, side-by-side onstage, were acting out a good cop/bad cop routine. At one point, Godard accused everyone assembled in the Grande Salle, and cinema in general, of having failed to represent the revolutionary moment: 'There's not a single film that shows the problems that workers and students are going through. Not one. Whether made by Forman, by me, by Polanski or François. We've missed the boat!'

It's true that Godard spoke from a position of some authority. His 1967 film *La Chinoise* (inspired by his relationship with Anne Wiazemsky, lead model in Bresson's *Au Hasard, Balthazar* and a student at Nanterre at the time) is widely regarded as remarkably prescient in its depiction of a Maoist student cell holed up in an apartment debating the pros and cons of terrorism. To audience booing, Godard insisted, 'It's not a matter of continuing or not continuing to watch films. It's a matter of cinema showing solidarity with the student movement and the only practical way of doing this is to stop all the projections immediately.' At one point, Godard lost his composure and unleashed a barrage of invective at one unfortunate *cinéaste* who had dared sound a note of dissent. Quivering with rage, he yelled: 'You're talking about solidarity with the students and workers and you're speaking travelling shots and close-ups! You're a prick!' It's a strange moment to watch now. Godard himself appears taken aback by the ferocity of his own outburst and, standing alongside him, Truffaut looks pained. It is as though Godard's attack was a fervent public recanting of the *cinéphilic* faith that had bonded him with Truffaut for so long. It might be read as the moment when Godard renounced *cinéphilia* for radical politics. The years to come would see him abandon any pretence of commercial film-making. It also presaged the bitter dissolution of his friendship with Truffaut, who would unforgettably describe him as 'the Ursula Andress of militancy'.

In the audience during these exchanges was a young Irishman named Peter Lennon, then Paris correspondent for the *Guardian*. Lennon was present not in his journalistic capacity but as the director of *Rocky Road to Dublin*, a film denouncing the baleful influence of the Catholic Church, on which he had managed to recruit the services of the great cinematographer and long suffering Godard stalwart, Raoul Coutard. '*Rocky Road* was the last film shown in '68,' says Lennon:

> It was selected for Critics Week to show on 18 May. What actually happened was the lights went up and in came Godard and Lelouch. They told us the festival had ended. They closed things down so they could have a huge debate, which lasted about two days. When they got talking . . . talk about Fidel Castro! So we were all told to go into the Grand Salle to '*discutez*'. Everybody had to get up and talk. I was asked to get up and talk. It was like an endless brawl. You went in there for a few hours, then you went home, had something to eat and went to bed, got up at two in the morning, and they were still talking. And the next day they were still talking . . . It was wonderful.

Newsreel footage shows Lennon making a decent fist of getting a word in edgeways, in French, demanding to know why others should not be given the chance to screen their films as he had done. But Godard was having none of it. Almost forty years later, Lennon recalls:

BENEATH THE PAVING STONES . . . THE BEACH

Godard is a poisonous little bastard but he gets an idea into his head and he's hopelessly stubborn. His idea was stop all projections, and I said 'Surely the point is, if this is liberation, project everything!' We had the cinemas. We could have walked into the rue d'Antibes and taken over any cinema, because no one was going to stand up against this tide. We had the equipment, we had all the films. But they got into an ideological corner.

Despite his call falling on deaf ears, Lennon's film found its way into what he describes as 'the parallel exhibition and distribution system stretching from the university in Nice to Paris'.

Only revolutionarily appropriate films were put on the circuit. I was invited to the first revolutionary screening at Nice University that evening. Milos Forman and Louis Malle were on the platform. Louis Malle, whom I'd not met, insisted that I be brought out of the audience and up on to the stage with the other representatives of world cinema. It's extraordinary how a tiny gesture of goodwill can work in a man's favour for decades. I have never been able to think ill of any of his films since.

It is an instructive anecdote, illustrating how central cinema was to the student upheavals of May and why, if only momentarily, Cannes appeared irrelevant, irredeemably bourgeois and compromised by commerce when compared with what was taking place around it.

The attempts to close the festival were not without comedy. There was a priceless moment during the occupation of the Grande Salle. The public was vocally demanding the screening of Carlos Saura's *Peppermint Frappé*, starring Geraldine Chaplin, despite the fact that Saura had withdrawn the film from competition. The lights came down and the protestors onstage took the only action available to them. Assisted by the film's director and his leading lady, they hung on to the curtains obscuring the screen, keeping them firmly closed so that the film could not be seen properly by the spectators. Godard was

134

CANNES

slapped in the face and lost his glasses, and Truffaut was thrown to the floor by an angry audience member. The lights went up and Favre Le Bret made a second announcement cancelling afternoon and evening screenings. By now, things had reached a stage of crisis management. Favre Le Bret had been informed by police intelligence of contingents 'having nothing to do with the film industry' intending to descend on Cannes to cause further disruption. Having asked the mayor of Cannes to use his powers to clear the protestors from the Palais, and having being refused, Favre Le Bret and his team realised it was imperative that a remake of 'The Night of the Barricades' be avoided on the Croisette. At midday on Sunday 19 May, Favre Le Bret declared the Cannes Festival closed. Sandy Lieberson observes that there was a good reason why the festival shutdown made sense:

> You have to remember the festival had control of the Palais. They had the police there. But they had the world's press there too, waiting to write about movies. I think they were worried about how it was going to be reported. So they stood back and learned from what had happened in Paris. They couldn't let that happen in Cannes. It was much more: 'Okay, close it down, let them have their speeches', rather than trying to arrest them, throwing tear gas and all the rest. And, fortunately, they didn't have a violent confrontation.

The Aftermath

'It was a great moment,' Louis Malle said of 1968. 'Suddenly the whole country stopped, people started to think about their lives and the society they were living in and to imagine all sorts of solutions, few of them feasible. When it was all over I thought: "One should make it an institution. May '68 should happen every four years. It'd be a better catharsis than the Olympic Games."' Gilles Jacob, then a film critic and yet to join the festival, wondered if '68 had changed anything at Cannes – yes and no, judging from the evidence of the following year's

BENEATH THE PAVING STONES . . . THE BEACH

festival. 'There's still the same starchy atmosphere, the same uneven selection', he wrote. Considering the role of Robert Favre Le Bret, Jacob described him sardonically as 'alone on the throne of a short-lived principality, handily sheltered behind the administrative council, he still reigns, the general administrator who with each passing year draws new strength from the promise to leave his post . . . next year.' However, he recognised that Favre Le Bret had been sufficiently smart to 'recuperate' the protestors by inviting Louis Malle's *Calcutta* to compete and by welcoming the Société des Réalisateurs de Film (SRF) into the festival's margins.

These were tactics that could be compared to the way the BBC recuperated the pirate DJs of Radio Caroline in 1967. In Britain, it was pop music above all that addressed the young. In France it was film. Also, the film-makers were available to be recuperated in as much as they had specific demands regarding the film industry in general and Cannes in particular, and had formed organisations through which these could be expressed. Foremost among these was the SRF, which had emerged from the Estates General of French Cinema. The film-makers involved did not want to destroy Cannes but to remake it in their image. Nevertheless, they threatened to create their own international festival and to boycott Cannes while demanding changes that would 'democratise' the festival and 'divest it of its worldly and diplomatic aspects in order to professionalise it'. Among their demands was that screenings be free of charge, compulsory evening dress be abolished, and awards be voted for by the public. What was achieved in compromise was the creation of the *Quinzaine des Réalisateurs*, or 'Directors Fortnight'. Operating within rather than against the festival, the Quinzaine was conceived as non-competitive, free of censorship and beyond any diplomatic considerations; 'a showcase for world cinema', as its organisers described it.

A native of Cannes, Jean-Gabriel Albicocco (1936–2001) was a young film-maker and one of the militants who disrupted the festival in 1968. A former assistant to Jules Dassin and the director of a 1967 film adaptation of the much-loved Alain-Fournier novel *Le Grand Meaulnes*, Albicocco would play a leading role in the SRF and, along with Pierre Kast and Jacques Doniol-Valcroze (a co-founder of *Cahiers du cinéma*), was one of those behind the inception of the Quinzaine. Albicocco described the objectives of the protestors at Cannes in '68 as being

> to open up the selection to include independently made films, because the selection was for the most part made up of titles proposed by producers' organisations, if not by state bodies belonging to the all-powerful International Federation of Film Producers Associations (FIAPF). We wanted the festival's programming to expand to represent the independent *auteur* cinema that was happening everywhere and giving birth to a new wave of directors that went way beyond 'official cinema' and was expressing the political, cultural and social aspirations of their countries, often struggling against systems of political and financial repression.

How did the process of recuperation work? Albicocco was brought on to the administrative council of the festival in order to make the SRF's case for a parallel strand. 'Favre Le Bret wasn't ignorant of the fact that the principal obstacle was my presence on the council,' he recalled, 'which was seen as a consequence of the events of May and raised the fear of the festival being pushed in a left-wing, *tiers mondiste* direction.' A lunch meeting was organised between Albicocco and the head of FIAPF, Edmond Tenoudji, who, according to Albicocco, 'asked in a very paternalistic way what I was complaining about. After all, I'd had a film in the official selection. He saw me only as the representative of a bunch of leftist thugs.'

> I didn't hide the fact that we planned to organise a counter-festival which would certainly oblige Cannes' administrative council to raise their bids in the selection of official films. I threatened them with the prospect that it would reveal the film-makers of tomorrow,

BENEATH THE PAVING STONES . . . THE BEACH 137

who would know to whom they owed the revelation of their talents and ideas. Those at lunch were stupefied by the idea and reacted as violently as I had done. They would never allow such an event to take place as part of the Cannes Festival and would fight the idea to the end.

Albicocco told this story in 1994 when the Quinzaine was celebrating its twenty-fifth anniversary, and he could allow himself a certain satisfaction. Not only had the idea been incorporated into the festival, it had gone on to do exactly what he predicted it would, screening the early work of directors such as Mrinal Sen, Theo Angelopoulos, Ken Loach, Atom Egoyan, Idrissa Ouedraogo, Glauber Rocha, Spike Lee, and Jim Jarmusch, among others. The list of those film-makers first screened in the Quinzaine who would later win major prizes in the official competition is both extensive and impressive. In the case of the Quinzaine, '68 had a real impact on the festival. Albicocco went as far as claiming that it 'saved the Cannes Festival for the next 30 years'. As for the post-'68 festivals, it's tempting to speculate to what extent the Quinzaine might have raised the selection committee's game and influenced the decision to select films that would not make the official selection look staid and, in the argot of the time, 'square', when compared with the new kid on (or, more accurately, *off*) the Croisette.

The Quinzaine's first edition in 1969 was subtitled 'Cinéma en Liberté' and was held in the Rex cinema, some distance away from the Palais, with an extra screening at the Olympia every night at midnight. Among the sixty-strong selection of films were works by Bernardo Bertolucci, Nagisa Oshima, and André Téchiné, as well as two that were very much of the moment – Peter Fonda in Roger Corman's psychedelic extravaganza *The Trip*, and *Head*, Bob Rafelson's light-hearted bid to lend the Monkees a touch of counter-cultural credibility. Both carried a writing credit for a young little-known actor named Jack Nicholson who was also starring in a competition film, *Easy*

Rider. However, things ran far from smoothly on the Cannes fringe, as Doniol-Valcroze recalls:

> On the first day, the opening film hadn't arrived for our inaugural screening at ten in the morning. We hesitated. There was only a dozen people in the auditorium. That's not many but we couldn't send them away. That would have been our Waterloo. Gaby [Jean-Gabriel Albicocco] and Pierre-Henri [Deleau, Quinzaine co-founder] climbed into the projection booth where there were heaps of bags containing reels of film. They took a lucky dip so the screening could start on time. It was a Cuban film, *The First Charge of the Machete* by Manuel Octavio Gómez. A masterpiece. When the screening was over, a Japanese gentleman approached us wearing a big smile and said 'I'll buy it'. The Quinzaine was born.

Robert Enrico, president of the SRF, remembers the Quinzaine receiving a less welcoming reception: 'One morning during a working meeting of the festival administration I was taken aside by a representative of the mayor of Cannes. Scandal! People were peeing in the projection booth, in the corners of the theatre, behind the seats . . . I went to the Rex wearing evening dress because of my official duties. Of course, I was met by a general uproar. Firstly, because of what I was wearing. Secondly, when I explained the aim of my visit. It all ended with roars of laughter . . . Our own enquiry revealed that it had been a piece of malicious gossip put about by a cleaning lady who was furious that she hadn't received any tips.'

'Is cinema still an art, a spectacle, or a weapon?' asked Maurice Bessy (who would replace Favre Le Bret as general administrator in 1972) in an edition of the 1969 festival's daily bulletin. After 1968 it looked increasingly like the revolution was taking place onscreen and that Cannes had caught the counter-cultural bug in a major way. In the following three years, *If . . .* , *Easy Rider*, *Z*, *M*A*S*H*, *Investigation of a Citizen Under Suspicion* and *Johnny Got his Gun* were among the films that won major prizes. Was this was merely an early example of

1 'The 1939 festival was over as soon as it began. On 1 September, Germany took Poland by *blitzkrieg*. Two days later England and France declared war.' The painter Jean-Gabriel Domergue's poster art for the inaugural/cancelled Festival. Photograph © Jean-Gabriel Domergue.

2 The first Palais de Festival. 'Construction went on right up to the wire of opening at 9.30 pm on Friday 12 September, 1949. *Le Film Francais* reported that "a few hours before the opening we were still walking through debris and gravel".'

3 Jean Cocteau (centre), Jury President of 1954, with Festival Administrator Robert Favre Le Bret (left) and actress Gina Lollobrigida (right). 'After each screening,' said Favre Le Bret, '[Cocteau] would compliment the delegation of the relevant country so much that each would tell themselves, "We're going to get the Grand Prix".' Photograph © Bob Hawkins, courtesy of The Kobal Collection.

4 Actors Yves Montand and Charles Vanel presenting Henri-Georges Clouzot's *Le Salaires de la Peur* at Cannes in 1953. '*The Hollywood Reporter*, describing the film as anti-American, dubbed Montand a "communist actor". But ultimately Clouzot's film prevailed.' Photograph © Bob Hawkins, courtesy of The Kobal Collection.

5 'A hungry public, not long emerged from the deprivations of war, was eager to gobble up these glamorous images. Into this febrile atmosphere a teenage Brigitte Bardot would saunter merrily in 1953.' Photograph © Bob Hawkins, courtesy of The Kobal Collection.

6 Kirk Douglas plays with Bardot's hair on the beach at Cannes, 1953. 'Douglas was archetypal 1950s American manhood, straight out of a Charles Atlas ad, and twice Bardot's age.' Photograph © Bob Hawkins, courtesy of The Kobal Collection.

7 Cary Grant and Grace Kelly taking the Cannes waters during the making of Hitchcock's *To Catch A Thief*, 1954. 'Jean Cocteau mused that there was "nothing stranger than this Cote d'Azur seen in Technicolor by the Americans".' Photograph © Paramount, courtesy of The Kobal Collection.

8 Blonde on blonde: Bardot and Kim Novak incline toward different lenses during a red-carpet procession, 1956. Photograph © Bob Hawkins, courtesy of The Kobal Collection.

9 Francois Truffaut (front row, third from left) holding court among young French directors at Cannes, 1959. 'Truffaut once described the classic career trajectory of an *enfant terrible* as tracing an absolutely predictable arc: from scandal and controversy to "a house in the country and the Légion d'Honneur".'

10 Mike Leigh, Palme d'Or winner for *Secrets and Lies* in 1996, juror in 1997: 'One of the wheezes about being on a Cannes jury is that you walk down the Croisette and it's "Mike, how's it going, what do you think of . . . ?" You just go, "Sorry . . ."' Photograph © Stephane Fefer, courtesy of The Kobal Collection.

11 Three disparate directors who made prize-winning breakthroughs at Cannes: (a) Dennis Hopper (*Easy Rider*, 1969), (b) Michelangelo Antonioni (*L'Avventura*, 1960), (c) Abbas Kiarostami (*Taste of Cherry*, 1997).

12 David Cronenberg, three-time Cannes competitor, bold Jury President in 1999. 'We were very surprised at how shocked and upset everybody was with our choices. And I began to realise – talk about alternate realities – that the Croisette had already decided who was going to win the Palme D'Or.' Photograph © Foc Kan/WireImage.com.

what Tom Wolfe would later christen 'radical chic' or a sign of the festival's true renewal? Had word gone out to the festival's international correspondents to send the best of their countries' angriest, hippest youth revolt pictures? Or, if they couldn't come up with that, to send something searing and denunciatory that would have the assembled tuxedos trembling with right-on rage and feelgood solidarity? With its glaring juxtapositions of *luxe* and revolt, Cannes cannot be anything other than intensely self-conscious about its contradictions. After all, this is the temple dedicated to an art form that is brutally Darwinian in its practice of capitalism. The spectacle of political revolt, youthful rebellion and sympathy with the underdog *du jour* all contributes to dignifying the business of cinema and keeps the festival on the side of a vaguely humanistic idea of film-as-art. Which is not an especially cynical interpretation of the lesson that Cannes can be seen to have drawn from '68, as ironically encapsulated by Gilles Jacob's description of the atmosphere in the following year: 'one rushes to the aid of the oppressed minorities before going sunbathing'. For a moment, however, it looked as though a repeat of '68 might be afoot. There were ructions within the jury when two of the jurors, the French critic Claude Mauriac and his British opposite number Karl Foreman, resigned in protest against 'French censorship', soon to be followed by the Swedish actress Ingrid Thulin. Replacements were swiftly made and jury meltdown was averted.

What, then, of the prizewinning films? *Easy Rider* was the fruit of a soon-to-be-disputed collaboration between actors Peter Fonda and Dennis Hopper, guest-starring their young-ish associate Jack Nicholson. The trio arrived in Cannes as if in character, a troupe of bandana-wearing, counter-cultural emissaries in hippy regalia, and carried all before them. After the much-delayed breakthrough success of *Bonnie and Clyde* in 1967, Hollywood was in a process of renewal. A new generation of directors, actors, producers and writers had looked to the example of European cinema and found Old Hollywood wanting. Given the reverence in which Hollywood was held by the New Wave,

140 CANNES

the fortunate congruence of history enabled by the events of May '68 was to wake Cannes up – in the nick of time – to the sudden influx of talent from the US. Youth was the key. The artists were the coming generation who spoke to and made films for and about the young. On one hand, it was a matter of identifying a demographic, to use that hideous term. On the other, more keenly and viscerally felt, it was also a matter of the climate of revolt and political unrest that shadowed and informed these film-makers' every move. This was the first flush of American 'independent' cinema, a term that would become synonymous in the late 1980s with Miramax Pictures and the coronation at Cannes of Stephen Soderbergh's chamber-piece *sex, lies and videotape*.

'Independence' *à la* 1969, however, was of a more socially critical variety. Distributed by the major Hollywood studio Columbia, *Easy Rider* was an original amalgam of 'biker's pic' and picaresque road movie. If not exactly an elegy, it was a drug-addled, drink-soaked swansong to the spirit of the sixties. But it also encapsulated the promise of a new style of American cinema in which sex, violence and self-aware snapshots of the times finally became acceptable cinematic fare for the general public, and hence for the studios. Dennis Hopper won the prize for First Film. The overall winner was Lindsay Anderson's *If . . .* which might be described as 'Mao meets Jean Vigo'. A savage, oneiric account of a bloody student uprising in a prestigious boys' public school, offering a career-defining central performance by Malcolm McDowell (henceforth to specialise in feral-eyed malcontents), it caused a sensation: 'Even the chambermaids knew all about "*Eef . . .*",' *Sight and Sound* editor Penelope Houston reported. Some years later, Anderson observed,

Emotionally, the film is revolutionary but intellectually, I don't know. It won the Palme d'Or, which was very pleasant but a bit of a fluke, I think. The jury that year was headed by Luchino Visconti and he wanted the prize to go to *Z*, the film about the assassination of a Greek MP made by Costa-Gavras. Then there was *Adalen 31*,

BENEATH THE PAVING STONES ... THE BEACH 141

a sort of socialist film about a strike made by Bo Wideberg. I don't think the jury members could make up their minds between these two films and somebody probably said, 'Why not give it to *If . . .?*'

While *Easy Rider* and *If . . .* can be seen as fatalistic allegories of youth revolt, both culminating in failure and death, *Z* was based on current events in Europe. The military *coup d'etat* in Greece in April 1967 would see the country led by a succession of right-wing governments until 1974. Known as 'The Regime of the Colonels', the junta was responsible for widespread repression, imprisonment and torture and had its origins in the undercover 'Gladio' operations sponsored by CIA and NATO to counter communist influence in Italy and other European countries after the Second World War. Constantin Costa-Gavras's film dealt with the investigation into the assassination in 1963 of the popular left-wing MP Gregoris Lambrakis (played by Yves Montand). A doctor and athlete, Lambrakis had been a member of the anti-fascist resistance during the Nazi occupation of Greece and was elected to the Greek parliament in 1961. The investigator, played by Jean-Louis Trintignant, uncovers links between the police and military and far-right extremists. The film divided opinion. It would be a calumny to call Costa-Gavras the Oliver Stone of his day, but the controversies over Stone's style of political cinema, especially over *JFK*, would later replay disputes similar to those provoked by *Z*. Some saw the film as overly didactic and Montand-driven, others claimed it as a breakthrough in political cinema for a mass audience. Richard Roud reported that some Italian critics at Cannes described the film as being 'in the style both of the American thriller and the Soviet propaganda film, an unholy combination if ever there was one'. The correspondent for *Les Lettres Françaises* observed that it was widely seen as certain to win the Grand Prix and received a triumphant reception, 'a fair response but one which smacks of good conscience'. Nevertheless, *Z* took two prizes and went on to have great international success, winning an Academy Award for Best Foreign Film in 1970. Despite being a Franco-Algerian co-production, filmed mostly in the former French colony, *Z* had been chosen to represent France in competition. The Algerian government demanded its dual identity be acknowledged in its designation, but Favre Le Bret's request that the film represent France alone was approved by the French foreign office much to the chagrin of the Algerians.

Other names were to emerge from the festival. Glauber Rocha won the Best Director Prize for *Antonio das Mortes*, something of a coronation for the leading figure of Brazil's *cinema novo*, two of whose films had previously featured in competition. As further proof of cinematic resurgence in the troubled continent of Latin America, the Argentinian film-maker Fernando Solanas showed his *Hour of the Furnaces* in Critics Week. But critical consensus was that the major discovery of 1969 was a Russian film by Andrei Tarkovsky. A three-and-a-half-hour long epic ostensibly about the life of a fifteenth-century icon painter, *Andrei Rublev* had been completed three years earlier and Favre Le Bret had seen a work print in Moscow in 1967. The Soviet authorities had used the pretext of a new edit not to send it to the festival, while promising to submit it the following year. When it finally screened at Cannes in 1969 it did so not as the official Soviet entry but out of competition. Despite being shown at 4 a.m. on the last day of the festival, it was awarded the International Critics Prize, much to the fury of the Soviet authorities.

Elsewhere in the festival, changes were afoot that would become more marked in the coming decades. 'Films and sea blue at Cannes', the *Daily Telegraph* reported waggishly of the newly overt sexuality on display. TV rights to the closing night's award ceremony had been bought by a company called Eurovision and Favre Le Bret embargoed the announcement of the winners until broadcast (though according to the *New York Times*, a print journalist from Agence France Presse, one of those granted early disclosure for the sake of deadlines, but supposedly confined to a locked room all night, turned a page-list of winners into a little paper aeroplane and sailed it out of the window to a conspirator in the street below).

Constant Revolution?

Where *Bonnie and Clyde* had shocked audiences with the protracted bloodbath of its climactic shoot-out, Robert Altman's *M*A*S*H* submerged them outright in haemoglobin. An exercise in deliberate coarseness and vulgarity that countered the futility of its army medic anti-heroes' blood-staunching efforts, *M*A*S*H* was not so much a case of 'gallows humour' as 'surgical gown humour'. To complain of bad taste was to miss the point completely. As Mike Nichols, director of the 1970 screen version of Joseph Heller's *Catch-22* observed: 'We were waylaid by *M*A*S*H* which was much fresher and more alive, improvisational and funnier . . . It just cut us off at the knees.' Both the American titles selected for the Cannes competition in 1970, *M*A*S*H* and Stuart Hagmann's *The Strawberry Statement*, were responses to America's deeply unpopular war in Vietnam which, by late April, President Nixon had extended to Cambodia.

M*A*S*H was only Altman's second feature film after twenty years directing TV. Though set during America's war in Korea in 1950 it was taken as a barely veiled assault on military values in general and the war in Vietnam in particular. Altman recalls Cannes coming as a complete surprise: 'Fox said, "You're going to go on a publicity tour" and we went to Argentina and from there to Cannes. We didn't have any anticipations of winning anything. It just kind of overwhelmed us.' Did he think the film got such a strong reception because it was a film that had protest at its heart?

> Yes I do, I think that's what was developing at that time. The film that was considered the big favourite was *The Strawberry Statement*, then somehow it switched over to us. Fox wasn't even really interested in releasing *M*A*S*H*. They didn't like it. Had we not had that success in Cannes I promise you someone would have come in there with a pair of scissors and it would have been a different film. Or it would have just been thrown out – tossed away to the drive-ins at that time . . .

The Strawberry Statement also had anti-war protest as its ostensible subject matter but, as many observed, something jarred about the film's vision of the April 1968 student occupation of Columbia University. The MGM film was based on a first-hand account written by a nineteen-year-old student, and by a bloody stroke of historical irony its world premiere coincided with the massacre at Kent State University in Ohio. On 4 May, four students were shot dead and nine injured when the Ohio National Guard fired on students protesting the war on the campus. The horror of the event could only have served to emphasise The Strawberry Statement's vacuous modishness. Where M*A*S*H was anarchic in tone, freewheeling in style and genuinely scabrous in its contempt for authority, this was seen as false and overly aestheticised. Alexander Walker described it as being 'like a telly commercial for a product called Protest'. David Robinson smelt a cynical Hollywood: 'the companies are ready to sell radical politics to the predominantly youthful market just as they might sell any other viable commodity – sex or violence or whatever else may currently be in fashion'. Also at Cannes, screening out of competition, was Woodstock, produced by Warner Brothers. Dissent was already being turned into a commodity.

It is clear that Cannes in some sense acted belatedly as a focus – one of the many – for the 'youthquake' of the 1960s. It was modified from within by French cinema's own representatives of 'youth', the New Wave, whose film-makers were central both in shutting down the festival in 1968 and then in militating for the creation of parallel sections such as the Quinzaine. Both the Venice and Berlin festivals would follow suit. One of the crucial aspects of the way the 'big three' festivals responded to the contestations of the late 1960s lay in the desire of each to preserve their A-list status which they could only do by incorporating parallel festivals within them, in the belly of the whale. For several years, two festivals cohabited at Cannes: a traditional one and one born of 1968. In the process, a new festival was slouching toward the beach to be born.

VII

Adventures in Cinema

To the best of our abilities, and even if we often time fail, we must produce films that hurt, films that will disturb, films that will not let you rest. For the times are bad, and given times like these, it is a crime to rest.
Lino Brocka, 1985

The European film festival as we now know it was a product of the post-Second World War era in which culture was seen as a means of encouraging friendly relations between states that had formerly been adversaries. Festivals became sites of cultural exchange that aimed to encourage both the art of film and better understanding between peoples. While this laudable intention was frequently compromised by diplomatic tussles and the propagandist efforts of competitor countries, it has nevertheless remained one of the underlying reasons for Cannes' longevity. This imperative has also been interpreted in different ways at different times throughout the festival's history.

During the Cold War, ideological confrontations were the order of the day but it was preferable that these took place through cultural exchange rather than through the exchange of intercontinental ballistic missiles. During the counter-cultural upheavals of the late 1960s and the post-colonial period of national independence struggles, Cannes served as a place where the visions of such conflicts could be seen (although this proved less straightforward when it came to the fight for independence of the Algerian people, as we will see later). By the end of the 1970 and throughout the 1980s, Cannes began to exercise its power with a different emphasis, promoting human rights through the defence of film-makers working in adverse circumstances.

146 CANNES

The art of cinema was seen as a form of resistance against tyranny and oppression. The so-called 'unspoken function' (*fonction non-dite*) of the festival became explicit.

Losing the Plot

We have gestured elsewhere to the legendary hostility that greeted *L'Avventura* at Cannes in May 1960. Fellini's *La Dolce Vita* arrived having already caused a scandal in its home country. But it was Antonioni who represented Italy in competition with his sixth film. Where Fellini's work was vivacious, expansive and more than a little in love with the 'immorality' it aimed to dissect, Antonioni's was withdrawn, tangential and mysterious. One was as accessible as a cartoon strip, the other as opaque as a modernist work of art. Antonioni had been lucky to have the film ready in time for Cannes as the production had been seriously troubled. The shoot on a tiny Sicilian island was interrupted for several weeks when the film's original producer went bankrupt leaving cast and crew stranded without pay and Lea Massari, one of the lead actresses, suffered a heart attack during filming. Nevertheless, the 145-minute final cut unspooled at Cannes on the evening of 15 May.

One British critic phlegmatically reported that Antonioni had 'apparently overestimated the patience of his audience'. If so, they let him know in no uncertain terms by unleashing a chorus of boos and hisses that reduced the director to tears. The reaction galvanised a group of film-makers and critics to leap to his defence, including Roberto Rossellini, producer Anatole Dauman, critic Georges Sadoul and Nelly Kaplan, then assistant to Abel Gance. The festival newspaper of 17 May carried a short declaration in which twenty-six signatories announced themselves 'shocked by the display of hostility' and thoroughly in favour of a work of 'exceptional importance'. In fact, *L'Avventura* was awarded a special Jury Prize for its 'remarkable contribution to the search for a new cinematic language'. French critic Robert Benayoun claimed it to be 'the most important film since

World War II after "Citizen Kane"'. What was it about *L'Avventura* that provoked such disparate responses?

The story concerns a group of well-off idlers who take a boat trip. Among them are Anna (Lea Massari), her lover Sandro (Gabriele Ferzetti) and her less upper-class friend Claudia (Monica Vitti). When the group visits a barren volcanic island Anna disappears and Sandro and Claudia go looking for her. Gradually, though, they lose sight of their quest and become involved in a troubled relationship. The set-up of Anna's disappearance holds out the promise of a suspense narrative and an explanation as to how and why she vanished. But we never learn the answer to either of these questions. Antonioni lets this absence grow until it becomes the focus of the film as expressed through the uneasy and inauthentic relationship between Claudia and Anna's former lover Sandro.

One of the possible explanations for the audience's hostility is that their emotional and psychological investment in the film's story was not simply unsatisfied but actively denied by the narration. Along with the film's leisurely rhythm, its 'dead times' and lingering expressive shots of landscape and environment, Antonioni's approach to story-telling was part of the reason why *L'Avventura* was deemed to be a revolutionary work. The day after the screening Antonioni gave a press conference where he read a statement explaining his intentions. He spoke of searching in the film for a new way to describe a contemporary sensibility where 'Eros is sick, man is uneasy [and] under the sway of moral forces and myths which today, when we are at the threshold of reaching the moon, should not be the same as those that prevailed at the time of Homer, but nevertheless are.' That a film director should feel able to address such weighty themes and that he trusted in his medium to be the ideal way of expressing them was a feature of European cinema in the 1960s.

Antonioni would be seen as one of the key figures in what English speakers came to call 'art cinema' and he was associated with a somewhat intimidating intellectual array of topics such as 'alienation', 'incommunicability' and 'Antonioni-ennui', as Pauline Kael once snarkily put it. 'Art cinema' has an unfortunate ring to it and now seems both irredeemably dated and hopelessly imprecise. The French came up with a more practical way of describing the same sort of films that emphasised the newness of their conventions rather than the exclusivity of their appeal: *le cinéma moderne*. This was, in fact, the title of a 1964 book by Gilles Jacob, a young critic soon to be closely involved in the Cannes Festival. An indication of the usefulness of the term is that the French still use it today to define a form of film-making with specific historical roots in post-war Europe that endowed later film-makers with a host of cinematic strategies. One could say that *L'Avventura* represents a split between old and new cinema in the way it handles the audience expectations created by Anna's disappearance. The usual conventions of film narrative are not simply subverted but instead, like Anna, they go missing.

So, then: a cast of penguin-suited philistines in a paroxysmal flap at the spectacle of 'modern cinema'. The sensitive Italian *maestro* and his blonde muse Monica Vitti weeping in despair as their traumatically conceived masterpiece is traduced before their eyes. Then sweet vindication. It all fits together rather neatly as a photo-fit 'Battle of Hernani'. Which is not to say that Antonioni did not have a lot riding on the screening. It was his first feature selected to compete in Cannes and his so far rocky career had increasingly depended on recognition by French *ciné-savants*. But what if the screening had passed without incident? What if the film had solicited no catcalls, no supportive petitions and possibly no prizes? Would *L'Avventura* still have been seen as the benchmark work it is today? Its troubled reception was as important for the festival as it was for the film. The adventure of *L'Avventura* at Cannes in 1960 meant that the festival could henceforth lay claim to the crucial attribute of being a place where new tendencies in film language and new waves of film production could be discovered and defended. The idea of the festival as promoter of 'a certain idea of cinema' was being born.

The 'unspoken function' of Cannes

Today a silver-haired gent of ambassadorial bearing, Gilles Jacob (b.1930) presided over the festival as its general administrator from 1978 until he became president in 2000. During that time he shaped the festival into what it is today. In 1976 he worked alongside Maurice Bessy, whom he succeeded when the latter retired after the 1977 festival. This was a transitional period, for Jacob best symbolised by Wim Wenders's *Kings of the Road*. 'I was convinced that the film was something of a milestone,' he explains. 'Maurice Bessy was outraged by a scene where someone defecates, and refused to select it. I managed to get the film through. From then on they left me in charge of the festival's evolution.' Jacob is fond of describing Cannes as 'a family' and relates with a certain avuncular pride how 'when Lars von Trier writes to me he puts "Dear Dad". The Coen Brothers call me "Uncle". And I call them "Dear Nephew" or "Dear Son".'

Jacob's tenure at Cannes saw three factors – institutional, aesthetic and politico-cultural – coalesce. In institutional terms, the crucial date was 1971 when festival regulations were changed:

> It was felt the best films were not always selected, and that often the criteria used for selection such as personal, political, or professional connections had nothing to do with art or the intrinsic qualities of the films. Gradually, the festival added its own selections to those of the various countries as a means of compensating for certain perceived errors or injustices. From 1972 films, not countries, would be represented. Moreover, it would be the Festival Director and not national committees who would decide which films would be invited from around the world. Thus nationalist biases could no longer hold sway.

This change arguably gave Jacob greater power to shape the festival than his predecessors. The 'aesthetic' focus of the festival's selection coincided with a period in world cinema when the dominant idea was of the 'director as superstar' and all over the world nations were producing new

150 CANNES

auteur films in the dynamic spirit of the New Waves of the 1960s. These were the years that saw Cannes institutionalise '*auteur* cinema'. The politico-cultural factor comes into play when one considers the example of certain auteurs working in countries with repressive political regimes, such as Andrzej Wajda in Poland, Yilmaz Güney in Turkey, Andrei Tarkovsky in the USSR or Lino Brocka in the Philippines. (It's interesting to note that three of the four – Wajda, Tarkovsky and Güney – all spent time in exile, adapting their film-making to the demands of international co-productions.) The newly invigorated aesthetic focus of Cannes allowed the festival to use its reach and prestige to actively pursue a policy of defending such directors, guaranteeing their work an international audience when it was banned at home. 'We have always placed artists above states and even above their film industries,' asserts Jacob:

> Certainly, we've been in conflicts with states that have risked posing problems for France. When you have international agreements, commercial or economic, and it is learned that the Cannes Festival has shown a film by Tarkovsky, a film by Wajda, or a film by Zhang Yimou that can create difficulties. We go a long way to defend the rights of artists. For example, we showed *Mirror* by Tarkovsky, which we'd obtained a copy of through back-channel means. When we started the screening the Russian Delegation practically tried to break down the door to the projection booth in order to stop the projection. The door was barricaded which bought enough time for the film to be shown, after which we gave them back the copy. So it can even lead to some direct conflicts in certain cases and to some quite tough situations. Our position now is that a film can be seen even if, for whatever reason, it's banned in its home country. In the final reckoning, it's a struggle against censorship.

Consider Andrzej Wajda's *Man of Marble* (1978), set in the mid-1970s and telling of a young Polish press photographer, Agata (Krystyna Janda), who finds a marble statue of a 'labour hero' of the Stalinist 1950s bricklayer Mateusz Birkut (Jerzy Radziwilowicz). She attempts to trace the man himself and discovers that he was killed in 1970 in Gdansk (the shipyard where the Solidarity movement was founded) in a peaceful demonstration against the regime. The film had been slated by official critics in Poland for 'lying' about the country's history and had not been authorised to represent the country at international film festivals. It played at Cannes in 1978 without the knowledge of the Polish authorities and won the International Critics Prize. Jacob clarifies what such 'back-channel means' entailed here. A print was smuggled out of Poland for a surprise screening with the title on the reels changed to '*J'irai cracher sur vos tombes*' ('I spit on your graves').

However, Jacob is well aware that supporting dissident film-makers can be risky:

> There can be reprisals and one must be very careful. We must show the film but not place the artist in a situation where they can't return to their country. In 1979 I selected Milos Forman's film *Hair*. He told me, 'I want to be at the opening of the festival.' I said, 'Okay. Maybe. We'll see. But why?' 'I absolutely want to be at the opening.' He'd been kicked out of Czechoslovakia as a subversive, but he told me, 'I'm going back to see my mother and I've no idea if they'll let me leave the country again.' He knew that if he had Cannes on his side they wouldn't come looking for him. Which was how it worked out. He wasn't forbidden to travel. So the festival has helped artists, independently of films, in giving them a certain prestige that can make them untouchable afterwards.

In 1982, the Palme d'Or was awarded ex aequo to a pair of films denouncing dictatorships: Costa-Gavras's *Missing* and Yilmaz Güney's *Yol* ('Road'). *Missing* made ideologically enlightened use of Hollywood money and featured an award-winning performance by Jack Lemmon to explore the toppling of the democratically elected Chilean socialist Salvador Allende in a bloody coup assisted by the CIA. *Yol* was shot clandestinely in Turkey, its director communicating his instructions from prison. When the film was projected at Cannes,

CANNES

Güney escaped. On news of the prize, the Turkish authorities demanded the director's immediate extradition.

Film, like politics, thrives on stories of heroism. Consider film-makers like Herzog, Coppola and Cimino whose legends are fuelled by stories of self-surpassing endeavour, the director as Prometheus, where the risk of grandiose failure is alchemised into epics of wide-screen hubris. But they look like dilettantes compared to Yilmaz Güney (1937–1984). Once described as 'something like Clint Eastwood, James Dean and Che Guevara combined', Güney was a highly popular star of 1960s Turkish action pictures and was nicknamed 'the ugly king' for his roles in titles like 'I Swear by My Gun', 'Güney Spreads Death' and 'The Blood Will Flow Like Water'. By the late 1960s he was making his own forays into directing films, combining the rough-hewn genre appeal of rural revenge films with stark and sometimes lyrical realism. *Umut* ('Hope', 1971), regarded as his first masterpiece, was screened at Cannes in 1971 in Directors Fortnight. The 1970s are regarded as the high point of Güney's career but he spent most of it in prison.

In every decade since the 1960s, Turkey has experienced military coups and as a left-wing Kurdish nationalist, Güney was arrested in March 1972 for harbouring anarchist refugees accused of a political assassination. Released in a general amnesty in 1974, he was rearrested in September supposedly for murdering a judge. He would spend the rest of the decade and part of the early 1980s in captivity, producing some of his most notable films from jail, including *Suru* ('The Herd', 1978), *Busman* ('The Enemy', 1979) and *Yol* which he directed by proxy, smuggling out instructions to trusted surrogates (*Yol* for example was directed by Sorif Goren). It seems he was allowed to watch dailies, order re-shoots and even edit in prison.

Yol tells the epic story of five prisoners, several of them Kurds, given brief leave to visit their families, none of whom return. A coup in September 1980 bought a renewed period of political repression in Turkey and Güney fled prison in 1981 to complete *Yol* abroad. He appeared at Cannes in 1982 to accept his share of the Palme d'Or, then vanished into hiding. Now *persona non grata* in Turkey he was officially exiled in France where he shot his last film, *Le Mur* ('The Wall'), a gruelling depiction of life in Turkish prison. He died of stomach cancer in Paris in 1984. Although largely forgotten in the West he remains a folk hero in Turkey where his legend has been claimed by the left, by Kurdish nationalists and even by Turks who have dubbed him a 'Turkish' director and established a Güney Foundation.

The Importance of Being Pierre

As a longtime Cannes insider, Pierre Rissient is also well aware of what working with dissident film-makers can involve. Rissient deserves a brief introduction. Film people know him as a 'player' par excellence, the *éminence grise* of French cinema. Todd McCarthy of *Variety*, maker of a documentary about Rissient, described him as 'probably the least known man of tremendous influence in the history of cinema'. Fifty years of reputation-making and film-scouting at the four corners of the globe have left Rissient's fingerprints in the most unlikely reaches of film history. In Clint Eastwood's transmogrification from cardboard screen psycho-cop to American auteur. Or in the discovery during the 1980s of short films by a young Australian woman, and Jane Campion's subsequent Palme d'Or (the first woman to win it) in 1993 for *The Piano*.

Rissient haunted the Cinémathèque Française in the 1950s, and was assistant director on *A Bout de souffle*. In the sixties, as the critic-programmer Tony Rayns tells it,

> Pierre went into business as a publicist with Bertrand Tavernier, specialising in what you might call classical Hollywood films, and particular directors. These gentlemen, when they visited Paris, were in the care of Pierre, and he and Tavernier played the field very expertly in a way that is perhaps only possible in France. So if you, for instance, wanted access to Fritz Lang when he visited Paris, you had

to do Pierre certain favours. It wasn't done in a Machiavellian way, this was just the way it works in Paris. And if you were part of the group, then you could be relied upon to give good reviews to this film, or that film-maker, this was how the system was built up.

Rissient was instrumental in recovering the reputations of Lang, Losey, Hawks, Ford, and Walsh, but he also became a hands-on emissary for a host of major auteurs from Lino Brocka to Chen Kaige and Hou-Hsiou Hsien. Rissient's career provides a fascinating insight into how persistent background work matched with unerring good taste and a fat book of contacts can play a crucial role in forming the cinematic canon.

Like his Brazilian equivalent Glauber Rocha, the Filippino director Catalino Ortiz ('Lino') Brocka seems largely forgotten now in the West. Rocha died in 1981 but his remarkable films certainly deserve a major revival, especially in the context of the international renaissance of Latin American cinema since the 1990s. Brocka, who died in 1991 and made over fifty films in just over twenty years, can be said to have suffered from the vagaries of film festival fashion. While his work occasionally gets shown at festivals today these tend only to be in DVD projection. The high point of his international acclaim in the late 1970s coincided with a period of political instability in the Philippines during Ferdinand Marcos's corrupt military dictatorship. Brocka was born in 1939 in the southern Philippines. When Brocka was six his father, a relatively prosperous shipbuilder, was the victim of a suspected political killing and the family spent the following years leading a precarious and poverty-stricken existence. An early interest in theatre led Brocka to university in Manila where he dropped his law studies to specialise in the arts. After a brief spell as a Mormon missionary in Hawaii, including time spent in a leper colony, by the early 1970s he was making successful commercial films in the Philippine industry but frustration with interference by financiers led him to found his own production company in 1974. Despite a somewhat tumultuous production history of box-office success followed by flops, Brocka began a string of works that established him as a singular film-maker and began to attract international attention, including *Tinimbang ka nguni't kulang* ('Weighed But Found Wanting', 1974), *Maynila. Sa mga kuko ng liwanag* ('Manila. In the Claws of Light', 1975), *Insiang* (1977), *Jaguar* (1979) and *Bayan ko: Kapit sa patalim* ('My Country: Double-Edged Knife', 1984).

During this period, the Marcos government tried to persuade him to make films supporting the state and eulogising Marcos as a war hero, which Brocka resisted. This led him to found Concerned Artists of the Philippines (CAP) and he became increasingly involved in political activities and strike action following the assassination in 1983 of Benigno Aquino, a leading political opponent of Marcos, who had returned from self-imposed exile in the United States. Brocka served a short jail sentence for these activities and his films of this period, particularly *Insiang* (the heroine's name) and *Jaguar* (the nickname for bodyguard), increasingly concentrated on the brutal conditions of life in the Manila slums and how such an existence can pervert the lives of the poor. *Insiang* played at the Directors Fortnight in 1978 where it came as a revelation, films from the Philippines being completely off the map of international cinema at the time.

However, according to Rissient, such international appreciation was not to the liking of the Philippine authorities: 'Mrs Marcos was very upset at the film's success because it's a very violent drama set in the slums. She didn't want people thinking of the Philippine slums, she wanted beautiful landscapes . . .' By the time Brocka had completed *Jaguar*, Filipino films for export were subject to censorship. With money from a German TV sale in the offing needed to prepare the film for competition at Cannes, Rissient had to find a way of getting Brocka's film out of the country uncut. The convoluted behind-the-scenes manoeuvres involved in extracting work from under the nose of a repressive regime could even require the unlikely assistance of cinema's most famous secret agent, as Rissient recounts.

Lino said, 'The only person who could get it out would be Sean Connery' because Marcos had played golf with Connery in Marbella and had publicised the friendship to the Philippine people. Lino said that if Sean Connery asked for the picture to go out then Marcos would not refuse. I had met Connery briefly at John Boorman's place, so I sent a telex to John asking him if he could get in touch with Connery very quickly and I explained the situation. John sent us another telex saying, 'As soon as I am in contact with him I'm sure Sean will make a point of getting in touch with President Marcos, etc.' But we still didn't have what we needed. Lino said, 'Let me have that telex.' He took it and went to see the colonel in charge of film censorship. Lino told him, 'Look, you have just a few days left to let the film out!' The colonel said, 'I fear Mrs Marcos but less than Marcos himself. I'll let it go.' So James Bond freed *Jaguar* . . .

When Brocka arrived at the 1984 Cannes Festival to show his French co-production *My Country: Double-Edged Knife* he wore a 'barong tagalog' (loose Philippine shirt) with a blood red map of the Philippines printed on the front and emblazoned beneath it the word 'justice'. When accused of being overly theatrical he replied: 'Of course, that's the whole point. If I could have dragged a coffin in here with me, I would have.'

The Memory of War

Psychoanalysts talk of 'screen memory', meaning one constructed by the unconscious to 'screen out' a buried memory too traumatic to be recalled. Such is the memory of the Algerian War in France: still traumatic, still 'screened'. At Cannes in 2005, Michael Haneke won the Best Director Prize for *Caché* ('Hidden'), a film that glacially peels away the screens that Georges (Daniel Auteuil), a rather smug Parisian cultural commentator, has folded around a dirty family secret. As a child, Georges's parents adopted the son of Algerian friends who had disappeared, suspected killed, after a Paris demonstration in October 1961 in support of the Algerian pro-independence FLN (Front de Libération Nationale). When Georges starts to receive anonymous videotapes and threatening child-like scrawls in the post he suspects that his former half-brother Majid (Maurice Benichou), whom he had sent away for adoption as a boy, seeks revenge. In *Caché*, the memory of France's colonial war in Algeria remains hidden. It neither rises to the surface of the film nor is it addressed directly but continues to resonate in Georges's family memory as well as in omnipresent television images of present-day neo-colonial conflicts (Iraq, the Occupied Territories).

Officially denied for the eight years of its duration and still without a national day of remembrance, the Algerian War was 'the war without a name'. After more than a century in Algeria, the French colonial presence began to be challenged militarily after the Second World War. Such insurgencies were brutally repressed until the emergence of the FLN, which waged a long war of independence with the French army between 1954 and 1962, when Algeria finally claimed independence. Not only did the Algerian War topple the Fourth Republic, it terminated France's imperial status (already mortally wounded by its war in Indo-China). It divided the French people, saw bomb attacks on mainland France by renegade army officers, provoked desertions, and led to revelations of the use of torture by French troops which caused moral outrage. With the inauguration of de Gaulle's Fifth Republic in 1958 censorship became the order of the day, and any films dealing directly with the theme of war were systematically forbidden (which also included foreign films that had not been granted an exhibition visa, such as Stanley Kubrick's *Paths of Glory*). The 'dirty war' in Algeria was also one without an image.

From the early 1960s to the mid-1970s, the Algerian War remained a source of enduring controversy at Cannes. Being under the control of the state, Cannes was subject to the political edicts of the day and between 1958 and 1962 there was an increase in the numbers of plainclothes police at the festival and systematic surveillance of what administrative documents refer to as 'north African elements'. Censor-

158 CANNES

ship persisted at the festival even after it had been relaxed in France. Two films in particular suffered from this in the early 1960s. Godard's second feature *Le Petit soldat* (1960) had been filmed in Switzerland and so avoided the pre-censorship to which French film projects were susceptible. The film concerns a young French deserter, Bruno Forestier (Michel Subor), in hiding in Geneva who is being pursued by both the FLN and the OAS (Organisation de l'Armée Secrète, a group of renegade French army officers opposed to Algerian independence and led by General Salan, who was suspected of being behind an assassination attempt on de Gaulle). Bruno is tortured and his girlfriend Veronica Dreyer (Anna Karina) is executed. The film was due to be selected for competition in 1960 but was withdrawn, then banned in France until 1962 as constituting a 'justification for desertion'.

Alain Cavalier's *Le Combat dans l'île* (1962) was not permitted to compete at Cannes because the film was seen to contain allusions to the OAS, sufficient for it to qualify as 'an offence against France' over what was euphemistically referred to as 'the Algerian problem'. The film, about a right-wing extremist (Jean-Louis Trintignant) attempting to assassinate a left-wing politician, made no direct references to the Algerian War. The offending material featured in a scene set in a cinema showing newsreel footage of a demonstration in Paris on 8 February 1962 that had resulted in eight deaths and, though illegal, was protesting the OAS campaign of bombings on the French mainland. The film was not banned in France but excised from Cannes and was refused authorisation to be shown at any other film festivals.

The most celebrated film about the Algerian War was made by the Italian Gillo Pontecorvo in 1966. *The Battle of Algiers* narrates a key moment in the conflict, from October 1957, when French troops encircled the Algiers Casbah, up to December 1960 and the Algerian revolt. Every student knows the story of Black Panthers taking notes from the film's detailed explanation of how to form guerrilla cells, and in the era of street-to-street battles in Iraq, Gaza and Lebanon the film has accrued new relevance. In 1966, Italy chose the film to compete at

Cannes. Unexpectedly, the festival rejected the film, seeing its submission as an act of pure provocation. In September, it was shown at Venice instead and became the catalyst for worsening relations between the two festivals and their respective countries. The French ambassador in Rome advised against opposing the Venice screening of 'this mediocre film, which would give it unnecessary publicity'. When it won the highest prize, the Lion d'Or, the French delegation walked out in protest and the French press reported the award as 'a humiliation'. The participation of each country in the other's principal film festival was at risk and while the fracas was diffused through diplomatic manoeuvres it was clear that France was far from coming to terms with the Algerian War. *The Battle of Algiers* remained undistributed in France until 1971.

Nevertheless, films about the war began to appear at Cannes and one such, *Le vent des Aurès*, was shown only the year after the controversy over *The Battle of Algiers*. Made by Algerian director Mohammed Lakhdar-Hamina, it was an explicitly nationalistic story of an Algerian family during wartime, and had been sent to the festival by the Algerian government as its official competition entry. For the French Foreign Minister this was a diplomatically sensitive request and he passed the responsibility for the film's selection on to the festival. Following disagreements among the selection committee the film was accepted and won the Prix de la Première Oeuvre. Cannes took longer to accept French films about the war, but this was because, until 1972, no such works were made. For the tenth anniversary of Critics Week the selection included what is regarded as the first French film about the Algerian War, René Vautier's *Avoir 20 ans dans les Aurès*.

Vautier (b. 1928) is the archetypal *cinéaste engagé* and was so from a young age. After having fought in the Resistance and being awarded the Croix de Guerre at sixteen, he made his first film before he was twenty, a study of the effects of colonialism in Africa, *Afrique 50* (1948), which was banned. Vautier has remained a militant film-maker ever since. Between 1956 and 1957, when he had to leave France after

160   CANNES

being declared a 'threat to state security', Vautier went to Algeria where he filmed the war alongside the FLN. *Avoir 20 ans dans les Aurès* told the story of a young French conscript Noel (Alexandre Arcady) who deserts while serving in Algeria and tries to flee to Tunisia through the mountainous Aurès region. The story was heavily influenced by the real-life exploits of Noel Favrelière who published an account in 1960 of having deserted while serving as a paratrooper in Algeria. The film won the International Critics Prize and together with *Le Vent des Aurès* paved the way for the breakthrough film which would win the Palme d'Or three years later, Mohammed Lakhdar-Hamina's *Chronique des Années de Braise* ('Chronicle of the Years of Fire', 1975).

The year 1975 was a particularly turbulent one at Cannes, the atmosphere made especially tense by bombings and death threats connected to the presence of the Algerian film in the main competition. *Chronique des Années de Braise* told the story of two generations of Algerians who had successively fought with the French army in the Second World War then against it in the war of national independence. The film caused divisions within and beyond the selection committee, the mayor of Cannes expressing fears that it could stir up trouble in a region with a large population of repatriated French settlers (known as *pieds noirs*). The day before the festival opened two small bombs exploded, breaking several windows in the Palais, and during the festival several cinemas received anonymous hoax bomb threats which interrupted screenings. The film's projection took place on 12 May amid strict security. Jeanne Moreau was president of the jury which included English writer Anthony Burgess, Italian actress Lea Massari, the American director George Roy Hill, the Spanish actor Fernando Rey and Pierre Salinger, the journalist and former press secretary to US Presidents Kennedy and Johnson.

According to critic and juror Pierre Mazars, the Right thought 'the producers of the Algerian film were pulling the strings' while the Left saw 'the hand of vengeful *pieds noirs*' behind the attacks. No group was ever identified for placing the bombs. However, Mazars recalls no

ADVENTURES IN CINEMA 161

direct pressure being applied to the jury. Anthony Burgess remembers things a little differently:

> The big prize went with little difficulty to the Algerian entry. We were given an anonymous warning that a bomb would go off in the great *salle* if it did not win. It was no worse a film than the others, though it raised an interesting moral question. George Roy Hill and I tried to leave the showing during a scene in which, lavishly and in close view, the throat of a camel was cut. We were not permitted to leave, since the doors had been locked. Pierre Salinger, in his fluent but very American French, alleged that, in aesthetic terms, there was no difference between the *coupage fictive de la gorge d'un chameau* and the real thing. In cinematic art everything depended on the effect. How the director got his effect was his own business. This, I thought, was dangerous philosophy. And then the fictive rape of *Orange Mécanique* was brought up. Was not its impact the impact of real rape?

To add to the tumultuous climate, an unexpected festival of political film organised by the Socialist Party was held in the Lido cinema with representatives from Palestine, Chile and Cambodia attending a themed programme dealing with national liberation struggles. Outside the Palais, numerous groups distributed hundreds of anti-Cannes leaflets. The selection also raised a few eyebrows, the Semaine de la Critique including *Vase de Noce* (or 'One Man and his Pig' or 'The Pig Fucking Movie') by Belgian Thierry Zéno, a zoophilic piece about a young farmer who falls in love with a sow, marries it and raises a family of human-porcine mutants. Burgess recalls that 'the young pig had been brought as a kind of promising starlet to Cannes; it slept in the bathroom of the producer-director'.

On the night of the awards ceremony, a string of bomb alerts disrupted the festival; the Algerian delegation and festival representatives received anonymous death threats. But the victorious Lakhdar-Hamina claimed, 'This time the festival has become truly international. This prize recognises the existence of the third world.'

The award was symbolically significant, a recognition of the import of Third Cinema (Lakhdar-Hamina was the first 'third world filmmaker' to win the prize) as well as marking a symbolic recognition of both the Algerian struggle and the injustices of French colonialism. It also asserted the independence of the festival relative to political pressure, a factor that would be observable for the remainder of the 1970s and 1980s.

Cinéma sans Frontières

As politics in the USA and UK increasingly veered to the right in the 1980s, France seemingly went left. On 10 May 1981 François Mitterrand was elected as the first socialist president of the Fifth Republic. The Cannes Festival started three days later and, for the French at least, was somewhat overshadowed by events. As the new Minister of Culture Jack Lang put it that year, 'the main event was not at Cannes but in people's heads and on TV'. For the left-leaning daily *Libération* the festival was an 'epiphenomenon' compared with what was happening in domestic politics. Or rather, it was until the Palme d'Or was awarded to Wajda's *Man of Iron*.

Something rare happened at Cannes in 1981, as the festival became the focus for two major shifts in European politics: the election of the first left-wing government in France for twenty-three years and events in Poland involving the independent trade union Solidarity. With its award to Wajda's film and its auspicious dateline, Cannes in 1981 served up what the same newspaper called 'a privileged mélange of cinema and politics'.

Wajda (b.1926) was the son of a Polish cavalry officer killed in the Second World War and had fought the Nazis while still in his teens. He studied painting then joined the legendary Lodz film school and made a trilogy of films dealing with the war. *A Generation* (1955), *Kanal* (1956) and *Ashes and Diamonds* (1958) garnered international attention and established him as the pre-eminent cinematic chronicler of

ADVENTURES IN CINEMA 163

contemporary Polish history. *Man of Iron* concerned Solidarity's first success in getting the Polish government to recognise the workers' right to an independent union. The film tells the story of a young worker involved in the anti-communist labour union, and a journalist working for the communist regime whose job it is to discredit him. The young man is clearly meant to be a parallel to the Solidarity leader Lech Walesa who appears briefly at the end of the film (later to win the Nobel Peace Prize and become Polish president between 1990 and 1995). Neither the earlier *Man of Marble* nor *Man of Iron* are straightforward historical chronicles. Both films are keenly aware of the role that state media played in spinning facts into 'official' history. Where *Man of Marble* used the narrative alibi of a TV film-maker's deconstruction of Stalinist-era myth-making, in *Man of Iron* history was happening as the cameras rolled. Wajda remembers how he was inspired to make the film:

> At the Lenin Shipyards in Gdansk, talks had already been under way between the workers and the government for some time, but at the beginning only shreds of information were reaching Warsaw. At the time, the Association of Film-makers, of which I was president, had won the right to record important historical events for archival purposes, and a group of film-makers was already at the shipyard. The workers' guard at the gate recognised me at once and on my way to the meeting room one of the shipyard workers said 'Why don't you make a film about us?' 'What kind of film?' '*Man of Iron*' he answered without hesitation. I had never made a film to order but I could not ignore this call. The echo of *Man of Marble* returned to me. Its final scene had ended right here at the gates of the Gdansk shipyards. This could provide a good pretext for making a new film.

Man of Iron was made during the brief 'thaw' in communist censorship between the formation of Solidarity in August 1980 and its suppression in December 1981 with the declaration of martial law. It was highly critical of the regime but was able to be so because, as Wajda asserts, 'behind this film stood the many million strong Solidarity union which was prepared to defend it if necessary'. Thanks to such support *Man of Iron*, which even the state censor acknowledged was 'an outstanding work whose value and significance goes considerably beyond the criteria of aesthetic judgement', was released and not prevented from entering foreign film festivals. *The Times* described the film's Cannes premiere as 'without doubt the biggest historical event ever seen at the festival throughout its thirty-four-year existence, the rare phenomenon of a work directly born of current events and which itself has become part of them'. *Izvestia*, the official Soviet newspaper, was predictably less enthusiastic:

> The festival on the Côte d'Azur began in a heavily clouded atmosphere. Naturally, the organisers had to dream up something which would assure it a particularly political colouring. And so they prepared a sensation. *Man of Iron* was included in competition although contrary to tradition it had not been viewed in its final version by any representative of the direction. *Man of Iron* was a surefire winner of the first prize in advance. We can now state with certainty that the decision of the jury was a purely political act. And this is, above all, because Wajda's anti-socialist film, made to serve the needs of political convenience, has all the characteristics of a political pamphlet.

Jeane Kirkpatrick, nominated in 1981 by the new US President Reagan as America's first female ambassador to the United Nations, made herself famous by formulating a distinction between authoritarian (US-favoured) dictatorships and totalitarian (pro-communist) ones. For Cannes to garland Wajda's film was to demonstrate support for the Solidarity movement, and, perhaps, to suggest that the new French administration was 'anti-totalitarian' in its leanings. The discourse of 'human rights' and 'democracy' become the only game in town during the 1980s, a means by which 'post-Socialist' France could reorientate itself towards a renascent Republicanism especially through the

ADVENTURES IN CINEMA

founding declaration of the 'Rights of Man'. The defence of dissident film-makers throughout the 1980s at Cannes can be seen to have been part of the ideology of the Mitterrand years.

Man of Iron was front-line, front-page film-making from a director fully engaged with and committed to his subject and as such it fulfilled a vision of cinema as being both a witness to and an agent of the historical process under way in Poland. Wajda and his collaborators brandished their Palme d'Or wreathed in Solidarity banners. After the declaration of martial law in Poland, Wajda's production company was shut down and he went into exile. His next film, *Danton* (1983), starring Gérard Depardieu, was a lavish French production, thoroughly presenting a degeneration in the course of the French Revolution after 1789: *thermidor* after *thermidor*, and the Pyrrhic triumph of frosty Robespierre over life-loving Danton.

The memory of 1789 was not a purely academic matter in France during the 1980s. The bicentenary of the French Revolution loomed and, with a new left-wing government, the question of what it meant to espouse socialist ideas was a pressing one. In May 1989, Cannes hosted a colloquium entitled 'Cinema and Freedom' which brought together a hundred film-makers from five continents to discuss working conditions in their parts of the world. Among those present were Wajda, John Boorman, Roman Polanski, Otar Iosseliani, Emir Kusturica, and Jack Lang. But *Le Monde* saw certain paternalistic habits at work in the discourse of European film-makers for whom censorship was largely an economic matter: 'America is the bogeyman of the Europeans who they look to combat in the Third World. Africa, therefore, has two bogeymen.' Nevertheless, a declaration was issued, stating: 'On this symbolic day how can the Cannes Festival not celebrate the extraordinary connection between cinema and human rights, the better to remember the immense role cinema has played for freedom of expression and its still threatened propagation?' But the prognosis from the newly liberalised East was not promising. For the French-exiled Georgian director Otar Iosseliani the new pressures of commercialism would become overwhelming: 'The way is wide open for all the bastards, speculators and schemers.' For Andrzej Zulawski, it was already too late: 'Coca-Cola barbarism has taken over Poland. The best cinemas are showing porn.' In short, if Cannes found perhaps less cause for celebration than it hoped, it could at least boast its continued success in staying alive to its interesting times.

VIII

The Jury Speaks

A pattern was established . . . of Cannes as a place where jurors were blind to the great films in their midst.

Andrew Sarris

The Cannes jury has always been an inner sanctum, a secret society.

Jeremy Thomas

How can there be a winner?

Robert Altman

It would be difficult to conceive of a more fertile breeding-ground for rumour, gossip and feverish speculation than the judging of the main competition films at Cannes. That fabled inner sanctum, the competition jury, consists of anywhere between nine to twelve people, each renowned in a field of artistic, critical or technical endeavour (principally – but not exclusively – film), who are sworn to secrecy for the festival's duration. Nevertheless, those jurors can circulate during the festival as they please, attending competition films at times of their own choosing, as well as dinners, parties and other functions. Outside this charmed circle swarm directors, producers, financiers, distributors, sales agents and many others whose stock stands to rise or fall on account of the jury's deliberations.

Ponder, if you will, what might be riding on those decisions – fat profits, worldwide distribution deals, funding for your next film, career longevity, a place in cinema history . . . Small wonder, then, that scraps of overheard conversation, supposed leaks and insider information frequently do the rounds of the eager hordes awaiting the

168 CANNES

announcements. No surprise, either, that the final night's award ceremony in the Palais often plays host to a minor explosion, as several thousand exhausted and wound-up *festivaliers* vociferate either their delighted endorsement or their deep displeasure.

With so much at stake, and so many involved, it's inevitable that the jury awards are a prime source of the controversies for which Cannes is by now a byword. Accusations of jury-fixing and corruption have been rife down the years, not least, as we have seen, in the Cold War era when political considerations would occasionally override aesthetic ones. The ceremony is also a prime platform for outbursts of waspish pique and petulance. Remember Lars von Trier disdaining the minor palm awarded to his *Europa* by referring to president Roman Polanski as a 'midget'. Intense friction between audience and director may also be observed – remember, too, the late Maurice Pialat's notorious reception in 1987, as his *Sous le soleil de Satan* claimed top prize. Prizegiving, then, can be boisterous entertainment, but above all a serious business, a vital element in the whole Cannes rigmarole.

Gilles Jacob was mindful always that the films laurelled by Cannes should go on to justify their selection on theatrical release – 'that they are spoken of as *les grands films de Cannes*, this shows that we have indeed done our job'. But he had also to be alert to the satisfaction or otherwise of the critical establishment. 'The awards', says Jacob, 'don't need to *exactly* reflect the consensus of the press, but more that the principal films considered as the five or six best are the ones from which the Palme d'Or winner is chosen. If not, too bad, but the job hasn't been done. That's to say, if you have a good selection and awards that are deceptive, some dissatisfaction remains . . .' There are certain arguments about the merits of films rewarded by Cannes juries that are raging still today. Posterity is a tough judge, and *cinéphiles* glancing through the annals are bound to wonder what Cannes was thinking of in, say, 1957, when Wyler's *Friendly Persuasion* took top prize over Bresson's *A Man Escaped* and Bergman's *The Seventh Seal*. As John Boorman notes,

THE JURY SPEAKS 169

If you look at the history of Cannes, you'll see that the films that have survived with reputations are not often the ones that got the top prizes – the same as the Oscars. There may be a critic on the jury, but mostly you've got people who aren't used to seeing three films in a day and assessing them. What often happens is that half the jury espouses one film, the other half another, they can't agree, so a compromise film gets the top award. The whole atmosphere is somehow so frenetic that views get distorted . . .

Rather than revisiting the insoluble controversies of which film *should* have won what and when, we will take our cue from Boorman's insight and turn now to the actual process of how the jury arrives at its verdicts. What goes on behind those closed doors as the jury deliberates cuts to the heart of the festival's operation. It's the point at which the festival director and president step back, relinquish control, and place the fates of the films they've selected in the hands of a few good men and women. All the festival's hard work up to this point may be undone by a bizarre or wilful decision, a ridiculous compromise, or a plain misjudgement. The impulse to try to influence the course of events must indeed be powerful and sometimes – it appears – irresistible.

One point on which Jacob defends his festival most vehemently from charges of bias is in the relative paucity of French winners of the top prize. 'Because we are a French festival', he insists, 'we are very vigilant to not privilege French cinema. You'll notice that successive juries, even while there has been no shortage of French jurors, have rarely awarded the Palme d'Or to France.' This statement, though, seems to contain a contradiction. How can the festival be 'vigilant' on this issue and still grant the jury complete independence? Surely it's a matter of chance that the juries have awarded few prizes to France? Or are they actually instructed in advance not to favour French films? Or – to advance a yet wilier thesis – might there be an attempt to shape the likely distribution of awards in the selection of jury members? One

170 CANNES

thing, at least, is clear: those who take up the invitation to adjudicate at Cannes enter a hothouse environment. Amongst a Cannes jury, powerful bonds can be forged but also strong animosities, as we'll shortly see.

All the President's Men and Women

For better or worse, the president bestrides the Cannes jury. These days he or she is always the first figure (read: figurehead) to be installed, and eminence – aura, stature, credibility – must be assured in the choosing. The president need not have a multitude of Palmes in the trophy cabinet at home – though this does not hurt – but they must at least be a substantive icon of *le cinéma*. Or as film producer and scholar Colin MacCabe aptly phrases it, 'What they've absolutely *got* to do is get someone of whom *everyone* thinks, "*That's* the president of a Cannes jury . . ."'

Until 1960 jurors and presidents had been mainly drawn from the ranks of academicians, rather than film-makers and other artists. Thereafter the festival was shrewd in taking upon itself the selection and invitation of a president rather than leaving the jury to elevate one of their number by vote. In 1964 it was Fritz Lang, in 1969 Luchino Visconti. Wenders, Polanski, Bertolucci, Coppola, Scorsese, Lynch, Cronenberg, Kusturica, Tarantino, Wong Kar Wai . . . all these auteurs have taken a turn at the presidency in the last two decades. And no one would dispute the entitlement of Clint Eastwood, Jeanne Moreau, Gérard Depardieu or Liv Ullmann to have held the office within that same period.

Bernardo Bertolucci can remember his summons to preside over the forty-third festival in 1990, and also the stipulation he imposed on his acceptance: 'Gilles called and said, "I'm very pleased to invite you, blah-blah-blah", and I said, "Why not?" I had one condition – I had to have at least four or five ladies on the jury. Gilles was very pleased and accepted. So we had Fanny Ardant, Angelica Huston, Françoise Giroud, and I also came with the name of a new director who had

THE JURY SPEAKS   171

made only one film, *Salaam Bombay!*, which I loved. So we invited
Mira Nair, who I think was super-pleased to be asked.'

While Bertolucci brought his own ideas of gender representation to
the table, it is also very clearly an aim of the festival in choosing its
jury to concoct a would-be harmonious blend of men and women,
French and non-French, youth and experience, glamour and gravitas –
even camera and pen. Novelist Kazuo Ishiguro served on Eastwood's
competition jury in 1994, and was of a mind that he was filling a well-
defined berth. He observes:

> Because it's a French festival they've always had this tradition of
> having writers on the jury – that's a very French way of thinking.
> They want an author there, preferably a literary author, to lend
> the thing gravitas. If you look back at past juries, in the sixties you
> find people such as Eric Segal, the author of *Love Story*. So it's
> been a kind of tradition. I think they do like to know that the per-
> son is an enthusiast of film, they want some sort of link with cin-
> ema. The movie of my book *The Remains of the Day* had been
> around the previous year. Then *The English Patient* comes around
> as a movie and you find Michael Ondaatje on the jury the follow-
> ing year.

Mike Leigh, a fellow juror of Ondaatje's in 1997 – under the presidency of Isabelle Adjani, and alongside, inter alia, Paul Auster, Gong Li,
Mira Sorvino, Nanni Moretti, and Tim Burton – has largely positive
memories of the experience, shaded but slightly by a number of con-
tretemps with the president, disputes that are probably not uncommon in a gathering of artists and *artistes*. As Leigh recalls it,

> I have seldom been with a more harmonious, intelligent, sharp set of
> people. We all communicated and there was a good sense of
> humour, it was sophisticated, we were fair and open. Except for the
> president, who is – I would say on record – one of the greatest bone-
> heads that I have ever had the misfortune . . . a most disingenuous

bullshitter of the first order. And I make no apology, because she knows what I think.

The gifted Adjani has, of course, been a treasure of French cinema since her performance in Truffaut's *L'Histoire d'Adèle H* (1976), and won the Best Actress prize at Cannes in 1981 for the dual force of her work in Andrezj Zulawski's *Possession* and James Ivory's *Quartet*. But, evidently, whatever the massed credentials of those who take up seats round the jury table, they may yet find themselves beside or opposite someone they find they can't quite abide. Then again, the experience may also come as a delightful surprise. Jeremy Thomas, producer for Roeg, Oshima, Bertolucci and Cronenberg among others, served on Yves Montand's jury of 1987 in the company of Norman Mailer, not to mention heavyweight directors Klimov, Skolimowski and Angelopoulos. 'Norman Mailer was a director too,' Thomas recalls. 'He had a film in Un Certain Regard that year, *Tough Guys Don't Dance*. But he was a fabulous guy to spend a couple of weeks with. They were *all* fabulous. That's the great thing about a jury, you've got a fascinating group of people that you see on a regular basis and debate and discuss films – what a fantastic thing to do . . .'

The Casting of Lots

Each year the jury is expected to award a Palme d'Or, a Grand Prix (effectively a second prize, and often for a piece thought less accessible), a Jury Prize (which could be considered a bronze medal), and prizes for Best Director, Actor, Actress, and Screenplay. The Cannes authorities prefer a spread of prizes nowadays, so as to prevent too much ill feeling and foster the sense of inclusiveness on which they are intent. Since Roman Polanski's 1991 jury bestowed three prizes upon *Barton Fink*, the regulations now deem a film can take away only two. If one is the Golden Palm, then the second can only be Best Actor or Actress. (In 2003 Patrice Chéreau's jury violated the rules by giving Gus van Sant's *Elephant* both Palme d'Or and Best Direction, but

Chéreau brought off his coup by threatening to resign.)

Historically, the day-to-day mechanics of jury duty – how often jurors meet, how votes are cast and so on – is determined by the president. As Mike Leigh states it, 'This is the convention at most film festivals, it's the president's prerogative to have meetings whenever he or she wants, to have them however he or she wants, and to conduct the proceedings.' This too was Ishiguro's experience with Clint Eastwood:

> When we first met he described how he saw the process, and I guess it was a typical Clint Eastwood approach – very lean and straight-forward, minimal dialogue, you know . . . The idea was that we would meet every two or three days and discuss the films we had seen. Actually, as it turned out, most of us saw the films together, we went around in a pack, so inevitably there was informal discussion. But we had those meetings anyway, and we'd go round the table and have a good go at saying what we thought, then we'd discuss the films, but not yet with a view to prizes.

There is a natural tendency to suppose that the president sets the tone and style of the proceedings. Of course, this may be in a passive key as much as an active one. The critic Michel Ciment, juror in 1978 under director Alan J. Pakula, recalls a very hands-off chairmanship: 'Pakula was both a gentleman and a gentle man, and he really left the discussions open very much. There were three or four people there – I dare to include myself – who had very strong opinions, but in fact Pakula was more like a moderator than a president.' Jeremy Thomas has similar memories of Yves Montand's handling of his fellows in 1987:

> Yves Montand wanted it to be democratically done, by the vote. Films were discarded early on that nobody felt for, then you got down to a hard core group of movies, which you voted for in a little paper bag, and the chairman counted up. That's how it worked, with people arguing and shouting at each other in the middle – there was real passion, particularly from the directors on the jury. But

Montand was a very easygoing sort of guy, he didn't try and influence us that much, just tried to ensure there was no bloodshed.

John Boorman, twice-winner of the Directing *palme*, took his turn as juror in 1992 under Gérard Depardieu, and he agrees with Thomas that a degree of winnowing-out of titles is desirable prior to the jury's final deliberations. 'On each film, if not more than one person wanted to keep it in, we eliminated it. It needed two people to champion it before it was kept in, so if you'd seen twenty films you probably ended up with about ten that you were going to reward, and you worked on those.'

It is likely, then, that the deliberations are aided by an agreed order being placed upon proceedings and adhered to. As Mike Leigh found, if the order breaks down then the outcome can be highly disagreeable: 'We watched twenty-one films in all, and for twenty of those we sat down and had a discussion whereby we went round the table in whatever order we happened to be sitting, but Isabelle Adjani would go last. When it came to the twenty-first film – Wong Kar Wai's *Happy Together*, a great film – she said, "I think I'd like to go first this time", and we said, "Great, go." So for the first and only time she kicked off, and her participation in the discussion was therefore innocent of what everybody else would think.'

As Leigh remembers it, the *President de Jury* was not of the view that *Happy Together* was such a great film, but having led the discussion she found herself in a party of one. 'There was a sort of stunned silence, and then, one by one, everybody in turn went round and said, in effect, "Well, I'm afraid I really can't agree with that . . ."' In the end Wong Kar Wai came away with the Best Director Prize. One might take this as evidence that, firstly, one person's cinematic caviar is another's leftovers, and secondly that even in a rarefied atmosphere of high-level aesthetic discernment there is a principle of a majority verdict that, finally, is likely to carry the day. But jury presidents know that they are strongly associated with their jury's decisions, and if their preferences are at least as passionately held as any other juryman's then they may not be immune to exercising certain wiles – as we will now see.

THE JURY SPEAKS 175

Top Dog

Happy is the jury such as that which sat in 1978, where sweet consensus prevailed in the final measure of excellence. Michel Ciment remembers, 'Unanimity came very quickly on Olmi's *The Tree of the Wooden Clogs*, which had screened, I think, on the fourth day of the festival. We had three or four meetings with temporary votes, *Wooden Clogs* was voted for by everyone at the first meeting, and by everyone at the last. So it got the Golden Palm. And this was not a kind of "diplomatic unanimity", as they sometimes say, one that masks really strong disagreements. It was really unanimous.' Agnès Varda shakes her head in mild amazement that similar harmony should have arisen on her watch as juror in 2005: 'All these incredible cleavages between people with absolutely coherent sets of values . . . but interestingly, we were almost all of us in agreement when it came to the prizes. There were one or two films where there was a relative disagreement – for Jarmusch [Grand Prix, *Broken Flowers*], there was less unanimity. But for *L'Enfant* by the Dardennes [Palme d'Or] and *Caché* by Haneke [Best Director], we were unanimous and unchangeable.'

What, though, if the president in his or her wisdom should have a strong preference that they expect nonetheless to meet with resistance from the jury? Earlier we saw the wiles practised by Georges Simenon in the elevation of *La Dolce Vita* in 1960. Interested parties might also take a play from the book of Bernardo Bertolucci, an ardent *cinéphile*, who in 1990 found himself irresistibly attracted to *Wild at Heart* above all other competition entries. He recalls:

That was quite a difficult mission because I loved the films of David Lynch and I wanted to have the film awarded, but not everybody was appreciating David Lynch as I did. The female elements in the jury, especially, were against the violence of the film. Then it's often the case with movies that are shown at the end of the festival that they can explode and win everything, and here we had *Cyrano*, which everybody liked – especially the ladies who didn't like David

Lynch. So, I had a Machiavellian idea. In life I can't be Machiavellian, only in juries . . . The day before the Palmarès I invited the jury to a meeting and said, 'We have to now decide the awards for Best Actor and Actress. Maybe they will have to come from Hong Kong or Los Angeles, and if we want to have them for the ceremony tomorrow night we'd better decide now.' Everybody agreed that the Best Actor was Gérard Depardieu in *Cyrano*. Now, because of what the director of the festival has told us, there is no pressure and no conditions for what we decide. The only thing we are asked to respect is to spread the awards across various movies, not to concentrate them all on the same title. So at that point, having given the award to Gérard, I knew that I was much closer to what I wanted. *Cyrano* was the strongest rival to David Lynch? Okay, *Cyrano* had the prize for Depardieu. So *Cyrano* was on the side, and it was easier to give the Palme d'Or to David . . .

Compromise . . .

Bertolucci's account of his own wily machinations makes room yet for the respectfully unobtrusive presence of Gilles Jacob, something that Kazuo Ishiguro also took note of: 'Gilles Jacob sits in on all the discussions and all the meetings but he doesn't say anything. He only speaks on technical matters – how many prizes we can award, or if we're actually about to do something that contravenes the rules. I think we might have asked him is it okay for a prize to be shared?'

In fact the jury of 1994 bestowed its Grand Prix jointly upon *Utomlyonnye solntsem* by Nikita Mikhalkov and *Huozhe* by Zhang Yimou. A quick glance at the record-books will point up many such compromising prize-shares. In Cannes parlance it's called awarding a prize ex aequo, which is rarely a satisfactory resolution for anyone involved, especially the prizewinners. (As John Boorman opined in presenting the Best Actress Prize of 1985 to one such illustrious joint

THE JURY SPEAKS

winner, '*Ma chère* Cher, so sorry you have to share . . .') A shared Palme d'Or, moreover, can couple some unlikely bedfellows: in 1980 Kurosawa's *Kagemusha* took top prize ex aequo with Fosse's *All That Jazz*, and Coppola's *Apocalypse Now* won in 1979 together with Schlöndorff's *The Tin Drum*. Again, though, such largesse may be the only means to get the jury members out of their closeted chamber without significant discord. The 1997 jury split the Palme d'Or between Kiarastami's *A Taste of Cherry* and Imamura's *The Eel*, and Mike Leigh found the decision sound but somehow unsatisfactory: 'Personally I love Abbas and his films, including *A Taste of Cherry*, but I wanted to give it to *The Eel*, because actually, ultimately, I think it was the profoundest and best of the films. There was even some daft debate about whether it was right for it to go to Imamura when he'd won it before. But I must say, I actually find that shared things spoil it really. I'm glad that when we got it for *Secrets and Lies* we didn't have to share it with somebody else. I've had a shared prize once at Berlin, and it sort of takes the gilt off the gingerbread . . .'

Michel Ciment remembers the ex aequo award-winners of 1978 expressing much the same disappointment as Mike Leigh notes:

> That year there were two ties. And I realised we should never give ties, because it makes people furious. We shared the Best Actress Prize between Jill Clayburgh and Isabelle Huppert, and the Grand Prix between two directors I admired and knew very well, Skolimowski and Ferreri. And at the final dinner I remember Skolimowski coming to my table where I was having dinner with the jury, and he whispered in my ear, 'How could you share the prize with this non-entity? He has a view of life, but he's not a film-maker. Michel, we have known each other for fifteen years, how could you do this . . .?' And Ferreri refused even to go to the final dinner, just stayed in bed in his room because he was insulted to be sharing a prize with what he called at the time a 'Polish plumber' . . .

Interventions

Several reputable jurors have attested here to feeling no duress from on high as to how they gave out prizes. But as we've seen previously, diplomatic manoeuvrings have occasionally determined the allocation of awards at Cannes, in an often chaotic atmosphere of threatened (and actual) walk-outs and mutual recriminations between competing national delegations. It certainly created an amusing spectacle, and kept the press and the watching world entertained. But it probably undermined and damaged the festival's long-term credibility too. The American critic Andrew Sarris, writing in 1982, summed it up thus: 'Through the overlapping reigns of festival directors Robert Favre Le Bret, Maurice Bessy and Gilles Jacob, Cannes has operated, as any Kafkaesque government agency, in an atmosphere of calculating deviousness and self-serving indirection. In any given year it may be the turn of Hollywood to be soothed, or the Italian film industry to be placated, or the Soviet bloc to be appeased, or the Third World to be thrown a crumb.'

Of course, Cannes and its juries are not impervious to the real world outside its boundaries. The impact of current affairs and the high passions aroused by cinema that speaks of its time can carry all before it without need of political intervention. John Boorman remembers, 'In 1981 I had *Excalibur* in competition, and the word was that it was going to get the top prize, until the very last moment. Wadja came with *Man of Iron*, Lech Walesa was in it, the Solidarity movement was at its height . . . it arrived amid tremendous emotion, and the jury gave it the prize. But it wasn't a particularly good film, and it certainly hasn't survived in any way.' Our friend posterity will also have much to say of the awarding of the 2004 Palme d'Or to Michael Moore's documentary *Fahrenheit 9/11*, a choice made without a shadow of a doubt by the jury of president Quentin Tarantino, but which could just as easily have been made by Jacques Chirac, or by any soul who favoured the election of John Kerry over George W. Bush as president of the United States in that year.

THE JURY SPEAKS   179

Of course it's ultimately to the festival's advantage to keep all the various national players onboard, in order to uphold its reputation as a truly international film festival. That was particularly so before the switch in 1972 from national nomination to festival invitation. But doubts have also been cast on the jury's impartiality long after that pivotal date, removing at a stroke the old excuse of diplomatic appeasement. There have been two especially prominent accusations of festival pressure and interference in a bid to influence the awards. The first was made by the writer Françoise Sagan in 1979, the second by actor Dirk Bogarde in 1984.

L'affaire Sagan

In 1979 Cannes hosted the world premiere of *Apocalypse Now*, an event that has since passed into the realm of legend. Reports of the film's swollen budget and disaster-prone production, not to mention Coppola's extravagant ambitions, had circulated far beyond the trade press throughout its making. There had even been rumours that the whole project would be aborted. So the announcement that it was finally (almost) ready for Cannes created an unprecedented buzz of anticipation. When Coppola and his entourage flew in to Cannes with an unfinished print, one of the biggest feeding-frenzies ever witnessed at the festival ensued. It was a brilliant piece of show-manship on Coppola's part. Nowadays directors quite frequently show unfinished works at Cannes (Wong Kar Wai's *2046* was the most recent high-profile example in 2004), but this was the first time it had ever happened, and it was a publicity masterstroke. Producer Sandy Lieberson has strong memories of the picture's very first morning screening: 'It was staggering. This was a film in the works, surround-ed by controversy, by catastrophe. And everybody was just blown away by it. It was such an emotional experience to come out of that screening – an unfinished film, and yet you'd seen something you knew was just fucking *great*.' In his press conference, Coppola was fairly

180   CANNES

emotional too, feeling understandably embattled after the long and gruelling campaign to complete the picture under simultaneous media bombardment. But he was clearly proud of his work, and sizeable segments of the Cannes audience felt he had every right to be. It all seemed to portend a popular triumph for Coppola, come prize-giving night.

There was but one small problem. The jury, presided over by novelist Françoise Sagan, was relatively unenthusiastic about *Apocalypse Now*. The world had to wait several months before Sagan made public her version of events in the Paris daily *Le Matin*. But there she claimed that, following Coppola's screening, all ten members of the jury – with the exception of former festival director Maurice Bessy – agreed informally that Volker Schlöndorff's *The Tin Drum* should get the main prize. The following day Sagan was summoned to a meeting with festival president Robert Favre Le Bret, who said he hoped she would not adopt a difficult attitude by defying public and press opinion. She and other jurors were shown newspapers with headlines touting *Apocalypse Now* as the surefire favourite to win the main prize. Favre Le Bret went on to point out that for the first time ever, the three main US TV networks, ABC, CBS and NBC, were all covering the festival. When the jury then sat down to the official vote, Sagan was shocked to discover that a majority had changed their minds in favour of Coppola over Schlöndorff. After heated discussion, they eventually agreed on a compromise – that the Palme d'Or should be shared between the two films.

Of course, the world premiere of *Apocalypse Now* was a massive coup for Cannes. As Sandy Lieberson phrases it, 'Do you think Francis Coppola and his whole retinue would have come to Cannes with an unfinished film unless they were assured that something was going to happen . . .?' Was Coppola lured to the festival with the guarantee of a prize? If so, he was likely not the first. And posterity, not to mention legions of film fans, would not query the laurelling of *Apocalypse Now*. (Michel Ciment claims critical prerogative: '*Apocalypse Now* is

THE JURY SPEAKS   181

a landmark in film-making, so if there was pressure it was good pressure.') But then a jury is either sovereign or it is not. In a final twist to this murky story, Favre Le Bret let it be known publically that Sagan had run up a phone bill of several thousand francs during her stint as president, one the festival refused to pay. Was this an attempt to smear Sagan, deflect attention from the prize-giving controversy? The principal antagonists are now both deceased, so we can only speculate.

L'affaire Bogarde

The waspish and exquisite Dirk Bogarde was, inevitably, a keen if jaded diarist, and his published journal *Backcloth* (1986) is a generous window upon his experience as the jury president of 1984. Joseph Losey, who directed Bogarde to huge acclaim in *The Servant* and *Accident*, had taken on the Cannes presidency in 1972, and he had a stern warning for his friend: 'It's a terrible job, terrible.' Undeterred, Bogarde accepted, despite strong reservations:

> The festival had fallen on sad times. Once a glamorous occasion, it had now become a rather tacky affair, a film market attracting a host of unattractive customers, porno films, bums and tits, dope and drugs. The glamour had begun to fade and the big stars, such as there were, stayed away. And, what was far more to the point, the film-makers kept their best films out of the festival – its increasing (perhaps apocryphal) reputation for splitting the vote, juggling of the jury votes, and general under-the-bar-counter chicanery to suit individual interests had frightened off many serious studios and directors.

Bogarde's concern for the motives of the Hollywood studios might have been misplaced, but undoubtedly Cannes was looking a tad worse for wear. At his first briefing, Bogarde was told to try to restore dignity to the festival. He was even further alarmed by what followed. 'The jury was not to vote for anything overtly political. No emotional hysteria as there had been for Wajda's *Man of Iron*. Whoever went to see

CANNES

that? We were to choose films that would please a Family Audience, not ones which would appeal to a "few students and a handful of faux intellectuals. Family Entertainment for all the world markets".'

In other words, Bogarde and his jury were caught up in a then-assiduous courting of Hollywood by the festival, advanced further in 1985 by the awarding of the Légion d'honneur to MPAA supremo Jack Valenti, a global enforcer for the presence of Hollywood product on foreign soil, and an unlikely honoree in light of France's famous cultural *amour propre*. But Valenti's prize was bestowed on him in Cannes by then-Culture Minister Jack Lang, who haunted the festival a good deal during his tenure, boasting how his friendships with high-profile Americans such as Martin Scorsese would lure them over to Cannes. When Roland Joffe's *The Mission* (another unfinished piece, distributed by Warner Brothers) won the 1986 Palme d'Or ahead of Tarkovsky, it did seem that the studios might find a renewed enthusiasm for Cannes to be in their best interests.

In 1984, according to Bogarde, this panicked need for big US names clearly affected the festival authorities' moral probity when it came to the jury's decisions, foremost among which were the favouring for top prize of a pensive, wistful three-hour road movie by Wim Wenders, set in the American West but unmistakeably a product of a European sensibility. 'What about the American films?' Bogarde was upbraided. 'There are no American awards? You think that this . . . *Paris Texas* is Family Entertainment?' Even worse was to follow when the name of Helen Mirren was put forward as Best Actress for her performance as a Catholic woman widowed by the IRA in *Cal*. '*Elle est nulle, elle est nulle*,' one prominent apparatchik was heard to screech. 'We'll change it tomorrow, it's not official,' it was suggested. Bogarde at this point put his no doubt very elegantly shod foot down, and Helen Mirren – most certainly not *nulle* in the eyes of any sane filmgoer – thankfully received her just desert.

The slightly pompous, self-congratulatory tone of Bogarde's recollections may grate, but they still make compelling reading. One does

THE JURY SPEAKS 183

not feel he has any sound motive to be making it up. When a Channel 4 documentary rehearsing the same allegations was later aired in Britain, it passed virtually without comment, but a beady-eyed French journalist spotted the item and broke the news in France, where it caused a minor scandal. With hindsight it seems clear that 1984 carried a hangover from the era of routine diplomatic machinations under Robert Favre Le Bret. It may be said that Gilles Jacob finally, and firmly, put that tendency to bed at some point in the late eighties.

Michel Ciment's understanding is that Jacob has been always 'absolutely impeccable'. John Boorman concurs: 'My experience of it is that there was absolutely no influence wielded over the jury by Gilles Jacob. The only thing he did was beg us not to give more than one prize to each film.' Mike Leigh is not someone who will stand to have his opinion traduced, and he states firmly:

> My experience – and no one will pull the wool over my eyes – is that the jury was unimpeachable. At no stage of the proceedings was there any pressure, suggestion or interference from Gilles Jacob or anyone else, so far as one could possibly be aware. A jury at Cannes is going to be, by definition, a group of intelligent, confident people. They're not nervous yes-men. It's a gang of people who are used to expressing their views. We are going to do it seriously, and no one's going to tell us what to do.

Jeremy Thomas can summon formidable witnesses of his own to this, including the foremost pugilist of American letters: 'It's mad to think that someone like Theo Angelopoulos or Norman Mailer could be railroaded by the French authorities. They would go the other way instead. Norman Mailer – can you imagine him being told what to do?'

The Jury of One's Peers

We might pause only to acknowledge that there are many and subtle forms of influence that can be brought to bear on aesthetic discernment,

184 CANNES

such as those of one's contemporaries – who may be locked out of the jury room, but can hardly be avoided on the promenade or at Cannes' better restaurants. Michel Ciment remembers a particular form of peer-group lobbying to which he and fellow jurors were subjected in 1978: 'Whenever we met people on the Croisette we could not speak, of course, but we would listen to them say, "Of course you can't give it to an Italian film because last year Rossellini gave the prize to *Padre Padrone*, and this is another film about Italian peasants, also produced by RAI. And Italy has to have it one year, but then it's France, then the States . . ." And we were laughing inwardly, because we knew after six or seven days that unless there was something truly exceptional coming, Olmi would get the Golden Palm.' Mike Leigh has a firm policy on such consorting with comrades, and it is based on thoroughgoing experience: 'I've been on other juries, and it's the same – you just completely keep your mouth shut and get on with it. Sure, one of the wheezes about being on a jury at Cannes is that you walk down the Croisette and it's "Mike, how's it going, what do you think of . . .?" You just go, "Sorry . . ."' Leigh was only disappointed that his president did not seem to exercise the same discretion: 'At the beginning we all agreed we would give no press and talk to nobody, in any shape or form, which is obvious. And indeed we were impeccable. Suddenly there were comments of hers turning up in the French press . . . I complained, and she apologised.'

Even if one is discreet by nature, this code of jury *omertà* still faces challenges at every turn, as Kazuo Ishiguro found in the festival's very natural encouragement of social interaction:

We were allowed to mingle freely. There are dinners and parties in the evening and, of course, jury members are perfectly free to go to these. You end up with a lot of invitations and the festival certainly doesn't say, 'You musn't go to them.' Naturally the film-makers come too, and that can sometimes be slightly awkward; I found myself sitting next to Alan Rudolph at a dinner and he had *Mrs*

Parker and the Vicious Circle in competition. But I think everybody tries to be sensible – they don't lobby. Because I didn't know many people in the film world I didn't find this a problem. Someone such as Catherine Deneuve, of course – they know many, many people there, and so I think perhaps this might have been more an issue for them. But for most of us, including Clint Eastwood, we naturally formed a kind of enclave.

A last word: the application of pressure doesn't always require a heavy hand. Those who staff the editorial side of newspapers owned by Rupert Murdoch have often defended themselves from charges of Murdoch-directed political bias by asserting that they never see the proprietor on the shopfloor. But, of course, they do not need to. There is such a thing as an interiorised allegiance that needs no further prompting. There are also financial considerations, though this is in no way to speak of bribery. Critics and *cinéphiles* like to think fondly of films as belonging to their directors, but the financiers of those films – the big production and distribution companies – have perhaps a yet more tangible stake in them. Each jury member who is also a film-maker is potentially situated within a complex network of relationships, allegiances and loyalties. Directors sitting on Cannes juries may be more or less partial to the work of Lars von Trier, say, or Roman Polanski. They may also be aware that the financiers of the work under discussion are those to whom they too will be lobbying for funds this year. Actors and actresses, meanwhile, may yet be thinking of the director whom they would next like to work with – or who, perhaps, turned them down for a big part in favour of the actress now much-favoured for a prize. Nothing can be entirely innocent in this universe.

Matters of Taste and Expertise

Even if the judging process has been conducted impeccably the outcome can yet prove interminably controversial if, *contra* Gilles Jacob's

CANNES

hopes, the prizewinning films clash horribly with the declared tastes of those connoisseurs among the accredited press. Mike Leigh, though, takes a down-to-earth view of all the critical chatter at Cannes:

> You get up at 7 a.m. and open the door of your hotel room, shovel all the press into the loo and have a crap while you go through them. What was fascinating and great fun in 1997 was, of course, all the predictions of the critics were way off beam. We started off that year seeing *Nil By Mouth* and *Welcome to Sarajevo*, which were much promoted. The truth was, the jury was pretty unimpressed by both of them. You could see each had merits . . . but there was going to have to be a lot of lousy films to follow for us to award them. And that was without prejudice.

Perhaps the most conspicuous cleavage between jury and critics in recent times came in 1999, a year when Pedro Almodóvar's *All About My Mother* was widely rated a masterpiece, not to say an ideal opportunity to give the Spanish master an overdue Palme d'Or. Yet David Cronenberg's jury plumped for another one of those pictures to screen unassumingly in the dwindling days of the competition schedule. *Rosetta*, written and directed by the brothers Luc and Jean-Pierre Dardenne, had undeniable claims to the prize for anyone with eyes to see. But a more provocative choice still was that of the Grand Prix for Bruno Dumont's *L'Humanité*, further coupled with the Actor Prize for the film's lead Emmanuel Schotté, and a share of that for Best Actress awarded to Séverine Caneele. Both were non-professional players, Schotté an unemployed ex-serviceman, Caneele having been discovered by Dumont while operating a forklift in a vegetable canning factory. (She later wrote a well-reviewed book, *Aux Marches du Palais*, about the strange upheaval *L'Humanité* and Cannes wrought upon her life.)

David Cronenberg is no stranger to controversy – indeed he has a well-turned appreciation of it – and he took the critical flak philosophically.

THE JURY SPEAKS

187

My experience was that some people are attracted to films that are quite different from the ones they make themselves, and so they're more likely to give an award to something that seems unusual than something that feels like 'them'. My example was *Rosetta*, because I said I loved it and I thought it was absolutely not a film I would make. But that didn't stop me from thinking it was the best film in the festival. With *L'Humanité*, there were maybe more similarities with that film, because it was, in a strange way, a little stylised, and sort of sexual and sensual. But this is the thing – we were very surprised at how shocked and upset everybody was with our choices. And I began to realise – talk about alternate realities – that the Croisette had already decided who was going to win the Palme D'Or. But that had nothing to do with what was going on in the jury room. We didn't read that stuff, we didn't care about what the journalists thought, because that wasn't our job. Then, when we don't give the awards the way the critics think it ought to be, it's like we've stolen it from them. *Rosetta* was the last film to be shown at the fest, and I think a lot of the journalists didn't go to it, because it was a very unheralded little film. They hadn't seen it, so they couldn't write about it, so they were mad at us . . .

Michel Ciment is clearly not of the 'mad' brigade, though he has certain criticisms of the class of 1999:

I am absolutely sure that Cronenberg had a very strong influence on the jury. When a director has a very strong personality and is very bright, as Cronenberg is . . . and I think he was very political, he wanted to make a statement. He was very much against Hollywood, he wanted to give prizes to directors with little financial means – who, of course, had a lot of talent also. But he made a very drastic choice. It's okay with me, I don't mind. I think in the case of *L'Humanité* what was perhaps a little too much was the Actor and Actress prizes, plus the Grand Prix – though I like *L'Humanité* very much.

The charge that non-professionals should not be favoured with Prix

CANNES

d'Interpretation is based on the premise that they are merely 'playing themselves'. Then again, the charge itself may point to a critical laziness – even a profound critical misunderstanding – of what is 'good' acting for cinema. David Cronenberg, at least, is content to rest on the laurels he and his jury distributed. 'Apparently the actress from *L'Humanité* has been in other films now,' he notes with interest, 'and they say she's wonderful . . .'

Decision Day

The conduct of the jury's last-day decision meeting observes a set of needful protocols, but we might say that it is seasoned too with elements of stagecraft, cloak-and-dagger and VIP high maintenance – vital elements all in the lustre of Cannes. As John Boorman tells it:

> They whisk you away to a villa and lock you in there to deliberate. All phones are taken away, there's all this secrecy. Gilles Jacob is in the house though he doesn't take part in the discussion. And they have a very clever idea, which is to get a very good chef up there to make a marvellous lunch. As you argue and discuss, and time goes on, and you're perhaps finding it difficult to get a consensus, then these very delicious smells begin to waft in from the kitchen, and suddenly you find it a lot easier to decide . . .

Kazuo Ishiguro had no problems with the sequestered aspect of the proceedings in 1994: 'There is the fear of the results being leaked beforehand. I guess there's also the fear that people will be put under pressure if they're allowed to come and go during the day of the decision-making. That's why the jury have to go straight from the villa to the Palais where the announcement is made.' But Ishiguro's experience of the final arguments as chaired by Clint Eastwood was entirely painless.

> Clint had a house that he'd rented just outside of Cannes – I think he'd had it for a while. So we drove out to Clint's villa, and it was

THE JURY SPEAKS 189

very relaxed. We had had our regular sessions where we all talked about the films anyway, so I guess by the time we got to that final day we had a fairly clear idea of what people were keen on. All Clint wanted to do was for us to write our choices for each prize on pieces of paper, put them in a hat anonymously, and then he'd look at them. For wider things like Best Actor or Actress, where you're talking about an almost unlimited number of people, I think we discussed that and produced a long list, then we all put in our secret ballot papers and picked a winner over two or three rounds. They'd reserved the whole day for us to decide, but we'd given out all the prizes before lunch . . . Then we just kind of hung around the house for the rest of the day, playing the piano, or playing with Clint's baby daughter. Towards the end of the afternoon we started to get dressed up in our dinner jackets. We took photos of each other, signed Cannes posters for each other – it was a sort of big 'goodbye'. Then, as the evening came on, we walked outside and there waiting for us was a motorcade of cops and festival limos. So you're then driven with flags waving and five or six police motorcycles riding either side of you, all the way to the Palais. And it all becomes very formal . . .

For the jury, the principal anxieties of their fortnight in Cannes are then more or less behind them. For the competing film-makers, the night of long nerves is only just beginning. Directors are not always much incommoded by staying for the duration of the festival, not least if they fancy their chances of a Palm. But they do have homes to go to, and projects afoot. Their actors, meanwhile, are liable to have paid only flying visits to the Croisette before returning to work or daily life. But if they are among the front-runners for final day glory, they must remain edgily on call to catch a plane. Once a juror, thrice a competitor, winner of Best Director for *Naked* and of the Palme d'Or for *Secrets and Lies*, Mike Leigh has witnessed every possible combination of inconvenience that the awards palaver can generate: 'It's very difficult. The jury

190 CANNES

don't make the decision until the end because you can't. You have to wait till you've seen all the films and then they have to be discussed. If as the film-maker you've screened the film and come home – you may have to go back, you may not.' The jury of 1997 on which Leigh sat chose his friend Kathy Burke as Best Actress for *Nil By Mouth*, but the actress herself was not especially forearmed. 'This is a Sunday, and Kathy was shopping at Sainsbury's in Islington, and her agent got her on her mobile . . . She had to be shuttled out to somewhere like Elstree aerodrome, to get a flight to somewhere in the south of France. But the pressure is on and you can't fuck about.' Leigh reflects:

> Before I'd been on the jury I'd experienced this from the other side of the fence. For *Naked* in 1993 – I was still with Alison Steadman at the time, we were in our house in North London, sitting on the bed, bags packed, a car outside. Finally we got in the car and set off round the North Circular Road, then we got a message saying, 'Don't come.' We thought, 'Fuck it, no, we'll go.' We got there and were checked into a hotel under Japanese names . . . With *Secrets and Lies* [1996], Brenda Blethyn was rehearsing with Sam Mendes in a play, but she carried a suitcase with her. Finally she had to go, and she won. With *All or Nothing* [2002], again, I was packed to fly from Stansted, tux packed, car outside. Lesley Manville was packed to go from Gatwick, Timothy Spall to go from Heathrow. We sat there and time ticked away. There's a certain moment beyond which it's going to be too late, because you're not on the plane. Finally Jonathan Rutter the publicist called us and said, 'Forget it.' And it's a very strange experience. You unpack the case and you think, 'Oh, here's a spare day then . . .' And that's that.

And finally . . . a sense of proportion?

Lest we forget, two weeks in Cannes will propose alternate realities according to what role the pilgrim has come to fulfil. As much as we

THE JURY SPEAKS

have here discussed the high-stakes game of jury service, it should be said that many who come to Cannes are entirely oblivious to these fascinating proceedings. Certainly this was how the festival struck the keen eye of Kazuo Ishiguro:

I have to say my impression was not that we were at the centre of things. This business about the competition and the prizes is very, very much a sideshow. Obviously, the makers of the films in competition are concerned, but you're only talking about twenty-five films there. And there must have been a little community of film buffs, critics, who were quite concerned, but I felt it was a kind of minority interest. The real feeling I had about Cannes day-to-day, walking around, was that, on the whole, it's a huge trade fair. There are many, many other films being sold or bought or screened, lots of other deals being done, audibly, all around you. And all those people don't really give a shit about the prizes – it's nothing to do with them. I was staying at the Ritz-Carlton, the central hotel, and I felt a very marginalised figure, in that everybody else there was setting up stands, and people would often ask me – in the elevator, in the lobby, at the bar – they'd say, 'So, are you selling or are you buying?' If I said 'No, I'm a jury member' their face would just go blank . . .

IX

Selection

Any reasonably seasoned cinema lover will tell you – possibly, with a groan – that there is a certain kind of movie that gets itself nominated for the Academy Award for Best Picture: a range of values must be present therein, a set of boxes ticked. With that discrimination in mind, can we say there is also such a thing as a typical competition entry at Cannes? Of course, the passage of time has wrought changes on the selection process, and still many variables come into play. Jeremy Thomas has been taking films to compete at Cannes for thirty years, from Skolimowski's *The Shout* in 1978 to Richard Linklater's *Fast Food Nation* in 2006. Thomas affirms:

> They're looking for a certain type of movie. Hopefully it's a film by a master film-maker – a beautiful film, about something interesting and challenging. For the audience there's a high expectation for each movie, you're going in there hoping to find a masterpiece. You don't lobby for selection, you just show the film to Cannes when you feel it's in the right condition, and before their close-by date. A group of people watch the film, and then you hear. But that group of people are the principal critics in Paris as well as people from the festival. And, of course, the festival director has a great deal of push in what is selected, because he wants certain films by certain film-makers . . .

Thus defined, could the process be any more transparent? Or any more daunting? At times, of course, there will be politics at work – minor bits of horse-trading and bartering, quid pro quo and exertion of influence. The fraught and crucial selection of opening and closing films breeds a lot of such manoeuvres. For instance it is widely believed that Gary Oldman's writing/directing debut *Nil By Mouth* was slated for the Un Certain Regard sidebar until the film's executive producer Luc Besson consented to give his big-budget sci-fi picture *The Fifth Element* as opening film – on the condition that Oldman graduate to competition. Of course, the film carried off the Best Actress Prize, and few would quarrel with its elevation.

Though Thomas is robustly of the view that Cannes wants only the crème de la crème for its screens, his comrade Bernardo Bertolucci has wrestled with a different notion down the years, as a frequent attendee of all the leading festivals. 'Being Italian', he concedes, 'I was maybe a bit brainwashed for a while, about the difference between Venice and Cannes. Venice was considered as being more interested in art and auteurs, and Cannes was seen as a festival more oriented towards commercial cinema. And I had this prejudice too. I had to change completely my idea of Cannes, especially in the seventies.' The prime mover in Bertolucci's change of heart was the festival's influential *délégué general*.

When I first met with Gilles Jacob I understood that what he was trying to do was a very elegant attempt to conjugate different aspects of cinema. So he would try to have avant-garde cinema alongside establishment cinema, but always with great care taken in the choice – it was hard to see a really bad movie in Cannes. I think Jacob was extraordinary, and he has done it better than anybody – better than Venice was able to do, because in the first fifty years of the Italian republic we had something like sixty different governments, and the director of Venice changed almost as often. But Jacob, because he stayed for a long time, was able to elaborate a festival that I think was unique.

The Endurance of Gilles

'What is a successful festival?' Jacob responded rhetorically when asked in 2006. 'It's not one that is simply content with showing good films and giving good awards, but rather a festival that has an *editorial policy*. And this must be followed by someone who represents it, across the years and decades. Cannes has had the good luck to have directors who have lasted: Robert Favre Le Bret lasted forty-three years. I've lasted almost twenty-five. Which allows one not to be constantly preoccupied by the thought of one's re-election, or by having to save one's career. It allows one to get things done.'

The fruits of what Jacob has done with his time are quite apparent, and his era in the top job embodies tremendous change in the festival's constitution, from the days when Robert Favre Le Bret and Maurice Bessy were the chief arbiters of selection, and were well received in every major film-producing nation. He says:

> They travelled much more then than now. Now it's nothing to send a DVD or a cassette to Cannes, but back then the films themselves travelled less. So Favre Le Bret or Bessy would visit these countries, talk with the high functionaries, producers, distributors, and then decide on which films in situ. It used to be a matter of seeing five hundred films, now it's fifteen hundred. And yet we still select the same number for competition – around twenty-two. After 1972, it was clear the director couldn't do everything himself and had need of advice, so a selection committee was created, principally from among journalists, critics, historians, and the major film specialists in *les pays conseillers* [adviser nations]. But the director decided in the final analysis. Maurice Bessy would tell journalists, 'Come in on Tuesday', and he showed them films, but then they didn't see him again for a fortnight. The journalists didn't have an overall vision because Bessy wanted to keep the final choice for himself. I consider that one can maintain final choice even while having people permanently at hand. So, from 1978, my

selection committees were appointed for the entire year and came daily to see all the films.

Of course, many hands make light work of enormous piles of submissions, but Jacob acknowledges the need for diverse forms of viewing expertise: 'In the final selection, I know, everyone makes mistakes and we have to have the right to. But we have to make them less than others because the festival has its competitors, each one fighting to have the best films in the world.'

Michel Ciment is one who found his views occasionally consulted by Jacob when it came to the Cannes selection: 'About a dozen times down the years he called me because he had doubts, and he said, "I'd like you to see this film." So I saw a number of films, and I would recommend them, say, "That should be in competition", or else I would give a negative opinion. Jacob made up his own mind, I'm not saying my advice had any big influence but at least he was listening to opinions.'

In these pages we have already encountered the mandarin figure of Pierre Rissient, who offers a conspicuous example of how Cannes has drawn strength from expert consultation. From his formative work as a Parisian press agent Rissient knew how to place a discerning movie in the marketplace, and that discernment had its uses to the Cannes selection also. 'What I was doing for the movies', Rissient recalls, 'was very carefully preparing the promotional materials and the subtitles, holding private screenings in Paris for some key people who I thought could write first about the film to create a mood. In 1968 I was in charge of Milos Forman's *The Fireman's Ball*, which went to Cannes. Then Coppola, Scorsese, Robert Altman, John Boorman – I brought their pictures to Cannes. That's probably why some people mention me as an *éminence grise*. I've been active for so many years, and I have been proved not too wrong in the films I've liked . . .'

In 1971 Rissient lobbied Robert Favre Le Bret diligently in favour of a Cannes slot for Dalton Trumbo's film of his own harrowing anti-war story *Johnny Got His Gun*. He summoned heavy artillery to the cause:

SELECTION 197

I knew Jean Renoir in a cordial way because I'd taken care of the reissues in Paris of *The Rules of the Game* and *La Bête Humaine*, so I thought I should show the film to him. I thought that if the man who made *La Grande illusion* recommended a picture about war, that would have some meaning. Sure enough, there came a letter from Renoir to Favre Le Bret, saying 'Why don't you show this film?' That then gave the idea to Dalton Trumbo, who knew Luis Buñuel, and Buñuel at one point had thought about adapting *Johnny Got His Gun* for cinema, Trumbo got in touch with Buñuel, who did the same as Renoir. So Favre Le Bret had in front of him letters of recommendation from Renoir and Buñuel. What could he do? The picture was an incredible success with the audience, and it won second prize.

Upon the inauguration of the selection committee in 1972, Rissient retooled his formidable strategies, in the first instance on behalf of the then-up-and-coming Sydney Pollack.

I had liked *They Shoot Horses, Don't They?* and Sidney Pollack showed me *Jeremiah Johnson* when Warner Brothers didn't believe in it. I said, 'Sydney, this is a terrific film, it should go to Cannes.' He said, 'A Western should go to Cannes?' But the picture was what would have been called at the time 'an adult Western'. Favre Le Bret knew that I was behind the film, and the people who were looking at it on the selection committee I called from California and said to them, 'Please pay attention to this film.' Two days later we had confirmed it was in Cannes.

Rissient's links to the best American directors were a matter of record, but he quickly broadened both his taste and his influence in respect of the selection: 'I guess I can say that I was the first one to go to Asia and bring films from Asia, outside of Mizoguchi and Kurosawa. At that time people were only thinking of certain Japanese films and Satyajit Ray's films – basically there was nothing more.' Asian film specialist Tony Rayns confirms that Rissient made his presence felt.

198

CANNES

Pierre started scouting talent in East Asia in the early seventies. He would look for directors he could represent, and he'd say to them, 'Let's work together, I'll promote you.' He was never officially part of the selection committee for Cannes, but he very frequently went to committee screenings at the Cannes office in Paris, and he was known to be very close to Gilles Jacob and some other members of the committee. So if there was a question of getting something into competition, or saying the right word and having some bearing on it, Pierre was very well placed to do that. So he acquired a certain position of pre-eminence.

The Tenure of Thierry Frémaux

Jacob has lately handed the reins of the festival to Thierry Frémaux, and inevitably the keen-eyed observer will now see a fresh twist to the stewardship and editorial policy of Cannes that Jacob has fostered and advanced. Frémaux has certainly pitched into the role with the needful zeal.

From January first until May I am exclusively in Paris, completely devoted to the Cannes Festival. From June to August I'm more often in Lyon, then after September the travelling starts and goes on until December, during which the pre-selection takes place. When I arrived at Cannes, I didn't want to change it – I kept the people who worked on the most important committee, looking at foreign films. Quite simply there is the matter of films to be seen. In 2005, we looked at 1,400 films out of which 1,250 were foreign films and 150 French films. It's around fifty-five films we choose from that number: twenty to twenty-two in competition, twenty-two in Un Certain Regard, ten out of competition – that's it. Many of the foreign films are seen in the individual countries by the festival's correspondents there, but in Paris alone we see between five hundred to seven hundred films. I believe very much in collective work, because if you put two people in front of a film you'll get two different opinions, more with three people or four. Our job isn't to say 'I like it' or 'I don't like it' but rather 'Do we take it or not?' They're not the same jobs. I can sometimes programme films which are not my favourites, but which I think are important to show at Cannes. I can also like certain films very much but think, 'No, it's not for Cannes.' So it's an extremely nuanced job, but it's very important to know that you can get it wrong, and also to have a very strong conviction in order to make the right selection. Whatever happens at Cannes the most important things are the films, and that people talk about cinema.

Indeed, people most certainly talk, whether the selection be wrong or right. Michel Ciment believes there is one significant difference to have emerged from the change of Cannes leadership: 'Gilles Jacob was a clever diplomat and if he didn't want a film it was always possible for him to say, "Well, my selection committee didn't like it very much." Thierry Frémaux exposes himself much more. He has decided that he will make the decision himself, which is perhaps a mistake, because then he can't protect himself.'

The Fall and Rise of *Vera Drake*

For several decades at Cannes it was observable and indisputable that those auteurs who had competed with distinction down the years – a select band – enjoyed a more or less open return ticket to the festival competition. This has seemed like part of Cannes' duty to the great directors and an extension of its role in their elevation. Critically speaking, the policy has worked a little to the festival's disadvantage. Through the 1990s, for instance, the late films of Kurosawa; certain mid-career pieces by Wenders, Schlöndorff, or Skolimowski; occasional works by surprise Palme d'Or winner Jerry Schatzberg . . . all of these were selected, some competed, and none were thought liable to trouble the jury's deliberations. Within that same decade Mike Leigh, lately restored to feature film-making after long years in British television, became a Cannes staple with prizes for *Naked* and *Secrets and Lies*. But as the Frémaux years commenced, Leigh found himself the unlikely first victim of a cull of the great and the good from Official Selection.

Leigh takes up the story:

> In the cases of *Naked* and *Secrets and Lies*, each was screened in Paris and Gilles was immediately on the telephone to say, 'You're invited to be in competition.' The same happened in 2002 with *All or Nothing*. In 2003 we made *Vera Drake*. 2003 was the first year that Thierry Frémaux was making the decisions. Like *All or Nothing* it was backed by Studio Canal and made with Alain Sarde. We went to Paris and showed it to Alain and they were blown away, they said, 'Wow, this is a shoo-in at Cannes.' We weren't going to be able to show Cannes a print, but they said, 'It'll be fine, just take it to the latest stage possible.' And it went over to Paris. Then there was a sort of hold-up, which went on for a day, then another, and it carried on. Well, of course we had moles. Jerome Genaud is the Parisian equivalent of [UK publicist] Jonathan Rutter, he always does our stuff and he knew people inside. He said, 'Thierry's looking after it now.' And it began to emerge that Thierry had a massive dither about the film. I picked up from the Parisian grapevine that Gilles was pressuring him to take the film, because Gilles had seen it, and Gilles's son, and others. But I think Thierry was entrenched. We began to formulate the clear view that this was probably not a reflection on the film, but to do with his notion of what he thought he should be showing.

Frémaux confirms his feelings of ambiguity:

> My decision was that, one, I didn't think that Cannes was the best place for the film. Mike Leigh had often been to Cannes, and we'd been criticised for that, people saying, 'It's always the same auteurs.'

SELECTION 201

That year, I said to myself, 'We're going to try and renew things.'
And perhaps *Vera Drake* was, for me, a film that wouldn't bring
Mike Leigh a prize, and I told myself he'd won the Palme d'Or . . .
et voilà. I hesitated a great deal over the decision, it was very difficult. And I have a regret about this in that I didn't call Mike Leigh
to let him know about my decision.

For Leigh, the living in the dark over the decision certainly compounded the unhappiness of the non-invitation:

Apparently Thierry's preoccupation at the time was that he wanted
to bring in young Asian and Third World film-makers. Whether he
actually did that I've no idea. I suppose my view ultimately is that
they can do what they want. But we were being told that he was saying things like 'Mike Leigh can't automatically have a film in
Cannes', and 'I don't want it to be full of same old same old' –
though, in fact, quite a few people were already in who were old
hands. That was the piss-off – 'Mike Leigh's won the Palme d'Or.'
But Wim was already in. I think that were it the case that if you've
won the Palme d'Or you're automatically in, I would reject that as
being ridiculous and unacceptable. I'm not really concerned with
the dynastical aspect of it. My concern was this – I don't know what
the definition of a quite good film is, but I would have thought with
all the humility in the world that *Vera Drake* would qualify as that,
and it got rejected. Anyway, after ten days, my producer very smart-
ly had a tape carried to Rome to the man who'd just taken over
Venice. He watched it, called us up and said, 'We'll have it in competition.' Some months later, I received the Golden Lion at Venice
from Sophia Loren. I'd thought, 'I'm not going to say anything, it's
a bit vulgar . . .' But then I'm making the speech off-the-cuff, and I
thought, 'I'm going to have a gag . . .' So I actually said, 'And finally I'd like to thank the Cannes Film Festival for rejecting this film in
order that we could be here tonight.' And, of course, it brought the
whole house down, and the Venice lot, they loved it. Thierry was

sitting at the next table at the dinner afterwards and he never came and said hello . . .

In retrospect Thierry Frémaux is philosophical, as he must be:

> Mike Leigh went around the world having a go at me – there are worse things in life, I dealt with it and I understood that he must be unhappy. So who was right? For myself, I know that nobody can say that he would have won at Cannes. And I think that one shouldn't say bad things about the Cannes Festival which had allowed him to have international recognition. Perhaps I made a mistake, perhaps . . . But anyway, I know that *Vera Drake* won at Venice, it went to the Oscars, it had a great career. What's the problem?

There are, it should be said, sometimes happier ways to play at Cannes than in the official selection. The competition and its critical scrutiny can be unforgiving, and certainly smaller films are often better geared to make their impact in the sidebars, where they may be stumbled upon by jaded critics and so permitted to build their own enviable buzz: take Baz Luhrmann's *Strictly Ballroom* (1992) or Alejandro González Iñárritu's *Amores Perros* (2000). John Boorman remembers, 'When I produced *Angel* (1981) for Neil Jordan, I took it to Cannes – it wasn't in competition, we just screened it in the market, but it became the film that was discovered that year, and it made Neil's career. The critics love to find something in the market and berate the festival directors for not having included it . . .'

Native Sons

Amid the consensual concern for the maestro directors, the new discoveries, the potential winners – what (if any) degree of special consideration remains, at this great French film festival, for French films? The homegrown selection has its own formal committee, which must weigh with sensitivity the warring claims of local producers. But the

SELECTION 203

international profile of Cannes militates against much in the way of favouritism. That said, there is no limit upon the number of French films that may be officially selected, and some years have seen grumbles of this sort. As Tony Rayns sees it, 'The French are, shall we say, not backward when it comes to nationalist sentiments, so there are normally quite a lot of French films in competition in Cannes. The quantity bears little relationship to the quality.'

The selection process, however, contains unusually nerve-straining elements for French producers. Michel Ciment outlines the problems in sympathy:

> In order to give everybody a chance, Cannes has to see all the French films that are ready. I advise on the selection of French films for Berlin, and I see the films at the same time as Cannes. If Thierry Frémaux said of one French film in November, 'I'll take that', then he saw another in December and decided to take it too in order that Berlin not get it – then all the other French candidates who had yet to do their final editing and mixing, expecting to be ready in April, they would feel their chances had been limited. Cannes did exactly this in 1999 with Leos Carax's *Pola X*. They loved it so much – which is difficult to understand – that they decided to pick it up in November, and it created a riot. Then the film was a disaster at Cannes. So I think that served as a warning, and they decided not to select any French films before April. Instead they wait. But that makes a problem for French films. They have to wait and wait and wait . . . For French cinema it's no longer the same process as for foreign films, where the festival can go to Thailand and say, 'I love that film', or go to Hollywood and say the same. Sometimes the French film-makers don't know until the press launch for the selection which films are going to be selected.

Has, then, the Cannes Festival forced French cinema to work twice as hard for less reward in order that it be properly represented there? This was certainly not the view of *Variety* journalist Steven Gaydos in a 2003 article entitled 'The French connection', wherein he presented some statistical work on the competition films over a number of years, concluding that the selection tended to favour films that had French money somewhere in the financing package. Even if these were not French films – were the work of US auteurs, say – the implication was that the French industry benefited. Thierry Frémaux is happy to rebut the thesis:

> It's bullshit. In this article, and others, it says that when a foreign film is produced by the French we'll take it. Yes, David Lynch is produced by a Frenchman. Scorsese's *Casino* was produced by TF1. We take them because it's Lynch and his film-making, or Scorsese, or others. Look, I see a thousand films a year and I select fifty. Do you really think that I have it in my head each time I see a film whether there's French money involved? Like everybody, I make mistakes. But if I make mistakes it's out of my love for things, not out of some perverse instinct that makes me consider things on the basis of some 'French Connection'. In fact, American cinema is the cinema which is the best represented at Cannes, much more so than French cinema. This is because the Americans produce films everywhere. Harvey Weinstein produced *City of God*, a Brazilian film. Was I not going to take *City of God* because there was American money involved? No, I took the American money . . .

The Dollar and its Discontents

The US industry has learned to love Cannes but gradually: some might say the romance was tentative on both sides. Clearly the relationship has deepened and matured, but in the early years of the festival Hollywood was sure of its own appeal and played hard to get. In the 1950s its major directors tended to stay away, and the big studio epics were usually sent, but only to occupy non-competing berths: the likes of *Gigi*, *Around the World in 80 Days*, *The Fall of the Roman Empire*, *Ben Hur*. Gilles Jacob was acquainted with the legends:

The studios only wanted to send their films for the opening or the closing of the festival, never for competition, because they said that in competition it was always some unknown Norwegian film made by somebody in their bathroom for ten thousand dollars, and consequently one couldn't compare it to the great films by Preminger or 'L'Histoire du Monde', 'La Grande Course vers l'Ouest', 'Jesus Christ' – the great myths of American cinema. There was also the fear that even films by the great American auteurs would be criticised by the French press in such a way that there would be a knock-on effect in the New York and Los Angeles press, and as a consequence could harm the American release. We didn't do badly in the 1970s, though, when there were really good American films by Altman, Coppola and Cimino.

True, in the much-vaunted golden age of 1967–1980 Cannes bestowed Palmes d'Or on Altman and Coppola, and redeemed Cimino's *Heaven's Gate* from its catastrophic US opening at least in terms of critical respect. But producer Sandy Lieberson, a Fox executive in that period, saw that the bottom-liners in the operation were not significantly more comfortable with the risk: 'The publicity and marketing departments would always say to me, "Do we want to expose ourselves at Cannes? What does it really mean to us?" You've got to remember if you're releasing your film in two thousand screens across the States, maybe more these days, and spending fifty million dollars, do you want to take the chance of getting a lot of bad reviews at Cannes?' Lieberson also makes the shrewd observation that the American cinema championed by Cannes tended to be that which cast a sceptical eye on its home nation, as typified by Cimino's epic Western on the subject of what we would now call ethnic cleansing. 'You've got to understand this political thing is very subtle,' says Lieberson. 'Gilles Jacob is steeped in American culture, but certain kinds of American culture. There's a subtle distinction. And I don't think an admiration for and identification with US cinema is in

206 CANNES

any way incompatible with not really respecting what the United States stands for.'

In any event, that Hollywood golden age turned yellow, and the corporatised blockbuster-oriented Tinseltown that emerged in the 1980s as a hard-nosed remedy to the unprofitable personal pictures of the 1970s seemed to make a less amenable fit with Cannes. There was the occasional uncomfortable accommodation, as London *Time Out* critic Geoff Andrew remembers with a wince: 'There was a period in the early 1990s when – and I'm not sure whether Gilles Jacob was just so desperate to get the big stars, or whether Hollywood was doing more to be in Cannes – but you'd get a film like *Cliffhanger* [1993] in the Official Selection. It would screen out of competition, but Sylvester Stallone would turn up. That seemed to be when the festival was transformed, more people started going, and the newspapers wanted to have stars in Cannes.'

Of course, the American cinema scene was re-upholstered in the same span of years owing to the much-discussed independent renaissance that saw consecutive Palmes d'Or for *sex, lies and videotape* (1989), *Wild at Heart* (1990), and *Barton Fink* (1991). We may now observe a sort of two-tier system of US representation at Cannes – the Coens, Lynch, Jarmusch, sometimes part-financed by Europe or Japan, properly hopeful of prizes; and then Hollywood and its tentpole pictures, primarily desirous of acres of unstoppable press coverage. According to Gilles Jacob:

> The American majors are very courteous and they come to Cannes because they know how to make use of the festival for the promotion of their films. They want to take away some of the prestige. For the auteurs, who have their own egos, it's a case of winning a prize or, if they're not in competition, to get significant press coverage which will save you from having to travel all over the world. Because, at Cannes, when you have four thousand journalists from all over the world, it saves six months of your time to do interviews for three days . . .

SELECTION   207

And what of mainstream Hollywood studio product? Thierry Frémaux is aware there is no escape from the scrutiny of the Hollywood trade papers which take a bottom-line view of the cinema's value. 'This is a discussion I've often had with the *Variety* people. The problem is that Cannes is the biggest festival in the world and they continue saying "Be careful, money is important." But money is the *Marché du Film*. Our problem is quality. The critical, aesthetic, historical and cinematic perspective on cinema is the selection.' Nevertheless, Tony Rayns believes it has found a new dispensation under the directorship of Thierry Frémaux:

> There's been a further shift in recent years whereby Hollywood is now seen as part of cinema's rich tapestry. The old notion of an opposition between alternate kinds of cinema and Hollywood mainstream entertainment has to a degree broken down. I'm not saying we're going to see *Van Helsing* or *The Mummy* in competition in Cannes, but *Shrek 2* yes, they were happy to play that. They felt it was arty enough to justify it, but also commercial enough to make them able to say, 'We're in touch with what's happening.' The motor for that particular development was Berlin, which, under Moritz de Hadeln [director, 1980–2001], began to routinely show up to six US films in competition, almost always films that were nominated for Oscars – so Berlin was seen as the European showcase for the alleged cream of that year's US cinema.

Frémaux is blithely open about the shift Rayns identifies:

> It's true that the relationship between Cannes and Hollywood has got a lot better in the last five, ten years. Since we've played *Moulin Rouge*, *The Matrix*, *Troy*, big films such as those, now it's fine. We've had *Star Wars*, twice. Now, Cannes is American Cinema and everything's okay. *Moulin Rouge* was the only one of those films in competition. But *Matrix*, *Troy*, *Star Wars* – we don't show them because it's a showcase but because we want to show the films. Yes,

208 CANNES

there are programming strategies. No one has anything to gain – not the festival, nor the jury, nor the competition – from having *Star Wars* compete. But showing *Star Wars: Episode III* (2005) was a celebration. George Lucas called me, saying, 'I signed my first contract at Cannes thirty years ago and I want to complete the *Star Wars* cycle at Cannes.' He came, we became friends, and we still speak a lot. That's it . . .

Making it New

As we have seen, Cannes does not select in a vacuum, at liberty, or in its own sweet time. Berlin and Venice are lurking over its shoulder, looking to steal a march, trying to make use of their smaller scale of operation in order to be more nimble. Bold programming of new works, new directors, new nations neglected by the competitor is one obvious ruse. Tony Rayns argues:

Berlin was the first festival to go looking in areas that Cannes was overlooking and ignoring. They would look for Vietnamese films, Indonesian films, Korean films. Im Kwon-Taek the great Korean director was in competition in Berlin from about 1980 onwards. Cannes has certainly become more aware of it, but it's been forced on them to some degree. There is a greater awareness of other areas of cinema on the part of their constituency now. But also their traditional sources have tended to dry up. Italy's annual production tends to be around thirty features now, this is a country that routinely made three hundred. Cannes has been forced to cast its net widely and it would be a laughing stock if it didn't. In 2003 everyone was saying 'Worst Cannes ever', and so in 2004 Frémaux made a desperate attempt to drag the Cannes competition back into the international arena by doing what Berlin and Venice had been doing for some years. He probably felt he went a bit too far. If your jury gives the first prize to Michael Moore [*Fahrenheit 9/11*] and the second prize to *Oldboy* [dir.

Chan Wook Park], you become a laughing-stock in certain French critical circles. I'm not a huge fan of the French critical film press, but they're not completely stupid, and if they see a piece of shit like *Oldboy* touted as one of the great films of the year, they ridicule it.

An Asian expert, Rayns takes a particularly swingeing line here, but his point is that Cannes should do better than respond to the latest fashions, having made its name on the long-term backing of (mainly European) directors:

Wong Kar Wai made six films before Cannes showed the slightest interest in anything he was doing. It only started to pay attention because of pre-sales to French distributors. If you look at Korean cinema now, I think by far the most interesting, established arthouse director is Hong Sang Soo. Cannes completely ignored his earlier work, which some would say was stronger, more radical, more extraordinary. They weren't showing Korean films at that time, they had no interest, completely failed to pick up on the fact that his first film picked up a prize in Vancouver and in Rotterdam. They showed no interest in his second, third or fourth film, and it's not until [the French distributor] MK2 enters the picture and there's a French connection that they take an interest. It's a certain kind of parochialism and arrogance. But thanks to Pierre Rissient's mediation Hong Sang Soo made a deal for two films with MK2. His last three films have been screened in Cannes. He hasn't won a prize, the films haven't had huge impact, international sales have not flooded – so it's not been a terrifically successful experiment. But Cannes has remained loyal to him having finally started showing his films

Not Guilty?

These disputations – to a degree – no longer occur on Gilles Jacob's watch. Yet still he speaks for the Cannes Festival and its history, and,

210   CANNES

by extension, for a share of its future. He argues that Cannes has kept its reflexes sharp and taken care to stay current:

> The policy of Cannes has been to say to itself that the great film-makers are starting to disappear. They're either retired, not filming, or simply dying out, so one must endlessly prepare for generational renewal. And we've tried to have a coherent attitude, which takes films even before they've been made and to continue all the way beyond their release. This was progressively behind the creation of the Caméra d'Or in 1978, to award the best first film from any section of the festival. Then we created the Ciné-Fondation, then the Residence de la Ciné-Fondation where students come to stay for four months to write a screenplay and we help them to set it up. In 2005 we created an atelier in which a number of screenplays are selected and are attempted to be sold to different companies and countries in order that the films get made. Then, there's *Tout le cinéma du monde* which is the recognition of the cinematic work in countries generally having difficulties, which is to give them the desire and the energy to continue. So, you see there's a kind of coherence which means that it's not just a matter that this year it's the Palme d'Or for this or that film, or so-and-so as president of the jury, but a general editorial line that's followed through over time and which delivers the results we know of. Because Cannes is considered to be the number one festival – excuse me for saying this, it's not me who's said it! – because of the numbers who come, because of what the press say, and because of the work it does year after year.

X

Festivalworld

Film festivals have become the circuits through which an idea of cinema other than that valorized by the market constantly circulates.
Jean-Michel Frodon, *Cahiers du cinéma*

For twelve days a year, Cannes recharges the batteries of world cinema.
Gilles Jacob

Cannes is both the pinnacle of cinema, a film fair and a big, slightly vulgar bazaar.
Agnès Varda

It won't have gone unnoticed by even the most casual observers of the international cinema scene that the number of film festivals has multiplied exponentially the world over in the last twenty years – to the point where the number of film prizes awarded each year is more than double the number of films actually being produced during the same period. Several political and economic factors have caused this explosion, but one major reason is that this diverse, interconnected, vibrant festival circuit (or network) acts, on one level, as a counter to Hollywood's grasping global dominance. As well as fulfilling a traditional role of shop-window, this enormous global festival network functions virtually as an alternative distribution system for films that otherwise would almost certainly struggle to find exhibition and audience. Film festivals have become privileged sites where the harsh economic laws of the studio-dictated marketplace are temporarily suspended, and where more challenging, non-mainstream work (although not exclusively such) can be screened for potential buyers.

This self-sustaining, self-referential festival network is a complex entity, which breeds fierce rivalry as well as a certain degree of collabo-

CANNES

ration and mutual interdependence. On the one hand, the unseemly scramble for a glamorous world premiere or the latest Wong Kar Wai can be anything but amicable. The red carpet is a hungry beast that needs regular feeding and, as we have just seen, it is the festival director's job to ensure that happens, if possible, with the choicest cuts available. But festivals have different profiles and agendas, and are graded accordingly for status by the regulating body FIAPF (Fédération Internationale des Associations de Producteurs des Films) – Cannes, Berlin and Venice are, for example, competitive A-list festivals. There is a tacit understanding, not only that many films will travel from festival to festival (gradually accruing the necessary cultural capital through prizes and critical acclaim to enable them to find distribution outlets and potentially turn a profit in the 'real' exhibition sector); but also that director-auteurs will inevitably rise through the festival hierarchy as their careers blossom and advance. Although they would probably baulk at the suggestion, one could to some extent regard the smaller festivals as feeders for their more ravenous A-list brethren. Often, owing to their more specialist or local knowledge and contacts, they will spot a promising talent very early on in their career and usher them into the limelight. That director will then circulate through the system, gaining ever more recognition, until finally they too may walk the red carpet at Cannes – still regarded, after all these years, as number one.

The stage-set of Cannes supplies both deserved recognition and reflected glory – we've seen it happen time and time again. Michel Ciment encapsulates it:

> What is great about Cannes is that everybody comes to see the stars, the big films from Hollywood or France, but what happens is that suddenly – out of the blue – comes a Turkish film like *Uzak* ('Distant'). I knew the director Nuri Bilge Ceylan before, I discovered him in Angers and then I saw him in Berlin. *Uzak* was his third feature and I told everybody it would be a big event. Only a handful of people knew of him, but I suspected he was going to be one of the

FESTIVALWORLD 213

great European directors. Suddenly at Cannes in 2003, Ceylan, surrounded by Tarantino and Clint Eastwood, comes up with his film and gets two prizes [Grand Prix and Best Actor]. And he's launched.

Although Cannes throughout its sixty-year history has been instrumental in bringing many major directors to the world's attention in mid-career, it has generally been less frequently an excavator of new talent at the outset of their careers – although it may seem the reverse to those unfamiliar with the operations of the festival network. Rather, as in the case of Ceylan, it tends to validate and rubber-stamp – or 'anoint' in the quasi-religious parlance that Gilles Jacob and his acolytes favour. A debut feature appears in Cannes competition only in exceptional circumstances; the example of British director Andrea Arnold's *Red Road* is instructive. In 2006 artistic director Thierry Frémaux wanted the film to show in Directors Fortnight, but when the producers refused and threatened to take the film to another festival, he put it in competition, where it eventually won the Grand Jury Prize.

Simon Field, formerly an admired director of the Rotterdam Film Festival, argues that the competition can be overvalued when the sidebars have so much to offer: 'I think one of the really interesting phenomena at Cannes is that in the sixties you had the "Salon des refusés" which was Directors Fortnight and, gradually, what has happened is that distinctions between the different sections have dissolved. So films now can be in almost any section of the festival.' Producers, though, will always battle to get their films into Cannes competition. For all the merits of the other strands, they do not, as a rule, attract much press attention beyond France and international specialist magazines. And while Cannes certainly needs new lifeblood, as do all festivals, it also has a position of pre-eminence to maintain, one that requires weighty, well-established presences year in year out in competition, and which would be threatened if the festival were to show too many new directors there. That would be a risky business – what if they don't flourish as envisaged? Better to let smaller festivals incubate the

214   CANNES

talent and when it's proven, to pounce. What this means is that Gilles
Jacob and now Thierry Frémaux finesse a balancing act between
established and new, the dynastical and the upstart interloper, who
may well in time be inducted into that Cannes family alongside the
likes of Wim Wenders and Jim Jarmusch and the Coen Brothers.

That said, the picture has altered somewhat owing to recent initiatives at the grassroots level. Festivals such as Cannes, Rotterdam,
Berlin, as well as using their experience and connections to bring
together new creative talents and financiers, are also becoming
increasingly involved in actually producing films; that is to say, in providing a helping hand to talents right at the outset of their careers,
such as supplying funds for script development or post-production
completion, and then – if all goes well – possibly providing a slot in
one of the festival's competitive strands when the film is finished. A
recent example would be the young Romanian director Corneliu
Porumboiu and his debut feature film *12.08 East of Bucharest*.
Porumboiu was a beneficiary of the Cannes Residence du Festival, created under its Ciné-Fondation umbrella which, since 1998, has offered
a handful of budding directors four months' accommodation in Paris
where they can write and hone their feature script with free professional help. In Porumboiu's case the resulting film, shot in Romania
not long after, was invited into Un Certain Regard the following May,
where it not only won the prestigious Caméra d'Or for first feature,
but also picked up distribution in numerous sales territories across the
globe including Britain. The film then travelled to other film festivals
including Kluj in Porumboiu's native Romania, picking up further
awards. So not only is a promising new career kickstarted, but a lasting bond will unite an up-and-coming director with the Cannes brand;
a mutually beneficial situation.

Of course this doesn't happen to every budding director who is
invited on to the Residence (and spaces on it are very limited anyway)
but it does show that it can happen. It's not difficult to envisage a situation in the not-too-distant future where the bigger festivals become

FESTIVALWORLD 215

like the old Hollywood studios, with directors if not under contract then at least strongly associated with the one festival which has done most to advance his or her career from its earliest days. This initiative is not necessarily unique but Jacob sees it as a vital means to bring on a new generation of auteurs. 'If we have undertaken these initiatives,' says Jacob, 'it's because we think that it's not enough these day simply to show films. And the Director of Venice thinks the same. We are here to allow the art of cinema to progress and to help young talents.'

Critics of these new initiatives see them as entirely self-serving on the part of the festivals, a self-perpetuating strategy, and they use the pejorative term 'festival film' to attack what they perceive as an inward-looking, ghettoised system which will only generate, as US critic Jonathan Rosenbaum puts it, films 'destined to be seen by professionals, specialists or cultists but not by the general public'. Such films will tend to be much slower in pace and prioritise mood, atmosphere and character observation over plot mechanics. Be that as it may, if they scoop prizes at Cannes the acclaim and symbolic value can shift units internationally and put their directors in a much stronger position to realise future projects. Poromboiu maintains the Cannes award meant he was taken much more seriously back home in Romania, a similar outcome to the previous year when his compatriot and friend Cristi Puiu won the Prix Un Certain Regard for *The Death of Mr Lazarescu*.

For some directors, acceptance in the domestic sphere trails in the wake of festival awards and critical acclaim in other countries such as France. The neo-realists were rubbished by Italian critics, and it wasn't until the laurels showered on Rossellini in particular at Cannes that those negative appraisals back home were reassessed. The so-called New German cinema which emerged in the early 1970s, spearheaded by the likes of Wenders, Herzog and Fassbinder, achieved worldwide prominence thanks to Cannes, and in so doing overcame critical and commercial neglect in its homeland. On the other hand, critics of Kiarostami, Zhang Yimou, Wong Kar Wai and others maintain that

216   CANNES

their films don't find audiences in their own countries because they've become adept at fashioning their films for Western festival audiences. Tony Rayns takes a dissenting view: 'Utter rubbish. Zhang Yimou doesn't even speak English.' But in the instance of a director such as Kiarostami, the picture has been complicated by censorship.

The Kiarostami Case

Occasionally – *very* occasionally – there emerges a film-maker whose work lets the viewer discover a new world of cinema. Abbas Kiarostami is one such film-maker. He is justly lauded as one of the greatest living directors because, with the complete confidence and apparent simplicity that is the mark of a true artist, he offers another vision of the possibilities of film. And because he reinvents cinema he reinvents the viewer, too. His films propose new ways of seeing and for that achievement alone his name indisputably belongs alongside those of Bresson, Godard, Hitchcock and Eisenstein. But he is also important for another reason. His work allows the viewer to discover a new world *through* cinema, the world of post-revolutionary Iran. So his cinema is inherently and inescapably political, if only because it presents images of a country and a people that are a million miles away from the crude media stereotypes to which Iran has tended to be reduced since its Islamic Revolution of 1979. One can well understand why critics and festivals have enthusiastically promoted Kiarostami's work and that of other Iranian film-makers since the 1990s. Not only have rich and nuanced films emerged from the apparently hostile climate of a theocracy, they have proved that it is still possible for cinema to bring us news from elsewhere, to act as 'the world's conscience', as *Cahiers du cinéma* rather grandly phrased it. In the case of the discovery of Kiarostami's work, one could almost hear a collective echo of relief from the four corners of global *cinéphilia*. 'This', it sighed, 'is *Cinema*.'

Is it fair to hold up Kiarostami as the most representative 'festival film-maker' of the 1990s? Let the director himself answer. Interviewed during the Cannes Festival in 2005 (where he was president of the Caméra d'Or jury) he stated, 'the recognition I've received from film festivals has become my sole reason to continue making films'. And what recognition it has been! His work has received awards from festivals all over the world, including the Palme d'Or for *Taste of Cherry* in 1997. As well as being recognised as one of the world's foremost auteurs, he has exhibited his photography, created installations and made works with digital video. He has no problem acknowledging the role the festival circuit has played:

> My kind of film-making wouldn't have been able to continue without a certain amount of support. My cinema is not the sort that interests the [Iranian] public. In my country this sort of cinema is called 'festival cinema': films *for* festivals. And it's true that, at home, they have stamped my work as being for the festival circuit. There are many conflicts of interest in the way that the government regards my work but they forget that the responsibility and the viewpoint of a festival is to protect cinema in the broadest meaning of the word, that's the real responsibility of the world of film festivals. That's why the place of festivals is extremely important for film-makers like me who love cinema.

Kiarostami's status as a 'festival film-maker' is thoroughly paradoxical. He has gained a global audience at the expense of a domestic one yet remains a resolutely Iranian film-maker, intent on working in his home country. While his global renown allows him to travel widely it has also bought him international production funding. Since *The Wind Will Carry Us* (1999) his work has been produced by Paris-based Marin Karmitz. Prior to that, he made two films co-produced by the French company CiBy 2000, *Through the Olive Trees* (1994) and *Taste of Cherry* (1997). The 'discovery' of Kiarostami, in which the French have played a central role, runs parallel with the increasing worldwide recognition of the vitality of cinema from post-revolutionary Iran. Richard Pena, programme director of the New

York Film Festival, has enthused publically: 'What West German film had been in the Seventies, and Chinese film in the Eighties, Iranian cinema would become in the Nineties.' Kiarostami emerged on the festival scene with the full force of a 'discovery' for two reasons. Firstly, because of the sense that this was a director at the peak of his creative powers who had been working since the early 1970s and therefore had an extensive back catalogue of films, an already existing *oeuvre* that would serve to set his work in context and assist in providing the all-important retrospective programmes that are the lifeblood of festivals and *cinémathèques*. Secondly, because the landscape of his cinema was that of a country with which the West, particularly the USA and the UK (known as the 'Great Satan' and 'Old Fox' to hostile Iranians), had fraught relations since the Islamic Revolution of 1979 which had deposed the corrupt and brutal regime of Shah Reza Pahlavi and installed the grim Shi'ite Ayatollah Khomeini. Amazingly Kiarostami's career has straddled and survived both regimes. During the Revolution, zealous mujahideen torched cinemas. Twenty years later, Iranian film was being lauded around the world.

Kiarostami himself is a small, trim and dapper individual. He dresses unostentatiously in stylishly cut jackets and dark T-shirts and exudes the patient stillness of someone accustomed to waiting on location for the right light and the perfect shot. He favours tinted glasses (shades of Godard). His French is more than functional, his English less so (he also has some Czech) but he always speaks in Farsi. Born in 1940, he trained as a painter, worked as a graphic artist and came to cinema through making credit sequences and advertising films. In 1969 he was asked to join Kanun (Institute for Children and Adults Intellectual Development), a cultural organisation established by the wife of the Shah and which survived the Revolution. Kiarostami set up a cinema department where he would make over twenty films ranging from documentary shorts to pedagogical works and features. The prominence of children in his films was remarked on when he started to attract international attention, especially with the 'Koker trilogy'

FESTIVALWORLD 219

(named after the region of northern Iran where they were set), *Where is the Friend's House* (1986), *Life and Nothing More* (1992) and *Through the Olive Trees* (1994).

The latter two films were set in the aftermath of a cataclysmic earthquake in June 1990 and both feature a fictional film-maker who goes in search of the real-life youngsters who had taken part in an earlier film. The combination of documentary realism, location shooting, non-professional actors combined with a film-about-film reflexivity saw his work compared to certain European directors. The epithets of 'humanism', 'neo-realism' and 'modernism' were bandied about in an attempt to pin down the films. Associations further strengthened when he was awarded the 'Rossellini Prize' at Cannes in 1992 for *Life and Nothing More*. Gilles Jacob had created the award in 1986 to recognise film-makers whose work 'perpetuated the humanist tradition of the director of *Rome, Open City*'. In response to a succession of remarkable films, the tributes came thick and fast in the early 1990s. When Kiarostami's work was first screened in Japan in 1994, Akira Kurosawa delivered the following eulogy: 'I believe the films of Kiarostami are extraordinary. Words cannot convey my feelings about them and I simply advise you to see his films and you will see what I mean. When Satyajit Ray passed away I was very uspet. But having seen Kiarostami's films I thank God for giving us just the right person to take his place.'

Rossellini, Ray, Kurosawa . . . the Iranian was being spoken of in illustrious company. A consensus was emerging of Kiarostami as a great director, albeit in the internationally acceptable guise of a maker of 'humanist masterpieces'. Crucial to this process were the retrospectives that took place around this time and set his recent work in the context of twenty-plus years of film-making. Although the Rimini and Valladolid film festivals had both organised retrospectives in 1993 it was in 1995 at the Locarno Film Festival (then directed by Marco Muller, now head of the Venice Festival) that the most complete survey of his career was presented and *Cahiers du cinéma* took advantage of the occasion to publish a wide-ranging and important dossier on the director. In the same year, his films were screened at the New York and Chicago film festivals and *Through the Olive Trees* was released in the USA. The reaction to the film in Iran was telling. A new magazine published under the auspices of the Islamic Propaganda Organisation tore into the director for taking advantage of the earthquake to shoot a film that was capable of interesting no one but those 'few hundred spineless, rootless and sick pseudo-intellectuals, natives and foreigners alike who have discovered Kiarostami and are now putting him on a pedestal'. Such knee-jerk xenophobia was a characteristic strand of the official Iranian reaction to Kiarostami's films as he came to be loved by foreign audiences.

Kiarostami's seventh feature, *Taste of Cherry*, began shooting in spring 1996. It is his darkest film by far, about a man looking to end his life who, during a long car journey, auditions a number of people who might assist him in his own death. The film ends with a controversial and much discussed sequence shot in video. It was a film with an extended and traumatic production. Part of the negative was destroyed during processing which meant that certain sequences had to be entirely re-shot. In addition, Kiarostami was prevented from working for several months following a car crash. Nor could he decide how to end the film. All of which meant that it was not ready to be shown as planned at the Venice Festival, much to the chagrin of festival director Gillo Pontecorvo. Venice's loss was Cannes' gain, but there were obstacles to the film's inclusion. The Iranian authorities hesitated to let the film leave the country, less for censorship reasons relating to the film's story which concerns suicide (a sin in Islam) than for the more bureaucratic reason that it had not been first shown at the annual Fajr Film Festival in Tehran, which was then a technical necessity.

Long negotiations followed in which it is rumoured that the French Foreign Minister intervened, and eventually official authorisation was granted for the film to go to Cannes, where it appeared late in the day and without being mentioned in the festival catalogue. When asked

FESTIVALWORLD   221

about the authorities' change of heart, Kiarostami takes a positive view: 'I'd rather say that they let the film be shown, that's the most important thing. I don't want to think that they might have stopped it being shown since it didn't happen. It was the government that sent the film, after all.' Then an executive with the film's co-producer CiBy 2000, Pierre Rissient was well placed to record the inside story:

> I thought it was important to get the film in Cannes in 1997 and to get a prize for it. I brought *Through the Olive Trees* to Cannes and I was very much behind *Taste of Cherry*. But Abbas was late in getting the picture finished. I'd met Nanni Moretti once, very briefly – actually it was with Abbas in a restaurant in Cannes when he came for *Through the Olive Trees*. Everyone knew that Moretti is a great admirer of Abbas. Abbas was hesitating how to end *Taste of Cherry*, he came to Paris not long before and said, 'I don't think it can be ready for Cannes.' I said, 'Abbas, you'd *better* be ready for Cannes because Moretti is on the jury . . .'

Rissient was correct to identify Moretti as a potential supporter of the film. The Italian director (who won the Palme d'Or himself in 2001 for *The Son's Room*) runs a cinema in Rome and in 1996 made a short film, *The Opening Day of Close Up*, which is in part a tribute to Kiarostami's masterpiece as well a comical insight into the travails of running an art cinema, with *Close Up* opening head-to-head with Disney's *The Lion King*. Rissient picks up the story:

> Abbas thought of something for the end of the film. Some loved it and some hated it, the video sequence at the end. But he said, 'Let's do it. Let's go.' The picture was never seen by the selection committee because it was so late but during the first two or three days of Cannes, Abbas told me that he could come. So I told Gilles Jacob, 'We could have Abbas's film.' We had to put it at the end of the festival in a special screening. Gilles, his son Laurent and myself saw the picture once in a private screening and it was announced during the

festival that the picture was in. Of course, when Abbas was kissed by Catherine Deneuve, some people were very upset about that.

The congratulatory peck on the cheek from 'the most beautiful woman in the world' that Kiarostami received along with the Palme d'Or caused a scandal in Iran. Immediately after what he referred to as 'that disastrous kiss', Kiarostami called his son in Tehran:

> He told me I should not come back for a while because things did not look good. So I stayed for a week and when I went back I had to avoid the welcoming audience [at the airport] and go out of the backdoor. One of the fortunate things, though, was that this event coincided with the election of President Khatami and so the political atmosphere was changing in Iran. As a result it didn't take on the kind of significance that it could have without the political and social changes of the time.

The reaction in Iran to the award was overshadowed by the manufactured controversy of the kiss as well as the fact that the award was announced during an annual religious festival and on the eve of the presidential elections. Nor did it seem to do much for Kiarostami's career at home:

> Personally, to have won the Palme d'Or didn't open any doors in my country and hasn't made my work any easier since. On the contrary, there have been a lot of polemics and conflicts of interest around it because, up to now, a form of cinema that hadn't been supported in my country was seen as being so extraordinary that it could win such a prize on an international scale. It's got worse, in fact, because none of my films have been shown in Iran since I won the Palme d'Or.

Not strictly true. Both *Taste of Cherry* and *The Wind Will Carry Us* were released eventually but played for a short time to relatively small audiences and, like many of Kiarostami's other films, were received with hostility in some quarters. In this respect, his domestic career has

FESTIVALWORLD 223

suffered less from the direct intervention of state censorship than from an equally invidious form of market-based censorship, whereby exhibitors will not show the films because they are not seen as money-spinners. One reason given for the characteristically elliptical style of many Iranian film-makers is their need to outwit the custodians of Islamic law and so become agile practitioners of indirection, experts in the censor-bluffing feint. There are other factors that limit the Iranian audience, as Kiarostami describes:

> The number of cinemas has been diminishing more and more since before the revolution. The population has tripled from what it was twenty-five years ago and we have far fewer cinemas than before. There are fewer and fewer places where independent films like mine can be shown. Some say: 'Oh, he works for foreigners so he can easily find places to show his work, we're not going to bother with him here.' But for me it's so important that my own people can see my films.

Whatever effects the Palme d'Or did or did not have on Kiarostami's career at home, it effectively marked his inauguration as the leading light of Iranian cinema internationally and opened doors for the next generation of film-makers such as Jafar Panahi, Bahman Ghobadi and Samira Makhmalbaf, to name but a few. This became startlingly clear the following year at Cannes when Samira Makhmalbaf who, at eighteen, was the youngest person ever to have a film selected, screened her remarkably assured debut feature *The Apple* in Un Certain Regard. Samira Makhmalbaf comes from a family of film-makers. Her father is the famous Iranian director Mohsen Makhmalbaf who turned to cinema after having spent three years in prison in the late 1970s as a teenage Islamic radical involved in anti-Shah activism. The director of *The Cyclist*, *A Moment of Innocence* and *Gabbeh* and, in part, the inspiration for the story of *Close Up*, Makhmalbaf has joked that 'instead of making films I decided to make film-makers' and through the 'Makhmalbaf Film House' the entire family – wife Marziyeh, son

Maysan and daughters Samira and Hana – have all gone into the business. It has been Samira who has attracted most attention. Not only for the stark beauty and unflinching realism of her films – *Blackboard*, which won the Jury Prize at Cannes in 2000, would be a remarkable achievement by any director let alone someone barely in her twenties – but also for the image she presented before the world's press at Cannes. Diminutive, elegantly dressed in black, wearing a headscarf and speaking fluent English, Samira made a huge impression. As author of one of the best studies of post-revolutionary Iranian cinema Hamid Dabashi enthused, Samira Makhmalbaf 'changed for ever the image of Iran in the world media. After the stark and ascetic features of Ayatollah Khomeini in the 1970s, suddenly a young and beautiful face promised the rise of a whole new generation of hope in Iran.'

Just as Kiarostami cannot conceive of continuing to make films without the support of the festival circuit nor, as viewers, can we conceive of having had the chance to encounter Iranian cinema without it. Crucially, many films by Iranian directors, from the older generation to the newcomers, have not been limited exclusively to festivals. They continue to receive international distribution and are seen in cinemas by audiences worldwide. In this respect, Iranian cinema is one of the best recent examples of the festival circuit fulfilling what has become its present function: *to propose an alternative to the mainstream*. The 'Kiarostami Case' and, by extension, that of Iranian cinema must be set against two monolithic entities that constitute this mainstream: Hollywood and mass media. On one hand, Hollywood is both the hegemon of style, story and worldview made available to us through cinema and a commercial system whose vested interest lies in crushing the opposition. On the other hand, Iranian cinema emerges to give accounts of life in Iran that complicate, deepen and contradict the propagandist tenor of mass media images (which, to be fair, is far from being all one-sided). This is admittedly a somewhat crude representation of the calculus of power. But does that make it any less true? And it needs to be seen within the larger debate about 'globalisation'. Each

FESTIVALWORLD

of these components – Hollywood, mass media and the film festival circuit – represents an interlocking and competing aspect of a globalised media economy. And while the first two characterise the more pernicious and homogenising aspects of globalisation, what Benjamin R. Barber has dubbed 'McWorld', the other element introduced by the festival circuit militates against this. The adventure of Iranian cinema, the global recognition of this local industry in the 1990s, therefore can be seen to have high stakes. To produce another image of Iran in a cinema other than Hollywood acquires cultural weight and political significance.

Cannes is now one among many film festivals, though *primus inter pares*. It has the edge when it comes to attracting media coverage, but is just the grandest of the many points in the year-long, non-stop, overlapping timetable of the global festival circuit. 'Globalisation' is useful as a term only if it's understood as constituting both a promise and a threat. The unlimited movement of capital, people, goods and information promises and threatens to reduce the nation state to an irrelevance, which is one reason why theorists of globalisation tend to talk less in terms of the dimensions of 'national' and 'international' than 'local' and 'global', the terms being seen not as antithetical but interlocking. The film festival circuit can be seen as a system that routinely puts the 'local' into 'global' circulation and therefore provides an example of the promises and threats of globalisation. Hamid Dabashi sets them out clearly: 'Those who control the international film festivals at Cannes, Venice and Locarno favour aggressive exoticisation of the so-called Third World, so that these festivals become the cinematic version of *National Geographic*.' Jonathan Rosenbaum, who has written extensively on Kiarostami, makes a number of interesting and valuable points that extend the ideas of the 'local' and the 'global': 'For me, Kiarostami is first of all a global film-maker. Even though I'm interested in learning about Iran through Iranian cinema, and his films are certainly a part of that, I feel that I go to his films to learn about the world, not just Iran. There are surely other Iranian film-makers

226   CANNES

who could tell me more about Iran than he can, but I don't think there are any other Iranian film-makers now who could tell me as much about the world in general.'

Rosenbaum compares the director to Godard in the mid-1960s: 'If you wanted to know what was going on in the Western world at that time, you'd go to his movies – because he had this capacity to pick up on all these things that were current in the culture, and it wasn't necessarily because he was seeking this.' For example, he makes the fascinating observation of the way in which *The Wind Will Carry Us* spoke to him when it was released in the US (at the time of recounts of votes in the presidential elections in December 2000):

> How? Because there's an enormous rift between what's happening in the media and what's happening in everyday life – a rift that gets expressed through one's perception of time, one's body language, and all sorts of other things. If you turned to somebody on the street during that post-election period, you could immediately bond with them about what was going on, but if you turned on the TV all you'd encounter was people screaming at one another. This kind of discrepancy is captured perfectly in *The Wind Will Carry Us*, which shows such a division quite comically. So it shouldn't be surprising that what he's doing is appreciated and recognised as relevant by people across the world.

And he makes the following controversial assessment: 'My point is that Americans have no right to view Kiarostami principally as an Iranian artist if we don't know what being Iranian – as opposed to, say, Islamic (assuming we know that either) – really consists of.' Critic Godfrey Cheshire, who has also written authoritively about the director, claims 'if you wanted to reduce Kiarostami to a single idea, you would not be far wrong in saying that he has spent his career developing a cinematic equivalent to Iranian modernist poetry'. He takes issue with Rosenbaum: 'Pardon me, but I would say that Steven Spielberg and Majid Majidi are the ones addressing global culture. I think

Kiarostami is ultimately addressing himself – and perhaps a few other Gnostics.' Which has to count as one of the most hilariously elitist claims ever made for a film-maker by a critic since Truffaut declared that the audience for the film of the future would comprise the director and 'a few of his friends' (at least Truffaut's ideal audience was non-denominational). But a global audience – of Gnostics and others – has clearly taken to Kiarostami's work. So Rosenbaum's approach is more than simply a neat inversion of the local/global dichotomy. Whatever 'key' in which one chooses to read Kiarostami – whether in the 'global' register of humanism, neo-realism or the film festival circuit or the 'local' register of Gnosticism and Persian modernist poetry, let alone the always mysterious and private creative intentions of the director – none excludes the other. In their competing claims, though, lies some idea of the complexities involved in the trafficking of local cultures through the global network of the film festival circuit.

To be continued . . .

So-called 'festival films' are only part of what the big festivals are about. Gilles Jacob and Thierry Frémaux have cultivated deep and longstanding links with the Hollywood studios to ensure that their films are shown on the Croisette too. Their presence ensures plenty of glamour and glitz, and in turn big crowds, who might then happen to discover more rarefied gems. So, though in many respects a festival like Cannes and the network are part of an oppositional stance to Hollywood, this is only one element in a complex picture.

As we saw in Chapter 1, Cannes and other European film festivals developed partly in response to punitive post-war trade agreements which saw Hollywood flooding the European market with American films which had been stockpiled during the Second World War. The festivals represented a privileged non-commercial space where European films could at least be shown and accrue new, alternative kinds of prestige in the teeth of this Hollywood dominance. Since then, Cannes

228   CANNES

and Venice more than any of the other festivals have drawn upon star power, and were also swift to appropriate the branding techniques used by Hollywood, to help push more 'artistic films' toward mass awareness. In this way a market was created for Haneke and Almodóvar, Kieslowski and Kiarostami, who are all well-known names and big business now. Hollywood for its part now sees Cannes as the pre-eminent launch site for penetrating crucial European markets, creating a situation of mutual dependency.

The rise of the Miramax film in the nineties typifies this dynamic. Miramax was set up by the Weinstein brothers and their first big hit came with *sex, lies and videotape*, which won the Palme d'Or in 1989 (one of the very few debutants to have done so). That award was heavily exploited in the film's marketing (along, of course, with the actually rather minor sexual content), and inaugurated the era of 'The Miramax Film' which to some extent we still inhabit. That phrase refers to a particular kind of indie/arthouse crossover film, another mildly derogatory shorthand for a predictably formulaic, faux-intellectual item that appears a little too besotted with surface sheen and glossy despair, usually purveyed by very beautiful French actresses (did someone mention Kieslowski?) But 'Miramax' also denotes a particular savvy commercial exploitation of independent or art cinema, whose cultural legitimacy and stamp of quality is conferred to a large extent by marketing exploitation of awards scooped at Cannes, which became hugely important to the Weinsteins. Hollywood, of course, was quick to recuperate this lucrative niche market in the late nineties by setting up its own independent divisions, or buying the competition.

Commerce and art, art and commerce – this never-ending *pas de deux* has left its footprints all over this book. Film scholar Marijke de Valck rightly locates the European film festivals' roots in the avant-garde cultures of early twentieth-century Europe, of which they still bear traces in their cultural elitism and emphases on the genius director and enlightenment through art. 'The success of the international film festival might best be explained in terms of this peculiar position,

FESTIVALWORLD

sandwiched between the diametrically opposed antagonists Hollywood and the Avant-garde. The festival has one foot planted in the model of avant-garde artisanship, while the other strides forwards on the beat of market demands within the culture economy.' And like the film festivals where they're often launched, American and European cinemas have cross-fertilised in all kinds of interesting ways, in a history of reciprocity and mutual influence, a complex mirroring, which can't be reduced to a straightforward opposition.

It's tempting to see the opening of the new Palais in Cannes in 1983 as marking a symbolic rupture, when the festival's priorities shifted away from its avant-garde roots and more in the direction of commerce and the extravagant spectacle, what Agnès Varda describes at the head of the chapter as a 'big, slightly vulgar bazaar'. The year 1983 was also when the market was officially incorporated into the festival, in the lower depths of the Palais's structure. Henceforth business and glamour became indivisible, as de Valck has noted.

> Whereas the glamour of the 1950s had been mythical and constituted by the presence of stars and the scandals of starlets, the glamour of the 1980s turned commercial . . . the special festive atmosphere and the almost tangible relation to myth continues to be part of the reason why the Cannes market is so successful today. The stars, the red carpet, the parties and all other expressions of glamour, predispose film professionals to approach the film products not only rationally but also affectively. From the 1980s onwards, the glamour of Cannes was completely appropriated for business purposes.

The new box-like, heavily functional Palais could hardly be described as a glamorous or beautiful building. Liza Minnelli thought it looked like an Egyptian tomb, but it was the nickname 'The Bunker' which stuck early on. The contrast with the old Palais is so marked as to almost negate comment – it's a shift from pleasure to business. And the new Palais is being extended still further in the next few years to cope with the festival's continued growth.

Attracting buyers and sellers to the Cannes marketplace is another important part of the festival director's job, and that means creating a unique image and brand identity for the festival and marketing it skilfully. In that regard Cannes trades heavily on its past history and unique location. Gilles Jacob recently issued a DVD called *Au Coeur du Festival* ('At the Heart of the Festival') which taps into an almost mythically resonant sense of the festival's symbolic import and the idea of an annually renewable rite, unashamedly evoking a nostalgia for all those great stars who've passed through the Palais's portals, and hugely inflating the festival director's prestige and aura, while managing to retain a sense of his avuncular approachability. It's a highly self-conscious concoction, but extremely successful in setting up an affective bond with the viewer – so much so it's hard not to watch it without a glistening in the corners of one's eyes . . . It was produced with financial assistance from Agnes B and retails in their shops, immediately setting up a relationship with a particular well-heeled, influential demographic who buy into the Cannes notion of what constitutes art cinema.

Thus, amid a crowded festival network, does the figure of the festival director tread a delicate path through multiple agendas, different constituencies and the competing demands of art and commerce. The director has become a significant cultural figure in the last twenty years, not only in carving out a distinctive niche for his or her own festival but in forging lasting links with producers and assisting – some might say creating – directorial careers. They are arbiters, cultural gatekeepers, entrepreneurs, agenda-setters, even visionaries in the best cases. But they are only ever as good as the festivals they helm. Now that these festivals are firm fixtures of global culture it remains to be seen how their self-allotted mission to provide a sustainable alternative to mainstream cinema develops: just as it remains to be seen whether, in another ten, twenty – sixty? – years, Cannes is still the jewel in the festival circuit's crown.

Appendix I

Timeline

1937
Renoir's *La Grande Illusion* wins Jury Prize at Venice Film Festival (founded 1932); angers Hitler.

1938
Prizes at Venice for Riefenstahl's *Olympiad* and Alessandrini's *Luciano Serra: Pilote* prompts withdrawal of American and British delegates. French civil servant Philippe Erlanger and Minister Jean Zay conceive idea of a French counter-event, a 'festival of the free world'.

1939
17 July: official announcement that 'le Festival International du Film' (FIF) will open on 1 September.
1 September: FIF opens; Germany invades Poland.
3 September: England and France declare war. Festival aborted but rescheduled first for Christmas 1939, then for February, finally for Easter 1940, then abandoned.

1946
First official edition of FIF 20 September to 5 October with Robert Favre le Bret as festival director. Films include Hitchcock's *Notorious*, Wilder's *The Lost Weekend*; prizewinners include Rossellini's *Rome, Open City*, Clément's *La Bataille du Rail*.

1947
Hungary the only Eastern bloc country competing.

1948
Festival cancelled due to lack of funding.

232 CANNES

1949
The event is moved into a new facility, the Palais Croisette, where it will be held for next thirty-four years; no Eastern bloc presence.

1950
Festival cancelled due to lack of funding.

1951
From 1951, the event is held in April in order to compete more effectively with Berlin and Venice. Japan competing for the first time; USSR back in the fray; Buñuel's *Los Olvidados* and De Sica's *Miracle in Milan* among the winners; the Lettrist art-agitator Isidore Isou screens *Traité de bave et d'éternité* in the festival margins; in the audience is a teenage Guy-Ernest Debord who will go on to found the Situationist International.

1952
USSR and Eastern bloc countries absent; festival settles on May as its schedule; Robert Favre Le Bret appointed as general delegate; the Lettrists return uninvited, with three films and Debord now a member, to carry out a 'commando operation'.

1953
USSR and Eastern bloc countries absent; Jean Cocteau jury president; *I Confess* (Hitchcock), *El* (Buñuel), *Peter Pan* (Disney), *Les Vacances de M. Hulot* (Tati) among key films. *Le Salaire de la peur* (Clouzot) wins Grand Prix; little-known French teenage starlet Brigitte Bardot charms photographers – and Kirk Douglas – in a beachfront photo-session.

1954
USSR settles down to regular participation; Jean Cocteau jury president; British starlet Simone Silva causes a scandal by posing topless with Robert Mitchum.

1955
Vassiliev's *Heroes of Chipka* a prizewinner; the Palme d'Or awarded for the first time (to Delbert Mann's *Marty*); in *Arts* François Truffaut describes festival as 'a trade fair'.

1956
Scandal over the withdrawal of Resnais's *Nuit et brouillard*; Yutkevich's *Othello* a prizewinner; further hostile festival reports by Truffaut.

1957
Chukhrai's *The Forty-First* a prizewinner; annulment of 'article 5' of festival regulations; Jean Cocteau honorary president; Truffaut banned from festival, attends anyway and files extremely severe report. Bergman wins Special Jury Prize for *The Seventh Seal*.

APPENDIX I: TIMELINE   233

1958
Kalatozov's *The Cranes are Flying* only Soviet Palme d'Or winner; Truffaut wins Best Director Prize for *The 400 Blows*.

1959
The 'Marché du Film' (film market) officially incorporated into festival.

1960
Two Italian films, Fellini's *La Dolce Vita* and Antonioni's *L'Avventura*, provoke scandals and win major prizes against strong competition from Buñuel, Bergman and Chukhrai; Georges Simenon proves a strong-minded jury president.

1961
Buñuel's anti-clerical satire *Viridiana* wins Palme d'Or amid much scandal.

1962
Creation of the 'Semaine Internationale de la Critique' (International Critics Week).

1966
Sophia Loren first woman jury president; Rivette's *Suzanne Simonin: la Religieuse de Diderot* screens at Cannes despite being banned in France.

1967
Bardot returns to Cannes for the first time in over ten years accompanied by then-husband Gunter Sachs and causes a media sensation.

1968
10 May – festival opens as students clash with police in 'the Night of the Barricades' in Paris heralding two months of widespread social upheaval.
13 May – mass demonstrations in Paris; calls for festival to be suspended rebuffed.
18 May – New Wave figureheads Truffaut, Godard and Malle lead protestors in occupying one of the main screening rooms; jury resignations ensue; festival declared non-competitive.
19 May – festival suspended.

1969
First edition of the *Quinzaine des Réalisateurs* (Directors Fortnight) showcasing new 'young cinema' included as parallel strand to main competition to appease May '68 protestors. Dennis Hopper wins Best Director for *Easy Rider*. Lindsay Anderson wins Palme d'Or for *If . . .*

1970
Altman's *M*A*S*H* wins Palme d'Or.

234 CANNES

1972
Favre Le Bret appointed president of festival; Maurice Bessy made general delegate. Festival regulations change: countries no longer nominate films, the festival selects them.

1973
Awards for Ferreri's *La Grande Bouffe* and Eustache's *La Maman et la Putain* provoke tremendous outcries and questions are asked in the French Senate.

1975
Maurice Bessy creates three official out-of-competition categories: 'Les yeux fertiles' for films focusing on the arts; 'L'air de temps' for films based on contemporary events; 'Le passé composé' for compilation works. Algerian film *Chronicle of the Years of Fire* wins Palme d'Or.

1976
Roberto Rossellini is jury president, decides to hold a symposium open to all comers for duration of festival.

1978
Gilles Jacob appointed general delegate, regroups the three out-of-competition categories into Un Certain Regard and introduces the 'Caméra d'or' award for best first film in any section.

1979
Coppola's *Apocalypse Now* screens in an unfinished version (the first time an incomplete work had been invited) and shares Palme d'Or with Schlöndorff's *The Tin Drum*.

1983
Opening of the new purpose-built Palais des Festivals, instantly christened 'le bunker'.

1984
Pierre Viot appointed president; Favre Le Bret made honorary president.

1985
Creation of 'Roberto Rossellini Prize' awarded by a jury of French and Italian film-makers to a personality continuing Rossellini's 'humanistic' tradition. Godard gets 'flanned'.

1987
Fortieth anniversary. The festival presents a celebratory compilation film, *Le cinéma dans les yeux*, and a publication, *Les Années Cannes*. The Palme d'Or awarded to Pialat's *Sous le soleil de Satan* provokes a barrage of audience abuse to which the director responds in kind.

APPENDIX I: TIMELINE

1989
On the occasion of the fall of the Berlin Wall a symposium entitled 'Cinéma et Liberté' is held which attracts over a hundred directors from around the world. *sex, lies and videotape*, the first film by Steven Soderbergh, wins the Palme d'Or and inaugurates the American 'indie cinema' boom of the 1990s.

1991
Polanski's jury awards the Coen Brothers' *Barton Fink* three prizes (Palme d'Or, Direction and Actor); François Erlanbach appointed secretary general.

1992
Publication of *Les visiteurs de Cannes* to mark forty-fifth anniversary of festival. Creation of the official selection 'Cinéma de Toujours' combining tributes and retrospectives.

1993
The Palme d'Or awarded to Jane Campion for *The Piano*, first woman to win the prize.

1996
Cronenberg's film adaptation of J.G. Ballard's auto-erotic *Crash* causes a scandal.

1997
Fiftieth anniversary. The 'Palme de Palmes' awarded to Bergman by all Palme d'Or winners.
Kiarostami wins Palme d'Or (ex aequo) for *Taste of Cherry*; a congratulatory kiss bestowed by Catherine Deneuve is exploited by political scandalmongers in Iran.

1998
Eighteen-year-old Samira Makhmalbaf becomes the youngest person to be selected for the festival; *The Apple* plays in the Un Certain Regard selection. Creation of the Cinéfondation and a new official jury to award prizes to both shorts and three best Cinéfondation films.

1999
Creation of the Cinéfondation Association to further develop work undertaken at Cannes.

2000
Jacob made president of festival; Véronique Cayla appointed general manager; Thierry Frémaux appointed artistic delegate; Pierre Viot made president of Cinéfondation and honorary president of festival. Lars von Trier wins Palme d'Or for *Dancer in the Dark* (his star Björk winning Best Actress award). Launch of official festival website. In October in Paris, the Festival Residence opens welcoming

young film-makers from all over the world to write their first features. Samira Makhmalbaf wins Jury Prize for *Blackboard*.

2002
The Festival International de Film officially adopts the title 'Festival de Cannes'.

2003
Jury president Patrice Chéreau bucks festival regulation in awarding Gus Van Sant's *Elephant* two prizes (Palme d'Or and Direction).

2004
Michael Moore wins Palme d'Or for his anti-Bush polemic *Fahrenheit 9/11*. Festival publishes a three-part DVD 'Au Coeur du Festival', an anthology of the festival's greatest moments assembled by Gilles Jacob. Creation of the 'Cannes Classics' section dedicated to heritage films and unreleased works on the cinema. Launch of 'Actors Masterclass', Producers Network and a market dedicated to short films.

2005
Creation of festival workshop organised by Ciné-fondation – eighteen film-makers from all over the world with scripts assisted in getting films produced. A new programme created, 'All the Cinemas of the World', dedicated to a wide range of world cinema.

2007
Sixtieth anniversary.

Appendix II

List of Palme d'Or Winners

(The palm leaf motif was adopted for the festival's top award in 1954. The former top award, the 'Grand Prix International', was renamed the 'Palme d'Or'.)

2006
The Wind that Shakes the Barley
(Ken Loach,
UK/Ireland/German/Italy/Spain/France)

2005
The Child
(Jean-Pierre Dardenne & Luc Dardenne, Belgium/France)

2004
Fahrenheit 9/11
(Michael Moore, USA)

2003
Elephant
(Gus Van Sant, USA)

2002
The Pianist
(Roman Polanski,
France/Germany/UK)

2001
The Son's Room
(Nanni Moretti, Italy)

2000
Dancer in the Dark
(Lars von Trier, Denmark)

1999
Rosetta
(Jean-Pierre Dardenne & Luc Dardenne, Belgium/France)

1998
Eternity and a Day
(Theo Angelopoulos, Greece)

1997
The Eel
(Imamura Shohei, Japan) &
Taste of Cherry
(Abbas Kiarostami, Iran)

1996
Secrets and Lies
(Mike Leigh, UK)

1995
Underground
(Emir Kusturica, Yugoslavia)

238 CANNES

1994
Pulp Fiction
(Quentin Tarantino, USA)

1993
Farewell My Concubine
(Chen Kaige, China) &
The Piano
(Jane Campion, New Zealand)

1992
The Best Intentions
(Bille August, Sweden)

1991
Barton Fink
(Ethan Coen & Joel Cohen, USA)

1990
Wild at Heart
(David Lynch, USA)

1989
sex, lies and videotape
(Steven Soderbergh, USA)

1988
Pelle the Conqueror
(Bille August, Denmark/Sweden)

1987
Sous le soleil de Satan (*Under Satan's Sun*)
(Maurice Pialat, France)

1986
The Mission
(Roland Joffé, UK)

1985
When Father Was Away on Business
(Emir Kusturica, Yugoslavia)

1984
Paris, Texas
(Wim Wenders, France/W. Germany)

1983
The Ballad of Narayama
(Shohei Imamura, Japan)

1982
Yol
(Yilmaz Güney, Turkey) &
Missing
(Costa-Gavras, USA)

1981
Man of Iron
(Andrzej Wajda, Poland)

1980
Kagemusha
(Akira Kurosawa, Japan) &
All That Jazz
(Bob Fosse, USA)

1979
Apocalypse Now
(Francis Ford Coppola, USA) &
The Tin Drum
(Volker Schlöndorff, Germany)

1978
The Tree of Wooden Clogs
(Ermanno Olmi, Italy/France)

1977
Padre Padrone
(Paolo Taviani & Vittorio Taviani, Italy)

1976
Taxi Driver
(Martin Scorsese, USA)

1975
Chronicle of the Years of Fire
(Mohammed Lakhdar-Hamina, Algeria)

1974
The Conversation
(Francis Ford Coppola, USA)

APPENDIX II: PALME D'OR WINNERS

239

1973
Scarecrow
(Jerry Schatzberg, USA) &
The Hireling
(Alan Bridges, USA)

1972
The Working Class Goes to Heaven
(Elio Petri, Italy) &
The Mattei Affair
(Francesco Rosi, Italy)

1971
The Go-Between
(Joseph Losey, UK)

1970
*M*A*S*H*
(Robert Altman, USA)

1969
If...
(Lindsay Anderson, UK)

1967
Blow-Up
(Michelangelo Antonioni, UK/Italy)

1966
A Man and a Woman
(Claude Lelouch, France) &
The Birds, the Bees, and the Italians
(Pietro Germi, Italy/France)

1965
The Knack ... and how to get it
(Richard Lester, UK)

1964
The Umbrellas of Cherbourg
(Jacques Demy, France)

1963
The Leopard
(Luchino Visconti, Italy)

1962
Keeper of Promises
(Anselmo Duarte, Brazil/Portugal)

1961
The Long Absence
(Henri Colpi, France/Italy)
Viridiana
(Luis Buñuel, Spain)

1960
La Dolce Vita
(Federico Fellini, Italy)

1959
Black Orpheus
(Marcel Camus, Brazil)

1958
The Cranes are Flying
(Mikhail Kalatozov, USSR)

1957
Friendly Persuasion
(William Wyler, USA)

1956
The Silent World
(Jacques-Yves Cousteau & Louis
Malle, Italy/France)

1955
Marty
(Delbert Mann, USA)

1954
Gate of Hell
(Teinosuke Kinugasa, Japan)

1953
The Wages of Fear
(Henri-Georges Clouzot, France)

1952
Two Cents Worth of Hope
(Renato Castellani, Italy) &

240 CANNES

Othello
(Orson Welles, USA)

1951
Miss Julie
(Alf Sjöberg, Sweden) &
Miracle in Milan
(Vittorio De Sica, Italy)

1949
The Third Man
(Carol Reed, UK)

1947
Antoine and Antoinette
(Jacques Becker, France)
Dumbo
(Walt Disney, USA)
Ziegfeld Follies
(Vincente Minelli, USA)
The Damned
(René Clément, France)
Crossfire
(Edward Dmytryk, USA)

1946
Lost Weekend
(Billy Wilder, USA)
The Red Earth
(Bodil Ipsen & Lau Jr. Lauritzen,
Hungary)

Lowly City
(Chetan Anand, India)
Brief Encounter
(David Lean, UK)
María Candélaria
(Emilio Fernández, Mexico)
The Turning Point
(Fridrikh Markovitch Ermler, USSR)
La Symphonie Pastorale
(Jean Delannoy, France)
The Last Chance
(Leopold Lintberg, Switzerland)
Men Without Wings
(Frantisek Cap, France)
Rome, Open City
(Roberto Rossellini, Italy)
La Bataille du Rail
(Réné Clément, France)
Girl No. 217
(Mikhail Romm, USSR)
The Stone Flower
(Aleksandr Ptushko, USSR)
Figueroa
(Miguel Delgado, Mexico)
The Music Box
(Walt Disney, USA)

Notes

I To Serve the Cinema

11 'He asks not to be expected . . .' Doré Silverman, 'Film Festival in France', *World Review*, December 1946, p.48

11 'The festival must be a victory for France' FIF (Festival International de Film) archive document 4B1, 17 July 1939 (all translations from French by CD unless specified)

11 'ill mannered and extraordinarily undisciplined . . .' FIF archive document 23/14, 12 November 1946, p.8

12 'Hollywood Please Note' *People*, 22 September 1946

12 'the first festival . . . of agriculture!' Loredana Latil, *Le Festival de Cannes sur la scène Internationale* (Nouveau Monde Editions, France 2005), p.75

13 'The major American . . .' FIF document 1B1, 26 October 1938

14 'If the festival is a success . . .' FIF document 1B1, 1938

15 ' . . . to combat other such events that already exist . . .' FIF document 4B1, 17 July 1939

16 ' . . . the term being currently unsuitable' FIF archive document 'Projet pour année mai 1942 d'une exposition cinématographique de Cannes'

16 ' . . . a grand demonstration of friendship between nations . . .' FIF document, 18 April 1945

17 'It appears that the decision of the Italian government . . .' FIF document, Organising Committee meeting, 22 May 1946

17 'as much with terror as pride and joy' FIF document 23/14, p.6

18 ' . . . on the whole a salutary rule . . .' Dilys Powell, 'Films at Cannes', *Sunday Times*, 29 December 1946

19 ' . . . surely a set from . . . Lunch cost the French Government £2.8s a head . . .' Silverman, *World Review*, December 1946, p.47

20 'Why do you open wide . . . the only films that count are American' ibid., p.48

242 CANNES

20 'I gave it as my opinion that . . .' ibid., p.46

21 'If I had to sacrifice the interests . . .' Jens Ulf-Møller, *Hollywood's Film Wars with France: Film Trade Diplomacy and the Emergence of the French Film Quota Policy* (Rochester and Woodbridge: University of Rochester Press), pp.143–7

22 'the formidable machinery of Hollywood . . .' André Bazin, 'Le Festival de Cannes 1946' in *Le Cinéma de l'occupation et de la résistance* (UGE, Paris 1975), p.170

22 'nothing should be taken seriously . . .' Henry Magnan *Le Monde*, 8 October 1946

22 'suspended in a stratosphere . . .' Bazin, 'Le Festival de Cannes 1946', p.169

23 'Rossellini had sold the American rights . . .' Cari Beauchamp & Henri Behar, *Hollywood on the Riviera: The Inside Story of the Cannes Film Festival* (William Morrow, New York 1992), p.28

23 ' . . . a few hours before the opening . . . '*Le Film Français* no 145, 19 September 1947 in *Cahiers du cinéma* special issue 'Histoires de Cannes, 1939–1996', April 1997, p.14

II Avoiding Offence

25 'The French are too damned independent!' . . . Information and Education Division of Occupying US Forces in Paris, 1945

http://www.miquelon.org/gripes/index/html (accessed January 2006)

26 ' . . . an incessant diplomatic ballet . . .' Latil, p.106

28 'a few days before the opening of the festival . . .' ibid., p.112

29 'Art and Mammon are usually fighting . . . an opiate for millions' Gavin Lambert, *Sight and Sound*, June 1951, pp.38–40

30 'to show, for example, that there were . . .' David Robinson, *Sight and Sound*, vol 27 no 5 Summer 1958, p.235

31 'I've always played thieves and criminals . . .' 9 April 1953 in Jean Cocteau, *Past Tense Volume II Diaries* (Methuen, London 1990, translation by Richard Howard), p.79

31 'No question about it . . .' ibid.

31 'He had a kind word for everyone . . .' Frédéric Strauss, 'Jean Cocteau, messager du cinéma' in Gérard Pangon, *Cannes: les années festival, 1953* (Editions Mille et une nuits/Arte editions, 1997), pp.29–40

32 'Incredible nerve of the government . . . our feelings' Cocteau, *Past Tense*, 12–13 April, p.86

33 'I had agreed to the presidency in order . . .' 1 May, ibid., p.96

33 'A newspaper has repeated . . .' 5 April, ibid., p.77

33 'An American trick . . .' 17 April, ibid., p.91

NOTES

33 'seeing in the character of the Yankee . . .' Latil, p.119

33 'They thought O'Brien's "shit to you" . . .' Cocteau, *Past Tense*, 18 April, p.93

34 'charming. Each time America is . . .' 23 April, ibid., p.95

34 'an informer for HUAC' Latil, p.119

34 'If I were the only judge . . .' Cocteau, *Past Tense*, 8 April, p.78

35 'an ideal prize . . .' 14 April, ibid., p.87

35 'the exhaustion of a festival . . .' 27 April, ibid., p.96

37 'One of the most boring festivals . . . disappointed' André Bazin, 'Pour un festival à trois dimensions', *Cahiers du cinéma*, May 1953, p.6

37 'a small number of people . . . in order to participate' ibid., p.7

38 'At the end of the day . . .' ibid., p.9

38 'don the correct outfit . . .' ibid., p.12

38 'the festival of diplomatic censorship . . . Resnais preferred to withdraw it' ibid., p.12

39 'be likely to wound . . .' Latil, p.117

40 'A doorman politely checked all guests . . .' Dudley Andrew, *André Bazin* (Oxford University Press, New York 1978), p.155

42 'to a Russian delegate . . .' Lindsay Anderson, *Observer* 15 May 1955

43 'We, the winners . . .' Betsy Blair, *The Memory of All That: Love and Politics in New York, Hollywood and Paris* (Alfred A. Knopf, New York 2003), pp.264–5

44 'Some guy from the American Embassy . . .' Patrick McGilligan & Paul Buhle, *Tender Comrades: A Backstory of the Hollywood Blacklist* (St Martin's Press, New York 1997), p.219

44 'Ben and I were invited . . .' ibid., p.220

45 'This choice was judged not to be the best . . .' Interview with Dauman, *France Culture* radio, 1994, on *Nuit et brouillard* DVD (Arte Video/Argos Films, 2006)

46 '. . . first and foremost, out of respect . . .' *Figaro*, 12 April 1956

46 'The film tells us a story . . .' Jean Cayrol, *Le Monde*, 11 April 1956

46 'Whose feelings might it hurt? . . . '*L'Echo de la liberté*, 19 April 1956

46 'false political susceptibilities . . .' ibid.

46 'might contribute to a revival . . .' ibid.

46 'On the contrary . . .' ibid.

47 'What I feared was . . .' Interview with Alain Resnais, 18 February 1986, in Richard Raskin, *Nuit et Brouillard: On the Making, Reception and Functions of a Major Documentary Film* (Aarhus University Press, Denmark 1987), p.51

47 'The deportees . . .' ibid., pp.62–3

47 '. . . a sensation . . .' Max Favielli, *Paris-Presse*, April/May 1956 in *Cahiers du cinéma* 'Histoires de Cannes', p.46

244 CANNES

III That Riviera Touch

49 'The evolution of the Cannes film festival . . .' Pierre Billard, *D'or et de palmes* (Gallimard, Paris 1997), p.24

49 ' . . . a great rite . . .' Edgar Morin, 'Se donner en images', *Les Temps Modernes* June/July 1955

49 ' . . . holy order . . .' André Bazin, 'Du festival considéré comme un ordre', *Cahiers du cinéma* no 48 June 1955 in *Cahiers du cinéma* special issue 'Histoires de Cannes, 1939–1996' April 1997

50 'The question asked . . .' Morin, ibid.

50 'Cannes belongs to two nations . . .' Stéphen Liégeard, *La Côte d'Azur* (Maison Quantin, Paris 1887), p.87

51 'this warm and ravishing . . .' Guy De Maupassant, *Afloat* (Peter Owen, London & Chester Springs 1995, translated by Marlo Johnston), p.36

52 'No other holiday resort . . .' Philippe Erlanger, *Cannes* (Editions Xavier Richer, Paris 1977), p.120

52 'nothing stranger than . . .' Cocteau, *Past Tense*, 21–22 April 1953, p.94

53 'the essential goal of the festival . . .' François Truffaut, 'Cannes: Un échec', *Arts* 22–28 May 1957, p.1

53 'culture parties on a grand scale . . .' James F. English, *The Economy of Prestige: Prizes, Awards and the Circulation of Cultural Value* (Harvard University Press, Cambridge, Mass. & London 2005), p.32

54 'It is so beautiful here . . .' Kenneth E. Silver, *Making Paradise: Art, Modernity and the Myth of the French Riviera* (MIT Press, Cambridge, Mass. & London 2001), p.33

55 'As long as sex is box-office . . .' *Sunday Pictorial*, 4 April 1954

56 'Robert Favre Le Bret went . . .' Gilles Jacob, authors' interview, September 2005

56 'Let them say . . .' *Sunday Pictorial*, 4 April 1954

57 'in America there was hostility . . .' *Photoplay*, August 1955

59 'One shouldn't forget . . .' Cari Beauchamp & Henri Behar, *Hollywood on the Riviera: The Inside Story of the Cannes Film Festival* (William Morrow, New York 1992), p.28

59 'It was sort of posed . . .' Rita Tushingham, authors' interview, February 2006

60 ' . . . did all it could . . .' in Jean Bresson & Mario Brun, *Les Vingts marches aux étoiles: la fabuleuse histoire du festival de Cannes* (Editions Alain Lefeuvre, 1982), p.132

62 'There was a second of silence . . .' Catherine Rihoit, *Brigitte Bardot, un mythe français* (Editions Olivier Orban, Paris 1986), pp.99–100

64 'Brigitte does not act . . .' Simone de Beauvoir, *Brigitte Bardot and the Lolita*

NOTES

245

Syndrome (New English Library, London 1962, translated by Bernard Fretchman), p.18

64 'When I'm in front of the camera . . .' ibid.

64 'Of course . . .' Ginette Vincendeau, *Stars and Stardom in French Cinema* (Continuum, London & New York 2000), p.93

67 'French beauties . . .' Pascale Lamche, *French Beauties*, documentary for BBC4/Arte, 2005

68 'She considered it her duty . . .' Roger Vadim, *Bardot, Deneuve, Fonda: the memoirs of Roger Vadim*, p.27

69 ' . . . have no shame . . .' Kazuo Ishiguro, authors' interview, September 2005

70 'I understand what it is . . .' Rihoit, *Brigitte Bardot, un mythe français*, p.81

IV Sacred Monsters

71 'I want this picture . . .' *Sullivan's Travels* (1941), written and directed by Preston Sturges

73 'The first week . . .' John Gillett, *Sight and Sound*, vol 29 no 3 Summer 1960, p.120

74 'There are about ten rows . . .' Richard Roud, 'Festival Audiences', *Tribune*, 10 June 1960

75 ' . . . a scene I have never before witnessed . . .' Peter Baker, *Films and Filming*, July 1960, p.13

76 'What is most destructive . . .' Thomas L. Rowe, '1960 Cannes Festival Combines All Elements of Paradoxical Cinema', *Far East Film News*, June 1960, p.14

76 'Cannes this year . . .' Penelope Houston, *Sight and Sound*, vol 29 no 3 Summer 1960, p.122

77 'Fellini loves his characters . . .' Jean-Pierre Dubois, 'La dolce vita: scandale à l'italienne' in '50 films qui ont fait scandale', *CinémAction*, no 103, 2002, p.73

79 ' . . . it's no longer possible . . .' John Baxter, *Buñuel* (Fourth Estate, London 1994), p.5

80 'Ironically, its implacable prohibition . . .' Luis Buñuel, *My Last Breath* (Jonathan Cape, London 1984), p.48

81 'Until now we have had . . .' Baxter, *Buñuel*, ibid., p.3

83 'The spectators emerged . . .' Loredana Latil, 'L'age d'or' in *CinémAction*, no 103, 2002, p.27

83 'From the moment . . .' Luis Buñuel, *Viridiana* (Pierre Lherminier Editions, Paris 1984), p.144

84 'There is no record . . .' David Robinson, *Financial Times*, 6 April 1962

85 'But how . . .' Baxter, *Buñuel*, ibid., p.255

87 'Many of us . . .' Sarris, *Village Voice*, 21 May 1961

246 CANNES

88 'it was a time when ... "doing a Vadim"' Hélène Frappat, *Jacques Rivette, secret compris* (Editions Cahiers du cinéma, Paris 2001), p.129
89 'blasphemous and degrading ...' Bernard Bastide, 'Suzanne Simonin, la religieuse de Diderot' in *CinémAction*, no 103, 2002, p.90
90 'this film is deeply offensive ...' *Le Monde*, 1 April 1966 in *Cahiers du cinéma*, April 1966, p.8
91 'I only knew Fascism from books ...' *Le Monde*, 2 April 1966, ibid.
91 'I am not very sure in any case ... from Free France?' *Le Nouvel Observateur*, 6 April 1966 in Tom Milne, *Godard on Godard* (Secker & Warburg, London 1972, translated by Tom Milne), pp. 237–8
93 'the cinéphiles now knew ...' Antoine de Baecque, *La cinéphilie: invention d'un regard, histoire d'une culture* (Fayard, Paris 2003), p.346

V 'Our mere presence here makes them die'

95 'These hardened old men must die! ...' in Stig Björkman, *Trier on Trier* (Faber & Faber, London 1999), p.61
96 'Cinema is too rich ...' Thomas Y. Levin, 'Dismantling the Spectacle: The Cinema of Guy Debord' in Elizabeth Sussman (ed.), *On the Passage of a few People Through a Rather Brief Moment in Time: The Situationist International 1957–1972* (MIT Press, Cambridge, Mass. and London, 1989), pp.80–1
97 'We want to go beyond ...' ibid., p.81
98 'It is sometimes surprising ...' Andrew Hussey, *The Game of War: The Life and Death of Guy Debord* (Jonathan Cape, London 2001), p.57
99 'that young thug ...' Antoine de Baecque & Serge Toubiana, *Truffaut: A Biography*, translated by Catherine Temerson (University of California Press, Los Angeles 2000), p.111
99 'The *auteur* theory ...' ibid., p.100
99 'trade fairs and nothing else ...' Truffaut, 'Cannes: Palmarès anticipé selon les règles du jeu', *Arts*, 27 April–3 May 1955
99 'The forty films ...' ibid.
100 'When a jury ...' Truffaut, 'Un Palmarès Ridicule', *Arts*, 16–22 May 1956
100 'a failure ...' Truffaut, 'Cannes: Un échec dominé par les compromis, les combines et les faux pas', *Arts*, 22–28 May 1957
100 'It's he who ...' ibid.
101 'In order to get ...' ibid.
102 'Without radical changes ...' Truffaut, 'Si des modifications radicals n'interviennent pas: le prochain festival est condamné', *Arts*, 21–27 May 1958
102 'Those films produced ...' ibid.
102 'applauding shots of landscapes ...' Bertrand Tavernier, authors' interview, March 2006

NOTES

247

103 'a slightly intestinal festival' Molly Haskell, *Village Voice*, 7 June 1973

104 'At Cannes . . .' Michel Piccoli, *Dialogues Egoistes* (Marabout, Paris 1977), p.223

104 'nobody wanted to gamble . . .' ibid., p.224

105 'Provocation was his creed . . .' Evane Hanska, *Mes années Eustache*, (Flammarion, Paris 2001), p.53

106 'overwhelming . . .' Haskell, *Village Voice*

107 'a *corrida* . . .' Bernadette Lafont, *La fiancée du cinéma* (Editions Olivier Orban, Paris 1978), p.158

107 'If you've gone to all that trouble . . .' Haskell, *Village Voice*

107 'Grandmother, can you hear me? . . .' Lafont, *La fiancée du cinéma*, p.158

107 'guarantee that the films . . .' Robert Chazal, *Michel Piccoli: le provocateur*, (Editions France-Empire, Paris 1989), p.128

107 'a Festival should be a place . . .' ibid., p.129

108 'the beginning of the harvest . . .' René Prédal, *Le cinéma français contemporain* (Editions du Cerf, Paris 1984), p.113

108 'One day during May '68 . . .' Jean Eustache, *La Maman et la Putain: Scénario* (Editions Cahiers du cinéma, Paris 1986), p.75

108 'The bourgeoisie . . .' Haskell, *Village Voice*

109 'Practically every film . . .' ibid.

109 'the porno films in the *marché* . . . ' ibid.

110 'This liberal wants to make . . .' Michel Bosquet, *Nouvel Observateur*, 17 June 1974 in Jean-Pierre Jeancolas, *Le cinéma des Français: La Ve République 1958–1978* (Editions Stock, Paris 1979), pp.239–40

110 'It's silent cinema's revenge . . . '*Godard à la télé, 1960–2000* (Michel Royer, 1999)

110 'We are no longer human beings . . .' ibid.

111 'The only drawback . . . full in the face' Noel Godin, *Godin on Godin* (Editions Yellow Now, Belgium 2001), pp.20–1, 32–3, 35–6

112 'I flan people in the spirit . . .' Robert Chalmers, *Observer* 'Life' Magazine 2 July 1995

112 'one of the few . . .' Serge Daney, *Ciné Journal* (Editions Cahiers du cinéma, Paris 1986), p.282

112 'Godard's privilege . . .' ibid., p.283

113 'I don't think much of his films . . . '*Godard à la télé, 1960–2000*

113 'it is impossible at Cannes . . .' in Gilles Jacob, *Au Coeur du festival*, DVD Gaumont/Festival International du Film, 2004

113 'There is a sort of general weakening . . .' Jacob, authors' interview

113 'If you say that Cannes . . .' Jeremy Thomas, authors' interview, November 2005

115 'All your boos and hisses . . .' in Jacob, *Au Coeur du festival*

115 'The French don't like winning . . .' ibid.

248   CANNES

115 'The audience adopts the role . . .' Serge Daney, 'Cannes, quarante, dernière', *Cahiers du cinéma*, June 1987 in *Cahiers du cinéma* 'Histoires de Cannes', p.126
115 'he managed to construct . . .' Björkman, *Trier on von Trier*, p.167
116 'No one really cared how my films looked . . .' ibid., p.1
119 'I felt like I was in a porno film for *adult babies*' Jack Stevenson, *Lars Von Trier* (BFI Publishing, London 2002), p.120

VI 'Beneath the paving stones . . . the beach'

121 'The cinema had taught us . . .' François Truffaut, *Letters*, edited by Gilles Jacob & Claude de Givray, translated and edited by Gilbert Adair (Faber & Faber, London 1989) p.x
122 'May '68 had been one of the first . . .' Jean-Pierre Jeancolas, *Le cinéma des français: La Ve République* (Editions Stock, Paris 1979), p.170
123 'having the atmosphere of Cuba . . .' Claude Miller interviewed for *Cannes et l'histoire*, TV documentary (Directed by André Halimi) TX 14 May 2005
123 'the extremely thick wall . . . ' ibid.
124 'put me on the side of the students . . .' Philip French (ed.), *Malle on Malle* (Faber & Faber, London 1993), p.182
124 'the funereal boredom . . .' in Latil, p.228
125 'the old dragon . . .' in Richard Roud, *A Passion for Films: Henri Langlois and the Cinémathèque Française* (Secker & Warburg, London 1983), p.xxv
125 'one felt great sympathy . . .' ibid., p.viii
125 'One could see there . . .' Rivette, *Cahiers du cinéma*, no 199, March 1968
127 'I realise that though it's impossible . . .' in Antoine de Baecque, *Cahiers du cinéma: Histoire d'une revue II Cinéma, tours détours* (Editions Cahiers du cinéma, Paris 1991), p.183
127 'With the passing of time . . .' in Roud, *A Passion for Films*, ibid., p.viii
127 'It looks as if . . .' Richard Roud, *Guardian*, 14 May 1968
127 'there was definitely . . .' Roud, *Guardian*, 25 May 1968
128 'to protest against the . . .' Latil, p.228
129 'Films roll like heads . . .' Peter Forster, 'Fiasco at Cannes', *Evening Standard*, 20 May 1968
129 'Everything you say . . .' RTBV TV footage, Cannes, May 1968
129 'little kids playing . . . '*Variety*, 12 June 1968
129 'My role was to encourage the festival jury to resign . . .' French (ed.), *Malle on Malle*, ibid., p.183
130 'the directors of the Berlin and Venice festivals . . .' David Robinson, 'Fin de Fiesta', *Financial Times*, 21 May 1968
130 'I became *persona non grata* . . . ' French (ed.), *Malle on Malle*, ibid., p.183

NOTES

130 'They were shocked by it . . .' Sandy Lieberson, authors' interview, September 2005

131 'There's not a single film . . .' RTBV TV footage, Cannes, May 1968

131 'It's not a matter of . . .' ibid.

131 'You're talking about solidarity . . .' ibid.

132 'the Ursula Andress of militancy' Truffaut, *Letters*, ibid., p.390

132 'It was selected for . . .' Peter Lennon, authors' interview, November 2005

133 'Godard is a poisonous little bastard . . .' ibid.

133 'Only revolutionarily appropriate films . . .' Peter Lennon, *Foreign Correspondent: Paris in the Sixties* (Picador, London 1994), pp.208–9

134 'having nothing to do . . .' Latil, p.233

134 'You have to remember . . .' Lieberson, authors' interview.

134 'It was a great moment . . .' French (ed.), *Malle on Malle*, ibid., p.184

135 'There's still the same starchy atmosphere . . .' Jacob, 'La revolution récupérée', *Les Nouvelles Littéraires*, 15 May 1969 in *Cahiers du cinéma*, 'Histoires de Cannes', p.81

135 'divest it of its . . .' Latil, p.238

136 'to open up the selection . . .' Pierre-Henri Deleau (ed.), *La Quinzaine des réalisateurs a Cannes, cinéma en liberté: 1969–1993* (Editions de la Martinière, Paris 1993), p.16

136 'Favre Le Bret wasn't ignorant . . . leftist thugs' ibid., pp.17–8

136 'I didn't hide the fact . . .' ibid., p.18

137 'saved the Cannes Festival . . .' Albicocco interviewed for *Cannes et L'Histoire*

138 'On the first day . . .' Pierre-Henri Deleau, *La Quinzaine des réalisateurs*, ibid., p.27

138 'One morning . . .' ibid., pp.29–30

138 'Is cinema still an art . . .' Maurice Bessy, 'Peau Neuve', *Le Bulletin du Festival International de Cannes*, 8 May 1969

139 'one rushes to the aid . . .' Jacob, 'La revolution récupérée', *Les Nouvelles Littéraires*, 15 May 1969 in *Cahiers du cinéma*, 'Histoires de Cannes', p.81

140 'Even the chambermaids . . .' Penelope Houston, 'Ifs and buts at Cannes', *Spectator*, 30 May 1969

140 'Emotionally, the film is revolutionary . . .' Lindsay Anderson, *Never Apologise: Collected Writings*, edited by Paul Ryan (Plexus, London, 2004), p.119

141 'in the style both of . . .' Richard Roud, *Guardian*, 24 May 1969

141 'a fair response . . .' Michel Capdenac, 'Le triomphe des rebelles', *Les Lettres françaises*, 25 May 1969

143 'We were waylaid . . .' Peter Biskind, *Easy Riders and Raging Bulls: How the Sex 'n' Drugs 'n' Rock 'n' Roll Generation Saved Hollywood* (Bloomsbury, London, 1998), p.81

143 'Fox said, "You're going . . ." . . . tossed away to the drive-ins at that time . . .' Robert Altman, authors' interview, February 2006

250   CANNES

144 'like a telly commercial . . .' Alexander Walker, 'Mao and MGM . . .',
Evening Standard, 14 May 1970
144 'the companies are ready . . .' David Robinson, 'The two Americas', *Financial Times*, 15 May 1970

VII Adventures in Cinema

145 'To the best of our abilities . . .' *The Ramon Magsaysay Award in Journalism, Literature and Creative Communication Arts to Lino Brocka* (Ramon Magsaysay Award Foundation, Manila 1985), p.9
146 'apparently overestimated . . .' John Gillet, *Guardian*, 23 May 1960
146 'shocked by the display . . .' Festival Bulletin, 17 May 1960
146 'the most important film . . .' Geoffrey Nowell-Smith, *L'Avventura* (BFI Publishing, London 1997), p.54
147 'Eros is sick . . .' Seymour Chatman & Guido Fink (eds.), *L'Avventura, Michelangelo Antonioni, director* (Rutgers University Press, New Brunswick & London 1989), pp.178–9
149 'I was convinced . . .' Latil, p.258
149 'when Lars von Trier writes . . .' Jacob, authors' interview
149 'It was felt . . .' ibid.
150 'We have always placed . . . a struggle against censorship' ibid.
151 'There can be reprisals . . .' ibid.
152 'something like Clint Eastwood . . .' J. Hoberman, 'Listen, Turkey', *Village Voice*, 23 November 1982
153 'Pierre went into business . . .' Tony Rayns, authors' interview, November 2005
155 'Mrs Marcos was very upset . . .' Rissient, authors' interview, January 2006
156 'Lino said . . .' ibid.
156 'Of course . . .' *The Ramon Magsaysay Award*, ibid., p.25
159 'this mediocre film . . .' Armand Bérard, *Cinq années au Palais Farnèse: un ambassadeur se souvient* (Plon, Paris 1982), p.9
160 'the producers . . .' Latil, p.195
161 'The big prize went . . .' Anthony Burgess, *You've Had Your Time, Being the Second Part of the Confessions of Anthony Burgess* (Heinemann, London 1990), p.317
161 'the young pig . . .' ibid., p.317–18
161 'This time the festival . . .' Latil, p.196
162 'the main event . . .' Jack Lang interviewed for *Cannes et l'histoire*
162 'a privileged mélange . . .' Serge Le Péron, 'Les festivaliers (de gauche) sont contents', *Libération*, 26 May 1981
163 'At the Lenin Shipyards . . .' Andrzej Wajda, *Wajda Films 2* (Wydawnictwa Artystyczne I Filmowe, Warsaw 1996), p.135

NOTES 251

164 'The festival on the Côte d'Azur . . .' *Izvestia*, 6 June 1981, ibid., p.154
165 'America is the bogeyman . . .' *Le Monde*, 16 May 1989 in *Cahiers du cinéma*, 'Histoires de Cannes', p.131
166 'The way is wide open . . .' Otar Iosseliani, *Cannes et l'histoire*
166 'Coca-Cola barbarism . . .' Andrzej Zulawski, ibid.

VIII The Jury Speaks

167 'A pattern was established . . .' Andrew Sarris, 'The Last Word on Cannes', *American Film*, May 1982, p.30
167 'The Cannes jury . . .' Thomas, authors' interview, November 2005
167 'How can there . . .' Altman, authors' interview, February 2006
169 'If you look . . .' John Boorman, authors' interview, June 2005
168 'The awards . . .' Jacob, author's interview
169 'Because we are . . .' Jacob, authors' interview, September 2005
170 'What they've absolutely . . .' Colin MacCabe, authors' interview, August 2005
170 'Gilles called . . .' Bernardo Bertolucci, authors' interview, November 2005
171 'Because it's a . . .' Kazuo Ishiguro, authors' interview, September 2005
171 'I have seldom . . .' Mike Leigh, authors' interview, November 2005
172 'Norman Mailer was . . .' Thomas, authors' interview, November 2005
173 'This is the convention . . .' Leigh, authors' interview
173 'When we first met . . .' Ishiguro, authors' interview
173 'Pakula was both . . .' Michel Ciment, authors' interview, July 2005
173 'Yves Montand . . .' Thomas, authors' interview
174 'On each film . . .' Boorman, authors' interview
174 'We watched twenty-one . . .' Leigh, authors' interview
175 'Unanimity came very quickly . . .' Ciment, authors' interview
175 'All these incredible cleavages . . .' Agnès Varda, authors' interview, September 2005
175 'That was quite a difficult mission . . .' Bertolucci, authors' interview
176 'Gilles Jacob sits . . .' Ishiguro, authors' interview
177 'Personally I love Abbas . . .' Leigh, authors' interview
177 'That year there were two . . .' Ciment, authors' interview
178 'Through the overlapping reigns . . .' Andrew Sarris, 'The Last Word on Cannes', *American Film*, May 1982, p.30.
178 'In 1981 I had *Excalibur* . . .' Boorman, authors' interview
179 'It was staggering . . .' Lieberson, authors' interview
180 'Do you think . . .' ibid.
180 '*Apocalypse Now* is . . .' Ciment, authors' interview
181 'It's a terrible job . . . studios and directors' Dirk Bogarde, *Backcloth* (Viking, Middlesex 1986), p.291

252 CANNES

181 'The jury was not . . .' ibid., p.291–2
182 'What about the American films . . .' ibid., p.293–4
183 'My experience of it . . .' Boorman, authors' interview
183 'My experience . . .' Leigh, authors' interview
183 'It's mad to think . . .' Thomas, authors' interview
184 'Whenever we met people . . .' Ciment, authors' interview
184 'I've been on other juries . . .' Leigh, authors' interview
184 'We were allowed . . .' Ishiguro, authors' interview
186 'You get up at 7 a.m . . . .' Leigh, authors' interview
187 'My experience was . . .' David Cronenberg, interview with S.F. Said,
December 2002
187 'I am absolutely sure . . .' Ciment, interview
188 'Apparently the actress . . .' Cronenberg, interview with S.F. Said, December 2002
188 'They whisk you away . . .' Boorman, authors' interview
188 'Clint had a house . . .' Ishiguro, authors' interview
189 'It's very difficult . . . And that's that' Leigh, authors' interview
191 'I have to say . . .' Ishiguro, authors' interview

IX Selection

193 'They're looking for . . .' Thomas, authors' interview
194 'Being Italian . . . unique' Bertolucci, authors' interview
195 'What is . . . all the films' Jacob, authors' interview
196 'In the final selection . . .' ibid.
196 'About a dozen times . . .' Ciment, authors' interview
196 'What I was doing . . .' Rissient, authors' interview
197 'I knew Jean Renoir . . .' ibid.
197 'I had liked . . .' ibid.
197 'I guess I can say . . .' ibid.
198 'Pierre started scouting . . .' Rayns, authors' interview
198 'From January first . . .' Thierry Frémaux, authors' interview, February 2006
199 'Gilles Jacob was . . .' Ciment, authors' interview
200 'In the cases . . .' Leigh, authors' interview
200 'My decision was . . .' Frémaux, authors' interview
201 'Apparently Thierry's preoccupation . . .' Leigh, authors' interview
202 'Mike Leigh went . . .' Frémaux, authors' interview
202 'When I produced . . .' Boorman, authors' interview
203 'The French are . . .' Rayns, authors' interview
203 'In order to give . . .' Ciment, authors' interview

NOTES	253

204 'It's bullshit . . .' Frémaux, authors' interview
205 'The studios only wanted . . .' Jacob, authors' interview
205 'The publicity and marketing . . .' Lieberson, authors' interview
205 'You've got to understand . . .' ibid.
206 'There was a period . . .' Geoff Andrew, authors' interview, October 2005
206 'The American majors . . .' Jacob, authors' interview
207 'This is a discussion . . .' Frémaux, authors' interview
207 'There's been a further shift . . .' Rayns, authors' interview
207 'It's true that . . .' Frémaux, authors' interview
208 'Berlin was the first . . .' Rayns, authors' interview
209 'Wong Kar Wai made . . .' Rayns, authors' interview
210 'The policy of Cannes . . .' Jacob, authors' interview

X Festivalworld

211 'Film festivals have become . . .' Jean-Michel Frodon, 'Les festivals, l'exception culturelle, la mondialisation', *Cahiers du cinéma*, 601, May 2005, p.36
211 'For twelve days . . .' Jacob, authors' interview
211 'Cannes is both . . .' Varda, authors' interview
212 'What is great . . .' Ciment, authors' interview
213 'I think one of the . . .' Simon Field, authors' interview, August 2005
215 'If we have undertaken . . .' Jacob, authors' interview
215 'destined to be seen . . .' Jonathan Rosenbaum, *Movie Wars: How Hollywood and the Media Conspire to Limit What Film We Can See* (A Cappella, Chicago 2000), pp.160–1
216 'Utter rubbish . . .' Rayns, authors' interview
217 'the recognition I've received . . .' Abbas Kiarostami, 'Nous, les artistes, sommes la minorité', *Cahiers du cinéma* 601, May 2005, p.40
217 'My kind of film-making . . .' Kiarostami, authors' interview, January 2006
218 'What West German film . . .' Richard Pena, 'Iranian Cinema at the Festivals', *Cinéaste*, Summer 2006, p.40
219 'I believe the films . . .' Alberto Elena, *The Cinema of Abbas Kiarostami* (Saqi, London 2005), p.106
220 'few hundred spineless . . .' ibid. p.116
221 'I'd rather say . . .' Kiarostami, authors' interview
221 'I thought it was . . .' Rissient, authors' interview
221 'Abbas thought of something . . .' ibid.
222 'He told me . . .' Kiarostami interviewed by Bill Horrigan, Wexner Center for the Arts, Ohio State University, Columbus, Ohio, March 1998 *www.iranian.com/Arts/Aug98/Kiarostami* (accessed September 2006)
222 'Personally, to have won . . .' Kiarostami, authors' interview

254 CANNES

223 'The number of cinemas . . .' ibid.
223 'instead of making films . . .' Hamid Dabashi, *Close Up: Iranian Cinema Past, Present and Future* (Verso, London 2001), p.266
224 'changed for ever . . .' ibid., p.264
225 'Those who control . . .' Dabashi, ibid., p.259
225 'For me, Kiarostami . . .' Jonathan Rosenbaum & Merhrnaz Saeed-Vafa, *Abbas Kiarostami* (University of Illinois Press, Urbana Illinois 2003), p.81–2
226 'How? Because . . .' ibid., p.82
226 'My point is . . .' ibid., p.94
226 'if you wanted to . . .' Godfrey Cheshire, 'How to Read Kiarostami', *Cinéaste* vol 25 no 4, 2000, p.11
226 'Pardon me . . .' Cheshire, 'Poetry and Sufism: A guide to understanding Kiarostami's latest film', *Independent Weekly* (US), 13 December 2000
228 'The success of . . .' Marijke de Valck, *Film Festivals: History and Theory of a European Phenomenon that Became a Global Network* (Unpublished PhD thesis, Amsterdam University, Forthcoming Amsterdam University Press)
229 'Whereas the glamour . . .' ibid.

Bibliography

Absalom, Roger, *Flashpoints: The May Events 1968* (Longman, London 1971)

Acevedo-Munoz, Ernesto R., *Buñuel and Mexico: The Crisis of National Cinema* (University of California Press, Berkeley & L.A. 2003)

Atack, Margaret, *May '68 in French Fiction and Film* (Oxford University Press, 1999)

Aude, Françoise, *Ciné-Modeles, Cinéma d'Elles* (Editions L'Age d'Homme, Lausanne 1981)

Baecque, Antoine de, *Les Cahiers du cinéma Histoire d'une revue Tome II: Cinéma, tours détours 1959–1981* (Editions Cahiers du cinéma, Paris 1991)

Ballard, J.G., *Super-Cannes* (Flamingo, London 2000)

Barber, Benjamin R., *Jihad vs. McWorld* (Times Books, New York 1995)

Barker, Martin; Arthurs, Jane & Harindranath, Ramaswami, *The Crash Controversy: Censorship Campaigns and Film Reception* (Wallflower, London and New York 2001)

Biskind, Peter, *Down and Dirty Pictures: Miramax and the Rise of the Independent Film* (Bloomsbury, London 2004)

Bondanella, Peter, *The Cinema of Federico Fellini* (Princeton University Press, Princeton NJ 1992)

Bondanella, Peter, *Italian Cinema: From Neorealism to the Present* (Continuum, New York 2001)

Bresson, Jean & Brun, Mario, *Les Vingt Marches Aux Etoiles: La Fabuleuse Histoire du Festival de Cannes* (Editions Alain Lefeuvre, Paris 1982)

Bretton, Emile; Guilloux, Michel; Perron, Tangui & Roy, Jean, *Nous avons tant de voir ensemble – Cinéma et mouvement social* (VO Éditions, Montreuil 2000)

CinémAction: 'Christianisme et cinéma', May 1996

Cowie, Peter, *Revolution – The Explosion of World Cinema in the Sixties* (Faber & Faber, London 2004)

Cuman, Nathalie, *Cannes fait son cinéma* (Timée Editions, Boulogne 2005)

CANNES

Dine, Philip, *Images of the Algerian War: French Fiction and Film, 1954–1992* (Oxford University Press, US 1995)

Djian, Jean-Michel, *Politique culturelle: la fin d'un mythe* (Gallimard, Paris 2005)

Douin, Jean-Luc, *Dictionnaire de la Censure au cinéma* (Presses Universitaires de France, Paris 1998)

Ebert, Roger, *Two Weeks in the Midday Sun: A Cannes Notebook* (Andrews & McMeel, Kansas City 1988)

Elsaesser, Thomas, 'Film Festival Networks: The New Topographies of Cinema in Europe' in Elsaesser, T., *European Cinema: Face to Face with Hollywood* (Amsterdam University Press, Amsterdam 2005)

Ethis, Emmanuel, *Aux marches du palais: le festival de Cannes sous le regard des sciences sociales* (Documentation française, Paris 2001)

Evans, Peter William & Santaolalla, Isabel, *Luis Buñuel: New Readings* (BFI Publishing, London 2004)

Frodon, Jean-Michel, *Au Sud du Cinéma: Films d'Afrique, d'Asie et d'Amérique latine* (Cahiers du cinéma/ARTE Editions, Paris 2004)

Fumaroli, Marc, *l'Etat Culturel: essai sur une réligion moderne* (le livre de poche, Paris 1993)

Goldman, William, *Hype and Glory* (Futura, London 1991)

Haghighat, Mamad, *Histoire du cinéma iranien 1900–1999* (Editions BPI Centre Georges Pompidou, Paris 1999)

Harbord, Janet, 'Film festivals: media events and spaces of flow' in Harbord, J., *Film Cultures* (Sage, London 2002)

Harvey, Sylvia, *May '68 and Film Culture* (BFI Publishing, London 1978)

Higginbotham, Virginia, *Spanish Film under Franco* (University of Texas Press, Austin, Texas 1988)

Hoberman, J., *The Dream Life: Movies, Media and the Mythology of the Sixties* (The New Press, New York 2003)

Jacob, Gilles, *Les visiteurs de Cannes – cinéastes à l'œuvre* (Hatier, Paris 1992)

Kedward, Rod, *La Vie en Bleu: France and the French since 1900* (Allen Lane, London 2005)

MacCabe, Colin, *Godard: A Portrait of the Artist at 70* (Bloomsbury, London 2003)

Mirkine, Léo, *Festival de Cannes: 30 ans de photographie* (Contrejour, Paris 1981)

Moseley, Rachel (ed.), *Fashioning Film Stars: Dress, Culture, Identity* (BFI Publishing, London 2005)

Nichols, Bill, 'Global Image Consumption in Age of Late Capitalism', *East-West Film Journal*, vol 8 no 1, January 1994

Nichols, Bill, 'Discovering Form, Inferring Meaning: New Cinemas and the Film Festival Circuit', *Film Quarterly*, vol.47 no.3 Spring 1994

BIBLIOGRAPHY 257

Pasolini, Pier Paolo, 'The Catholic Irrationalism of Fellini', *Film Criticism* vol 9 no 1 October 1984

Perren, Alisa, 'Sex, lies and marketing: Miramax and the Development of the Quality Indie Blockbuster', *Film Quarterly*, vol 55 no 2, 2001

Perron, Tangui, *Accords, raccords, désaccords – Syndicalisme et cinéma* (Institut CGT d'Histoire Social, Seine-Saint-Denis 2002)

Philippe, Claude-Jean, *Cannes le festival* (Editions Fernand Nathan et Sipa-Press, Paris 1987)

Polanski, Roman, *Roman* (Heineman, London 1984)

Puttnam, David, *The Undeclared War: The Struggle for Control of the World's Film Industry* (HarperCollins, London 1997)

Roger, Philippe, *L'Ennemi Américain: Généalogie de l'antiaméricanisme français* (Editions Du Seuil, Paris 2002)

Servat, Henry Jean, *In the Spirit of Cannes: From A–Z* (Assouline, Paris 2004)

Server, Lee, *Robert Mitchum: Baby I Don't Care* (Faber & Faber, London 2001)

Sinclair, Iain, *Crash* (BFI Publishing, London 1999)

Sklar, Robert, 'Beyond Hoopla: The Cannes Film Festival and Cultural Significance', *Cinéaste*, vol 22 no 3, June 1996

Stringer, Julian, 'Global Cities and the International Film Festival Economy' in Shiel, M. & Fitzmaurice, T. (eds.), *Cinema and the City: Film and Urban Societies in a Global Context* (Blackwell, Oxford 2001)

Télérama magazine: *50 ans de Festival* (Paris, 1997)

Turan, Kenneth, *From Sundance to Sarajevo: Film Festivals and the World They Made* (University of California Press, Berkeley 2002)

Variety magazine: *Cannes – Fifty Years of Sun, Sex and Celluloid: Behind the Scenes at the World's Most Famous Film Festival* (Hyperion, New York 1997)

Vogel, Amos, *Film as a Subversive Art* (Weidenfeld and Nicolson, London 1974)

Walker, Stephen, *King of Cannes: A Journey into the Underbelly of the Movies* (Bloomsbury, London 2002)

Williams, Alan, *Republic of Images: A History of French Filmmaking* (Harvard University Press, 1992)

Documentaries

Paparazzi (dir: Jacques Rozier)

Visions series 1, Channel 4 23/5/1983, item on the Cannes Film Festival (courtesy of Large Door Ltd)

Visions series 3, Channel 4 28/5/1985, item on the Cannes Film Festival (courtesy of Large Door Ltd)

Cannes: The 400 Blows (dir: Gilles Nadeau)

Waiting For Harvey: A Beginner's Guide to Cannes (dir: Stephen Walker)

Websites

www.festival-cannes.fr
www.fiapf.org/intfilmfestivals.asp
www.quinzaine-realisateurs.com

Acknowledgements

The authors wish to thank those who kindly agreed to spill the beans (ever so diplomatically, of course) about Cannes: Robert Altman, Geoff Andrew, Bernardo Bertolucci, John Boorman, Jean-Pierre Burdin, Michel Ciment, Simon Field, Thierry Frémaux, Kazuo Ishiguro, Jean-Pierre Jeancolas, Gilles Jacob, Abbas Kiarostami, Mike Leigh, Peter Lennon, Sandy Lieberson, Colin MacCabe, Tony Rayns, Pierre Rissient, Ousmane Sembene, Bertrand Tavernier, Jeremy Thomas, Rita Tushingham and Agnès Varda .

Many thanks also to the following, without whose research assistance this book would not have been possible: Sean Delaney, Sarah Currant and the staff of the British Film Institute library, Marie-Pierre Hauville at the Cannes Festival office, Marijke de Valck and Thomas Elsaesser at the University of Amsterdam, Valdo Kneubuhler and the staff of the Bibliothèque de Film (BiFi) at the Cinémathèque Française; the staff of the British Library and the Kobal Picture Collection. Salutations to Richard T. Kelly at Faber for scrupulously shepherding the project from idea to execution.

And warmest thanks to Kaleem Aftab, Kevin Biderman, Paul Buck, Fiona Candlin, Lee Corless, Shelagh Cox, Paul Cronin, Simon Cropper, Gareth Evans, Simon Hattenstone, Pascale Lamche, Yann Perreau, Julien Planté, Peter Matthews, Dominique Martinez, Simon Payne, Jeremiah Quinn, S.F. Said, Libby Saxton, Verena Stackelberg, Paul Tickell and Jason Wood whose wise words, cold drinks and hot dinners kept us both going.

Index

A Bout de Souffle (Jean-Luc Godard), 64, 77, 153
Accident (Joseph Losey), 181
Act of Love (Anatole Litvak), 61
'Actors Masterclass', 236
Adalen 31 (Bo Wideberg), 140–1
Adjani, Isabelle, 174, 184
Afrique 50 (René Vautier), 159
Age d'Or, L' (Luis Buñuel), 79
Alain-Fournier, 136
Albicocco, Jean-Gabriel, 135–8
Albinus, Jens, 119
Alejandro, Julio, 81
Alessandrini, Goffredo, 13, 231
Algeria, 156–62
    Cannes 1961, 83
        Cannes and the war in, 145
        Lakhdar-Hamina's Palme D'Or, 7
        Nuit et brouillard and 47,
        political consciousness absent
    during war in, 93, 123
    Z and, 142
All About My Mother (Pedro Almodóvar), 186
All or Nothing (Mike Leigh), 190, 200
All That Jazz (Bob Fosse), 177, 238
'All the Cinemas of the World', 236
Allende, Salvador, 151

Almodóvar, Pedro, 84, 186, 228
Altman, Robert, 108, 143, 167, 205, 233
Amants réguliers, Les (Philippe Garrel), 127
Amis du Film, Les, 111
Amores Perros (González Inárritu), 202
And God Created Woman (Roger Vadim), 52, 62–6, 71
Anderson, Lindsay, 42, 140, 233
Andrei Rublev (Andrei Tarkovsky), 142
Andress, Ursula, 132
Andrew, Geoff, 206
Angel (Neil Jordan), 202
Angelopoulos, Theo, 116
Années Cannes, Les, 234
Anticoncept, L' (Gil Wolman), 97
Antoine and Antoinette (Jacques Becker), 240
Antonio das Mortes (Glauber Rocha), 142
Antonioni, Michelangelo, 73, 78, 123, 146–8, 233
Apocalypse Now (Francis Ford Coppola), 177, 179–81, 234, 238
Apple, The (Samira Makhmalbaf), 223, 235
Aquino, Benigno, 155

INDEX

Arcady, Alexandre, 160
Arnold, Andrea, 213
Arts, 99
Ashes and Diamonds (Andrzej Wajda), 162
Association of Film-makers (Poland), 163
Au Coeur du Festival (Gilles Jacob), 230, 236
Au Hasard, Balthazar (Robert Bresson), 112, 131
Aurenche, Jean, 40–1
Aussi Longue Absence, Une (Henri Colpi), 84
Autant-Lara, Claude, 99
Auteuil, Daniel, 156
Aux Marches du Palais (Séverine Caneele), 186
Avoir 20 ans dans les Aurès (René Vautier), 159–60
Avventura, L' (Michelangelo Antonioni), 73, 75, 113–15, 146–8, 233

Backcloth (Dirk Bogarde), 181
Bagdadi, Maroun, 116
Baker, Peter, 75
Ballad of a Soldier (Grigori Chukhrai), 75
Ballad of Narayama (Shohei Imamura), 238
Ballard, J.G., 235
Bande à part (Jean-Luc Godard), 113
Barber, Benjamin R., 225
Barbin, Pierre, 125
Bardot, Brigitte, 60–8
    Cannes' impact on her career, 59
    contradictions of image of, 8
    fame becomes a monster for, 70

    impact of, 2
    Kirk Douglas and, 55
    1967 return, 233
    photos with the Fleet, 76
Barton Fink (Coen Brothers), 172, 206, 235, 238
Barzman, Ben, 44
Bataille du Rail, La (René Clément), 23, 231, 240
Batalov, Alexei, 30
Battle in Heaven (Carlos Reygedas), 77
Battle of Algiers (Gillo Pontecorvo), 158–9
Baudelaire, Charles, 95
Baxter, John, 84
Baye, Nathalie, 110
Bazin, André, 21–3, 37–41, 49
Beau Serge, Le (Claude Chabrol), 102
Benayoun, Robert, 146
Benichou, Maurice, 157
Bercy, 124
Bergman, Ingmar, 6, 36, 75, 77, 232–3, 235
Bergman, Ingrid, 105
Berlin (Yuli Raizman), 19
Berlin Film Festival, 57–8, 144, 203, 207–8, 212, 214, 232
Berlin Wall, 235
Bernanos, Georges, 114
Bertolucci, Bernardo, 105, 111, 124, 127, 170–1, 194
Besson, Luc, 194
Bessy, Maurice, 60, 149, 178, 195, 234
Best Intentions (Bille August), 238
Bête Humaine, La (Jean Renoir), 197
Beverly Hills, 51
Biarritz, 40

INDEX

Bidone, Il (Federico Fellini), 73
Bienvenido, Monsieur Marshall (Luis García Berlanga), 34
Billard, Pierre, 49, 73
Björk, 235
Black Orpheus (Marcel Camus), 239
Black Panthers, 158
Blackboard (Samira Makhmalbaf), 224, 236
Blair, Betsy, 42–3
Blethyn, Brenda, 190
Blier, Bertrand, 110
Blow-Up (Michelangelo Antonioni), 239
Blum, Léon, 21
Blum-Byrnes Accord, 21, 22, 26, 67
Bo, Sonica, 97
Body and Soul (Robert Rossen), 43
Bogarde, Dirk, 116, 179, 181–3
Bonnaire, Sandrine, 114
Bonnie and Clyde (Arthur Penn), 139, 143
Boorman, John, 168, 174, 176, 183, 188, 202
Bory, Jean-Louis, 124
Bourges, Yvon, 89–90
Bowie, David, 115
Brasseur, Claude, 113
Breaking the Waves (Lars von Trier), 117, 118
Bresson, Robert, 87, 100, 101, 111, 114
Breton, André, 79
Brief Encounter (David Lean), 240
Brocka, Lino, 145, 150, 154–6
Broken Blossoms (D.W. Griffith), 125
Broken Flowers (Jim Jarmusch), 175
Brook, Peter, 127

Brougham, Henry, 50–1
Browning, Tod, 98
Bundestag, 46
Buñuel, Luis, 6, 29, 75, 79–87, 197, 233
Burgess, Anthony, 160, 161
Burke, Kathy, 174, 190
Burton, Richard, 131
Burton, Tim, 35
Busman (Yilmaz Güney), 152

Caché (Michael Haneke), 156–7, 175
Cahiers du cinéma
    auteur theory, 78
    Eustache, 106
      founders, 22, 136
      Kiarostami, 216, 219–20
      Langlois protest, 125
      Rivette, 88
      Truffaut, 99
Cal (Pat O'Connor), 182
Calcutta (Louis Malle), 130, 135
Caméra d'Or, 210, 217
Cammell, Donald, 130
Campion, Jane, 153, 235
Caneele, Séverine, 186
'Cannes Classics', 236
Carax, Leos, 203
Carlton Hotel, Cannes, 16, 60
Carmel, California, 69
Caron, Leslie, 52
Cartier, Raymond, 62
Casino (Martin Scorsese), 204
Catch 22 (Mike Nichols), 143
Catholic Church
    Buñuel, 79–80, 82
    censorship battles with, 6
    La Dolce Vita, 77, 82

INDEX

Lettrists, 96
mid fifties France, 63
La Religieuse, 88–9
Rocky Road to Dublin, 132
Cavalier, Alain, 158
Cayla, Véronique, 235
Cayrol, Jean, 45, 46
Celui qui doit mourir (Jules Dassin), 44
Centre National de la Cinématographie (CNC), 86
Ceylan, Nuri Bilge, 212–13
Cézanne, Paul, 54
Chabrol, Claude, 102
Chan Wook Park, 209
Chaplin, Geraldine, 133
Chelsea Girls (Andy Warhol), 125
Chère Louise (Philippe de Broca), 108
Chéreau, Patrice, 172, 236
Cheshire, Godfrey, 226
Chien Andalou, Un (Luis Buñuel), 79
Child, The (Jean-Pierre Dardenne & Luc Dardenne), 237
Chinatown (Roman Polanski), 117
Chinoise, La (Jean-Luc Godard), 131
Chirac, Jacques, 36, 178
Chronique des Années de Braise (Mohammed Lakhdar-Hamina), 160, 234, 238
Chukhrai, Grigori, 30, 75, 232, 233
CIA, 151
Ciment, Michel
on Cronenberg, 187
on Frémaux, 199
French films at Cannes, 203
on Jacob, 183, 196, 199
juries that declare ties, 177
on Pakula, 173

The Tree of Wooden Clogs, 175
the unexpected at Cannes, 212
Cimino, Michael, 205
Cinecittà, 72
Ciné-Fondation, 210, 214, 236
Cinema Paradiso (Giuseppe Tornatore), 65, 78
Cinémathèque Française, 124–8
Cinemonde, 59
City of God (Fernando Meirelles), 204
Clayburgh, Jill, 177
Clemenceau, Georges, 32
Clément, René, 23
Cliffhanger (Renny Harlin), 206
Clift, Montgomery, 28
Clooney, George, 61
Clouzot, Henri-Georges, 32–4
CNC, 86
Cocteau, Jean, 31–5
at Cannes, 6
jury president, 232
on Langlois, 125
Palme d'Or and, 37,
takes Godard etc under wing, 40
on Technicolor, 52
Coen Brothers, 149, 206, 214, 235
Cold War, 3, 6, 19, 25, 30, 145, 168
Colpi, Henri, 84
Columbia Pictures, 140
Columbia University, 144
Combat dans l'île (Alain Cavalier), 158
Commission de Contrôle Française, 85
Committee for the History of the Second World War, 45
Communist Party, 30
Concerned Artists of the Philippines, 155

Connery, Sean, 156
Conversation, The (Francis Ford Coppola), 238
Cook, the Thief, his Wife and her Lover, The (Peter Greenaway), 104
Cooper, Gary, 62
Coppola, Francis Ford, 35, 177, 179–80, 205, 234
Corman, Roger, 137
Costa-Gavras, Constantin, 140–2, 151
Cote d'Azur, 8, 10, 14, 50, 52, 54, 63
Cottrell, Pierre, 105
Coutard, Raoul, 132
Cranes Are Flying, The (Mikhail Kalatozov), 30, 233, 239
Crash (David Cronenberg), 113, 114, 235
Cream and Punishment (Noel Godin), 111
Croisette, Cannes, 2, 7, 58–9, 69, 77, 134
Cronenberg, David, 113, 186, 187–8, 235
Crossfire (Edward Dmytryk), 240
Cukor, George, 21
Cyrano De Bergerac (Jean-Paul Rappeneau), 175–6

Dabashi, Hamid, 224
Dada, 112
Dali, Salvador, 79
Damned, The (René Clément), 240
Dancer in the Dark (Lars von Trier), 118, 235, 237
Daney, Serge, 112, 115
Danton (Andrzej Wajda), 165
Dardenne brothers, 5, 175, 186

Dassin, Jules, 42, 43–4, 135
Dauman, Anatole, 45
de Baecque, Antoine, 93
de Beauvoir, Simone, 66
de Gaulle, Charles, 122
de Gaulle, Yvonne, 89
de Hadeln, Moritz, 207
de Havilland, Olivia, 78, 123
de Maupassant, Guy, 51
De Sica, Vittorio, 38
de Valck, Marijke, 228–9
Dean, James, 65
Death of Mr Lazarescu (Cristi Puiu), 215
Debord, Guy-Ernest, 97, 98, 232
Debray, Charles, 68
Deldick, Françoise, 60
Deleau, Pierre Henri, 138
Deneuve, Catherine, 114, 185, 222, 235
Depardieu, Gérard, 114, 165, 176
Détective (Jean-Luc Godard), 110, 113, 174
Diderot, Denis, 88–90, 93
Dionysus, 53
Do the Right Thing (Spike Lee), 9
Dogme 95, 118–19
Dogville (Lars von Trier), 118
Dolce Vita, La (Federico Fellini), 71–5, 77–8, 82, 84, 146, 233, 239
Domergue, Jean-Gabriel, 15
Doniol-Valcroze, Jacques, 136, 138
Dors, Diana, 60
Douglas, Kirk, 55, 61, 67, 232
Dreamers, The (Bernardo Bertolucci), 124
Du rififi chez les hommes (Jules Dassin), 43

266 INDEX

Dubcek, Alexander, 122
Dumbo (Walt Disney), 240
Dumont, Bruno, 186
Duras, Marguerite, 84

East of Eden (Elia Kazan), 42
Eastwood, Clint, 69, 113, 153, 173
Easy Rider (Dennis Hopper), 137,
    139, 141, 233
Ecole de Nice, 54
Eel, The (Imamura Shohei), 237
Eisner, Lotte, 125
Eissler, Hans, 45
Ekberg, Anita, 72–3
El (Luis Buñuel), 232
Element of Crime, The (Lars von
    Trier), 95, 116, 118
Elephant (Gus van Sant), 172, 236, 237
Endfield, Cy, 42
English, James F., 53
English Patient, The (Anthony
    Minghella), 171
Enrico, Robert, 138
Erlanger, Philippe
    Article 5, 45
    funding problems, 17
    as jury member, 31
        publishes book on Cannes
    town, 52
        recognises the Bardot factor, 59
        seeds of Cannes, 13, 15, 231
Ermler, Fridrikh, 18
Estates General of French Cinema,
    128, 135
Et Dieu créa la femme (Roger Vadim),
    52, 62–6, 71
Eternity and a Day (Theo Angelopou-
    los), 237

Europa (Lars von Trier), 116
Eustache, Jean, 103, 105–9, 234
Excalibur (John Boorman), 178
Exterminating Angel (Luis Buñuel), 84

Fahrenheit 9/11 (Michael Moore), 4,
    178, 237
Fajr Film Festival, 220
Farewell My Concubine (Chen Kaige),
    238
Fast Food Nation (Richard Linklater),
    193
Favre Le Bret, Robert
    Andrei Rublev, 142
    Apocalypse Now, 180
    Bardot's party, 67–8
    on Cocteau, 31
        dispute with Simenon, 74
        first appointments, 16, 231,
    232, 234
        long service of, 195
        1968 *evenements* and, 134–6
        Palme d'Or creation, 36–7
        replaced, 138
        Sagan and, 180–1
        Simone Silva backlash, 56
        Truffaut criticises, 100
        Trumbo, 196–7
        Viridiana, 83, 84, 86
        woos Americans, 33
Favreliére, Noel, 160
Fellini, Federico, 6, 71–5, 77, 233
Femme douce, Une (Robert Bresson),
    111
femme mariée, Une (Jean-Luc
    Godard), 91–2
Fernández, Emilio, 81
Ferréol, Andréa, 104

INDEX

Ferreri, Marco, 103–4, 107, 109, 119, 234

Ferzetti, Gabriele, 147

Festen (Thomas Vinterberg), 119

Festival du Film Maudit, 40

Festival International du Film (FIF), 231, 236

Feux de la chandeleur, Les (Serge Korber), 108

FIAPF, 136, 212

Field, Simon, 213

Fifth Element, The (Luc Besson), 194

Fifth Republic, 157

Figueroa (Miguel Delgado), 240

Film Français, Le, 23

Fireman's Ball, The (Milos Forman), 196

First Charge of the Machete (Manuel Octavio Gómez), 138

First World War, 32

Flor Silvestre (Emilio Fernández), 81

Fonda, Peter, 137, 139

Fondation Maeght, 54

Fontán, José Munoz, 83, 84, 85

Foreman, Karl, 139

Forman, Milos, 129, 133, 151, 196

Forty First, The (Grigori Chukhrai), 30, 232

Four in a Jeep (Leopold Lindtberg), 28

Fourth Republic, 26

Franco, General Francisco, 80, 81, 85–7

Freaks (Tod Browning), 98

Frémaux, Thierry, 3, 16, 198–204, 207, 213–14, 227, 235

French Beauty (Pascale Lamche), 67

French National Film School, 128

Friendly Persuasion (William Wyler), 100, 168, 239

Frodon, Jean-Michel, 211

From Here to Eternity (Fred Zinnemann), 41

Gance, Abel, 31

Garbo, Greta, 70

Garnier, Catherine, 106

Garrel, Philippe, 127

Gaslight (George Cukor), 21

Gate of Hell, The (Teinosuke Kinusaga), 41, 239

Gaydos, Steven, 203

Gdansk, 163

Genaud, Jerome, 200

Gendre, Henri, 14

Generation, A (Andrzej Wajda), 162

Gergely, François, 83

Germany, 32, 45–8, 215

Ghobadi, Bahman, 223

Gilda (King Vidor), 21

Gillett, John, 73

Giono, Jean, 84

Girardot, Annie, 108

Girl No. 217 (Mikhail Romm), 240

Giscard d'Estaing, Valéry, 109–10

Gnostics, 227

Go-Between, The (Joseph Losey), 239

Godard, Jean-Luc, 90–3, 110–15, 131–3

    Bardot and *Le Mépris*, 70

    Biarritz festival, 40

    censorship issues, 158

    on *The Idiots*, 119

      1968, 121

    nouvelle vague, 88

    Polanski's observation, 129

    Vadim sees his influence on, 64

Godard à la télé (Michel Royer), 112

INDEX

Godin, Noel, 111–12
Golstein, Jean-Isidore, 96–7, 98
Gómez, Manuel Octavio, 138
Gone with the Wind (Victor Fleming), 41, 71
Gould, Elliott, 111
Grand Hotel, 12, 14
Grand Meaulnes, Le (Jean-Gabriel Albicocco), 136
Grande Bouffe, La (Marco Ferreri), 103–5, 109, 119, 234
Grande Illusion, La (Jean Renoir), 13, 197, 231
Grant, Cary, 53
Greenaway, Peter, 104
Griffith, D.W., 19, 125
Gstaad, 51
Guerasimov, Sergei, 29
Guerre est Finie, La (Alain Resnais), 44
Güney, Yilmaz, 150–3

Hagmann, Stuart, 143
Hair (Milos Forman), 151
Hallyday, Johnny, 110
Haneke, Michael, 156, 175
Happy Together (Wong Kar Wai), 174
Haskell, Molly, 106, 108–9
Hays, Will, 25
Hays Code, 25, 65
Hays Office, 20
Head (Bob Rafelson), 137
Heaven's Gate (Michael Cimino), 205
Heller, Joseph, 143
Hellman, Lillian, 41
Hernani (Victor Hugo), 95, 148
Heroes of Chipka (Sergei Vassiliev), 30, 232
Hidden (Michael Haneke), 156–7, 175

Hill, George Roy, 160–1
Hilton, Paris, 5
Himmel Ohne Sterne (Helmut Kautner), 48
Hireling, The (Alan Bridges), 239
Hiroshima, mon amour (Alain Resnais), 44
Hitchcock, Alfred, 19, 21, 22, 53, 231
Hitler, Adolf, 13, 231
'Hollywood Ten', 41
Hommage to Kurosawa, 100
Home From the Hill (Vincente Minelli), 76
Hong Sang Soo, 209
Hopper, Dennis, 139, 140
Hopper, Hedda, 56
Hors la Vie (Maroun Bagdadi), 116
Hou-Hsiou Hsien, 154
Hour of the Furnaces (Fernando Solanas), 142
House Un-American Activities Committee (HUAC), 34, 41–2
Houston, Penelope, 140
Howe, James Wong, 43
Hugo, Victor, 15, 95
Humanité L' (Bruno Dumont), 186–7
Hunchback of Notre Dame (William Dieterle), 15
Hungary, 27, 231
Huozhe (Zhang Yimou), 176
Huppert, Isabelle, 177

I Confess (Alfred Hitchcock), 232
Idiots, The (Lars von Trier), 118–19
If . . . (Lindsay Anderson), 140, 141, 233, 239
Images (Robert Altman), 108
Inárritu, Alejandro González, 202

INDEX 269

Insiang (Lino Brocka), 155
Intolerance (D.W. Griffith), 19
Iosseliani, Otar, 165
Iran, 220, 222, 224
Ishiguro, Kazuo, 69, 171, 173, 176,
 184, 188, 191
Isou, Isidore, 96–7, 98, 232

Jacob, Gilles, 149–51, 194–6, 204–6,
 213–15
 appointed, 234
 book by, 148
 on Cannes, 209–11, 230
 criteria for awards, 168–9
 DVD (dedicated to Godard),
 112–13, 236
 hands over reins, 198
 Hollywood connections, 227
 Ishiguro on, 176
 1968, 134–5, 139
 praised, 183, 199
 Rossellini Prize, 219
 von Trier's apology, 117
Jagger, Bianca, 60
Jaguar (Lino Brocka), 155, 156
Janda, Krystyna, 150
Japan, 27, 231
Jarmusch, Jim, 175, 214
Jeancolas, Jean-Pierre, 122
Jeremiah Johnson (Sydney Pollack),
 197
Je t'aime, Je t'aime (Alain Resnais), 44
JFK (Oliver Stone), 141
Joffe, Roland, 182
Johnny Got His Gun (Dalton Trum-
 bo), 196–7
Johnston Office, 20
Jones, Terry, 87

Jordan, Neil, 202
Jules et Jim (François Truffaut), 106
Jürgens, Curd, 63
Jury Prize, 78, 87, 116, 119, 146,
 172, 224

Kael, Pauline, 148
Kagemusha (Akira Kurosawa), 177,
 238
Kalatozov, Mikhail, 20, 30
Kalfon, Jean-Pierre, 124
Kanal (Andrzej Wajda), 162
Kanun, 218
Kaplan, Nellie, 146
Karina, Anna, 88, 158
Karmitz, Marin, 217
Kast, Pierre, 127, 136
Kautner, Helmut, 48
Kaye, Danny, 53
Keeper of Promises (Anselmo Duarte),
 239
Kelly, Gene, 42
Kelly, Grace, 53, 56, 65
Kennedy, Robert, 122
Kensington and Chelsea, Royal Bor-
 ough of, 51
Kent State University, 144
Khatami, Mohammad, 222
Khomeini, Ayatollah, 224
Khrushchev, Nikita, 30
Kiarostami, Abbas, 177, 216–27
Kieslowski, Krzysztof, 228
King, Martin Luther, 122
Kings of the Road (Wim Wenders),
 149
Kinugasa, Teinosuke, 41
Kirkpatrick, Jeane, 164
Klein, Yves, 54

270 INDEX

Kluj Film Festival, 214
Knack . . . and how to get it, The
   (Richard Lester), 239
'Koker trilogy', 218
Korber, Serge, 108
Kubrick, Stanley, 157
Kundera, Milan, 9
Kurds, 152–3
Kurosawa, Akira, 177, 197, 199, 219
Kusturica, Emir, 35
Kwon-Taek, Im, 208

Lafont, Bernadette, 105–7
Lakhdar-Hamina, Mohammed, 7,
   159, 160, 161–2
Lambert, Gavin, 29
Lambrakis, Gregoris, 141
Lamche, Pascale, 67
Lang, Jack, 162, 182
Langlois, Henri, 93, 100, 124–7
Last Chance, The (Leopold Lintberg),
   240
Last Tango in Paris (Bernardo
   Bertolucci), 105
Latil, Loredana, 28
Laughton, Charles, 15
Léaud, Jean-Pierre, 106, 124
Lebrun, Françoise, 106
Lee, Spike, 9
Leigh, Mike, 5, 35, 171–4, 177,
   183–4, 186, 189–90, 199–202
Leigh, Vivien, 123
Lelouch, Claude, 128, 129, 132
Lemmon, Jack, 151
Lennon, John, 69
Lennon, Peter, 132–3
Leopard, The (Luchino Visconti), 78,
   239

Lerins, Ile de, 55
Lettrists, 96–9
Liaisons dangerueses, Les (Roger
   Vadim), 89
Liberated China (Sergei Guerasimov),
   29
Lieberson, Sandy, 130, 134, 179, 180,
   205
Liégeard, Stéphen, 50
Life and Nothing More (Abbas
   Kiarostami), 219
Lili (Charles Walters), 52
Lindtberg, Leopold, 28
Linklater, Richard, 193
Lion King, The (Walt Disney), 221
Liza (Marco Ferreri), 104
Locarno Film Festival, 219, 225
Lollobrigida, Gina, 30
Long Absence, The (Henry Colpi),
   239
Long Day's Journey Into Night (Sid-
   ney Lumet), 84
Loren, Sophia, 78, 201, 233
Losey, Joseph, 42, 181
Lost Weekend, The (Billy Wilder), 22,
   231, 240
Lowly City (Chetan Anand), 240
Lucas, George, 5, 208
Lucciano Serra: Pilote (Goffredo
   Alessandrini), 13, 231
Luhrmann, Baz, 202
Lumet, Sidney, 84
Lumière, Louis, 15
Lynch, David, 175–6, 204

MacCabe, Colin, 4, 170
Madonna, 66, 70
Magnan, Henry, 21–2

INDEX

Mailer, Norman, 172, 183
Majidi, Majid, 226
Makhmalbaf, Mohsen, 223
Makhmalbaf, Samira, 223–4, 235, 236
Malle, Louis, 64, 68, 124, 128–30, 133, 134–5
Malraux, André, 88, 90–3, 124, 126
Maman et la Putain, La (Jean Eustache), 103, 105–7, 109, 234
Man and a Woman, A (Claude Lelouch), 239
Man Between, The (Carol Reed), 55
Man Escaped, A (Robert Bresson), 168
Man of Iron (Andrzej Wajda), 162–5, 178, 181, 238
Man of Marble (Andrzej Wajda), 150–1, 163
Mann, Delbert, 42, 232
Mansfield, Jayne, 31
Manville, Lesley, 190
Marais, Jean, 35
Marché du Film, 7, 60, 207, 233
Marcos, Ferdinand, 154–6
María Candélaria (Emilio Fernández), 81, 240
Marker, Chris, 38
Marquand, Christian, 63
Marshall Plan, 34
Marty (Delbert Mann), 42, 232, 239
*M*A*S*H* (Robert Altman), 143, 144, 239
Massari, Lea, 146, 147, 160
Mastroianni, Marcello, 72, 78, 104
Maté, Rudolph, 21
Mauriac, Claude, 139
Maurois, André, 78
Mazars, Pierre, 160

McCarthy, Todd, 153
McDowell, Malcolm, 140
McLaren, Norman, 40
Meaning of Life, The (Terry Jones), 87, 104
Meerson, Mary, 125
Men Without Wings (Frantisek Cap), 240
Mendes, Sam, 190
Mépris, Le (Jean-Luc Godard), 70
Mexico, 80–1, 87
Midway (aircraft carrier), 62
Mikhalkov, Nikita, 176
Miller, Claude, 123
Miller, Henry, 74–5
Minnelli, Liza, 229
Minnelli, Vincente, 76
Miracle in Milan (Vittorio de Sica), 29, 232, 240
Miramax, 79, 140, 228
Mirren, Helen, 182
Mirror (Andrei Tarkovsky), 150
Miss Julie (Alf Sjoberg), 29, 240
Missing (Costas-Gavras), 151, 238
Mission, The (Roland Joffe), 182, 238
Mistons, Les (François Truffaut), 102
Mitchum, Robert, 55–7, 232
Mitterand, François, 23, 162, 165
MK2, 209
Monaco, 16
Monet, Claude, 54
Monkees, 137
Monroe, Marilyn, 56–7
Montand, Yves, 33–4, 141, 172, 173–4
Montez, Maria, 20
Monty Python's Life of Brian (Terry Jones), 87

272 INDEX

Moore, Grace, 12
Moore, Michael, 4, 178, 208, 236
Mordillat, Gérard, 123
Moreau, Jeanne, 36, 68, 107, 160, 170
Morecambe and Wise, 53
Moretti, Nanni, 221
Morin, Edgar, 49, 50
Mosley, Leonard, 61, 65
Mostra Internazionale d'Arte Cinematografico, 12
Motion Pictures and Producers Association of America (MPAA), 25
Moulin Rouge (Baz Luhrmann), 207
Mr Arkardin (Orson Welles), 100
Mrs Parker and the Vicious Circle (Alan Rudolph), 184–5
Muller, Marco, 219
Mur, Le (Yilmaz Güney), 153
Murdoch, Rupert, 185
Music Box, The (Walt Disney), 240
Mussolini, Benito, 2, 12
My Country: Double-Edged Knife (Lino Brocka), 156
My Lives (Edmund White), 4

Nair, Mira, 171
Naked (Mike Leigh), 5, 190, 200
Napoule, Gulf of, 50
National Geographic, 225
Nazarin (Luis Buñuel), 81
Neff, Hildegard, 55
New Wave, 64
Next Voice You Hear, The (William Wellman), 29
Nichols, Mike, 143
Nicholson, Jack, 137, 139
Nights of Cabiria (Federico Fellini), 73

Nil By Mouth (Gary Oldman), 186, 190
Noiret, Philippe, 104
Notorious (Alfred Hitchcock), 19, 20, 21, 231
Novak, Kim, 101
Nuit et brouillard (Alain Resnais), 38, 45, 100, 232

Office Catholique Français du Cinéma, 77
Oldboy (Chan Woo Park), 207
Oldman, Gary, 194
Olmi, Ermanno, 175
Olvidados, Los (Luis Buñuel), 81, 232
Olympia cinema, Cannes, 137
Olympiad (Leni Riefenstahl), 13, 231
On the Riviera (Walter Lang), 53
Opening Day of Close Up, The (Nanni Moretti), 221
Othello (Orson Welles), 240
Othello (Sergei Yutkevich), 30

Padre Padrone (Paolo Taviani & Vittorio Taviani), 184, 238
Pahlavi, Shah Reza, 218
Pakula, Alan J., 173
Palais, Cannes (Croisette), 23–4, 27, 229, 232
Palais, Cannes (Grand Palais), 7, 10, 24, 110, 229–30, 234
Palais de la Méditerranée, Nice, 19
Palazzo del Cinema, Venice, 13
Palin, Michael, 88
'Palme des Palmes', 235
Palme d'Or, 35–7, 175–8, 186–9, 237–40
    Buñuel, 84, 87

INDEX

273

chronologies, 232–5, 237–40
Cocteau, 37
Dancer in the Dark, 118
design of, 2
Dolce Vita, 75
Fahrenheit 9/11, 4
first woman winner, 153
French films and, 169
Güney, 152
Hollywood and, 182, 205–6
Jacob on, 168, 169
Kiarostami, 217, 222, 223
Lakhdar-Hamina, 7
Leigh, 201
Leopard, 78
list of winners, 237–40
Man of Iron, 162
Marty, 42
Miramax, 228
other awards and, 172
shared, 180
60th celebrations and, 1
Sous le Soleil de Satan, 114
Panahi, Jafar, 223
Paparazzi (Jacques Rozier), 70
Paris Opera, 16
Paris, Texas (Wim Wenders), 116, 238
Parsons, Louella, 56
Paths of Glory (Stanley Kubrick), 157
Pelle the Conqueror (Bille August), 238
Pena, Richard, 217
Peppermint Frappé (Carlos Saura), 133
Performance (Nicolas Roeg), 130
Pétain, Marshal, 16
Peter Pan (Walt Disney), 232
Petit soldat, le (Jean-Luc Godard), 91, 158

Peyrefitte, Alain, 89
Pialat, Maurice, 114–15, 234
Pianist, The (Roman Polanski), 237
Piano, The (Jane Campion), 153, 235, 238
Picasso, Pablo, 6
Piccolo, Michel, 104
Pierrot le fou (Jean-Luc Godard), 91
Piñal, Silvia, 83
Place in the Sun, A (George Stevens), 28
Pola X (Leos Carax), 203
Poland, 163, 165
Polanski, Roman, 117, 123, 129, 168, 172, 235
Pollack, Sydney, 197
Pompidou, Georges, 109
Pontecorvo, Gillo, 220
Poromboiu, Corneliu, 214, 215
Positif, 22
Powell, Dilys, 18–19
Prade, Georges, 14
'Prague Spring', 122
Prédal, René, 107–8
Preminger, Otto, 205
Prix de la Mise en Scène, 81
Prix de la Première Oeuvre, 159
Prix Un Certain Regard, 172, 198, 214, 215, 234, 235
Prouteau, Gilbert, 32
Provence, 50
Puiu, Cristi, 215
Pulp Fiction (Quentin Tarantino), 238

Quatre cents coups, Les (François Truffaut), 96, 102, 233
Quinzaine des Réalisateurs, 7, 135–8, 144, 233

274 INDEX

Radio Caroline, 135
Radziwilowicz, Jerzy, 150
Rafelson, Bob, 137
Raizman, Yuli, 19
Rassam, Jean-Pierre, 104
Ray, Satyajit, 197, 219
Rayns, Tony, 153, 197, 203, 207, 216
Rebel Without a Cause (Nicholas Ray), 65
Red Earth, The (Bodil Ipsen & Lau Jr. Lauritzen), 240
Red Road (Andrea Arnold), 213
Religieuse, La (Jacques Rivette), 88–93
Remains of the Day, The (James Ivory), 171
Renoir, Jean, 13, 114, 125, 197, 231
Resnais, Alain, 38, 44–7, 232
Rex cinema, Cannes, 137, 138
Rey, Fernando, 160
Reydegas, Carlos, 77
Richardson, Tony, 59
Riefenstahl, Leni, 13, 231
Rissient, Pierre, 153, 154, 196, 197, 209
Rivette, Jacques, 88–91, 93, 125, 233
Robinson, David, 30, 84, 144
Robinson, Edward G., 31, 33, 34
Rocha, Glauber, 7, 142, 154
Rocky Road to Dublin (Peter Lennon), 132
Roeg, Nicolas, 130
Romania, 214
Rome, 72
Rome, Open City (Roberto Rossellini), 22, 219, 231, 240
Room at the Top (Jack Clayton), 55
Rosenbaum, Jonathan, 215, 225–7

Rosetta (Luc and Jean-Pierre Dardenne), 186, 187, 237
Rossellini, Roberto, 22–3, 146, 184, 215, 231, 234
Rossellini Prize, 219, 234
Roud, Richard, 73, 127, 141
Rousseau, Jean-Jacques, 89
Rowe, Thomas L., 76
Royer, Michel, 112
Rozier, Jacques, 70
Rudolph, Alan, 184
Rules of the Game, The (Jean Renoir), 197
Russell, Jane, 57
Rutter, Jonathan, 190, 200

Sachs, Gunther, 68
Sadoul, Georges, 146
Sagan, Françoise, 180–1
Salaam Bombay! (Mira Nair), 171
Salaire de la Peur (Henri-Georges Clouzot), 32, 232, 239
Salinger, Pierre, 160, 161
Samojlova, Tatyana, 30
Sarde, Alain, 200
Sarris, Andrew, 87, 167, 178
Sartre, Jean-Paul, 86
Saura, Carlos, 133
Scarecrow (Jerry Schatzberg), 239
Schatzberg, Jerry, 199
Schlöndorff, Volker, 177, 180, 199, 234
Schotté, Emmanuel, 186
Schwarzenegger, Arnold, 5
Scorsese, Martin, 182, 204
Second World War, 1, 92, 160, 227
Secrets and Lies (Mike Leigh), 177, 189, 200, 237

INDEX 275

Segal, Eric, 171
Semaine International de la Critique, 233
Sembene, Ousmane, 7
Servant, The (Joseph Losey), 181
Seventh Seal, The (Ingmar Bergman), 77, 168, 232
sex, lies and videotape (Stephen Soderbergh), 228, 235, 238
Shout, The (Jerzy Skolimowski), 193
Signoret, Simone, 55
Silent World, The (Jacques-Yves Cousteau & Louis Malle), 239
Silva, Simone, 54–7, 232
Simenon, Georges, 74–5, 175, 233
Situationist International, 97
Sjoberg, Alf, 29
Skolimowski, Jerzy, 177, 193, 199
Smith, Harold, 20
Soderbergh, Stephen, 140, 235
Solanas, Fernando, 142
Solidarity, 162–4, 178
Son's Room, The (Nanna Moretti), 221, 237
Sous le soleil de Satan (Maurice Pialat), 114, 168, 234, 238
Soviet Union, 27, 28–30
Spain, 81
Spall, Timothy, 190
Spanish Civil War, 44, 80
Spielberg, Steven, 226
St Tropez, 52, 63
Stalin, Joseph, 30, 43
Stallone, Sylvester, 206
Star Wars (George Lucas), 207–8
Statues Meurent Aussi, Les (Alain Resnais), 38
Steadman, Alison, 190

Stevens, George, 28
Stone, Oliver, 141
Stone Flower, The (Aleksandr Ptushko), 240
Strada, La (Federico Fellini), 73
Strawberry Statement, The (Stuart Hagmann), 143–4
Strictly Ballroom (Baz Luhrmann), 202
Strindberg, August, 29
Studio Canal, 200
Subor, Michel, 158
Sueros, Monsignor Jésus, 85
Sullivan's Travels (Preston Sturges), 71
Suru (Yilmaz Güney), 152
Suzanne Simonin, la Religieuse de Diderot (Jacques Rivette), 89, 92, 233
Sweet Smell of Success (Alexander Mackendrick), 43
Symphonie Pastorale, La (Jean Delannoy), 240

Tarantino, Quentin, 178
Tarkovsky, Andrei, 87, 142, 150, 182
Taste of Cherry, A (Abbas Kiarostami), 177, 217, 220, 221, 222, 235
Taste of Honey, A (Tony Richardson), 59
Tati, Jacques, 11, 52
Tavernier, Bertrand, 102, 153
Taxi Driver (Martin Scorsese), 238
Taylor, Elizabeth, 28, 131
Technicolor, 52
Thibault, Jean-Marc, 52
Third Man, The (Carol Reed), 240
Thomas, Jeremy, 10, 113, 167, 172, 173, 183, 193–4

INDEX

Through the Olive Trees, The (Abbas Kiarostami), 217, 219, 220, 221
Thulin, Ingrid, 139
Tin Drum, The (Volker Schlöndorff), 177, 180, 234, 238
To Catch a Thief (Alfred Hitchcock), 53
Tognazzi, Ugo, 104
Tough Guys Don't Dance (Norman Mailer), 172
2046 (Wong Kar Wai), 179
Traité de bave et d'éternité (Jean-Isidore Golstein), 96, 232
Tree of Wooden Clogs, The (Ermanno Olmi), 175, 238
Trintignant, Jean-Louis, 63, 158
Truffaut, François, 99–102
    on Bardot, 64
    Bazin and, 41
    duties of Cannes, 53
    enfant terrible, 96–7, 119
    on future film audiences, 227
    1968, 126, 128–9, 131–2, 134, 233
        Quatre cents coups, 96, 233
Trumbo, Dalton, 42, 196–7
Truth or Dare (Alek Keshishian), 70
Turning Point, The (Fridrikh Markovitch Ermler), 18, 240
Tushingham, Rita, 59
12.08 East of Bucharest (Corneliu Poromboiu), 214
Two Cents Worth of Hope (Renato Castellani), 239

Umbrellas of Cherbourg, The (Jacques Demy), 239
Umut (Yilmaz Güney), 238
Underground (Emir Kusturica), 237

Utomlyonnye solntsem (Nikita Mikhalkov), 176
Uzak (Nuri Bilge Ceylan), 212
Vacances de M. Hulot, Les (Jacques Tati), 52, 232

Vadim, Roger, 60–5, 71
Valenti, Jack, 182
Valseueses, Les (Bertrand Blier), 110
Van Sant, Gus, 236
Vanel, Charles, 32–3
Varda, Agnès, 211, 229
Vase de Noce (Thierry Zéno), 161
Vassiliev, Sergei, 30, 232
Vautier, René, 159–60
Venice Film Festival, 12–14, 16–17
    awards of, 36
    Bertolucci on, 194
    Cannes and, a comparison, 194
    competition to Cannes, 6, 8, 23, 57–8, 130, 208
    Debord and, 98
    Fellini and, 73
    Hitler's anger, 231
    Hollywood and, 228
    Mussolini, 2
    Taste of Cherry, 220
Vent des Aurès, Le (Mohammed Lakhdar-Hamina), 159, 160
Vera Drake (Mike Leigh), 200
Via Veneto, Rome, 72
Vichy, 16
Victorine Studios, Nice, 19
Vie Passionée de Clemenceau, La (Gilbert Prouteau), 32
Vietnam, 127, 143
Vinterberg, Thomas, 118
Viot, Pierre, 234, 235

INDEX

277

Virgin Spring, The (Ingmar Bergman), 75

Viridiana (Luis Buñuel), 79, 81–7, 233, 239

Visconti, Luchino, 78, 140

Vitti, Monica, 123, 129, 147, 148

Vive les Vacances (Jean-Marc Thibault), 52

von Trier, Lars, 95, 115–19, 168, 235

Voyage to Cythera (Theo Angelopoulos), 116

Wajda, Andrzej, 150, 162–5, 181

Walesa, Lech, 163

Walker, Alexander, 144

Warhol, Andy, 125

Weak and the Wicked, The (J. Lee Thompson), 55

Weingarten, Isabelle, 106

Weinstein brothers, 228

Welcome to Sarajevo (Michael Winterbottom), 186

Welles, Orson, 40, 100

Wenders, Wim, 9, 149, 214

When Father Was Away on Business (Emir Kusturica), 238

Where is the Friend's House (Abbas Kiarostami), 219

White, Edmund, 4

Wiazemsky, Anne, 131

Wideberg, Bo, 141

Wild at Heart (David Lynch), 175, 206, 238

Wilder, Billy, 22, 231

Williams, Alan, 109

Wind that Shakes the Barley (Ken Loach), 237

Wind Will Carry Us, The (Abbas Kiarostami), 217, 222, 226

Winterbottom, Michael, 77

Wolman, Gil, 97

Wonderman (H. Bruce Humberstone), 20

Wong Kar Wai, 174, 179, 209

Woodstock (Michael Wadleigh), 144

Working Class Goes to Heaven, The (Elio Petri), 239

Wyler, William, 38, 100, 168

Yol (Yilmaz Güney), 151–2, 238

York, Susannah, 108

Young, Terence, 123, 129

Young One, The (Luis Buñuel), 75

Yutkevich, Sergei, 30, 232

Z (Costa-Gavras), 140–2

Zéno, Thierry, 161

Zentropa, 117

Ziegfeld Follies (Vincente Minelli), 240

Zhang Yimou, 150, 215–16

Zulawski, Andrzej, 166